Oscar Wilde and the theatre of the 1890s

Oscar Wilde and the
theatre of the 1890s

KERRY POWELL

Professor of English
Miami University, Oxford, Ohio

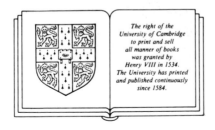

The right of the
University of Cambridge
to print and sell
all manner of books
was granted by
Henry VIII in 1534.
The University has printed
and published continuously
since 1584.

CAMBRIDGE UNIVERSITY PRESS

Cambridge
New York   Port Chester
Melbourne   Sydney

Published by the Press Syndicate of the University of Cambridge
The Pitt Building, Trumpington Street, Cambridge CB2 1RP
40 West 20th Street, New York, NY 10011, USA
10 Stamford Road, Oakleigh, Melbourne 3166, Australia

© Cambridge University Press 1990

First published 1990

Printed in Great Britain at the University Press, Cambridge

British Library cataloguing in publication data
Powell, Kerry
Oscar Wilde and the theatre of the 1890s.
1. London. Theatre. Productions, History. 2. Drama in English. Wilde, Oscar, 1854–1900
I. Title
792.9′5′09421

Library of Congress cataloguing in publication data
Powell, Kerry.
Oscar Wilde and the theatre of the 1890s/by Kerry Powell.
p.   cm.
Includes bibliographical references.
ISBN 0–521–38008–1
1. Wilde, Oscar. 1854–1900–Dramatic works. 2. Theater–England–History–
19th century. I. Title.
PR5827.D7P6   1990
822′.8–dc20   89–77386 CIP

ISBN 0 521 38008 1 hardback

To Sam and Martelle Powell
for never losing their sons

Contents

Illustrations

Plates 1–5 are reproduced by kind permission of the Raymond Mander and Joe Mitchenson Theatre Collection and Plate 6 by kind permission of the Victoria and Albert Picture Library, Victoria and Albert Museum.

Acknowledgments

This book has benefited from the generous assistance of many people. In particular I want to thank Martin Meisel and George Rowell for reading the manuscript and offering invaluable suggestions and encouragement. Their work on Victorian theatre, moreover, has in many respects made mine possible.

Some of those whose writing on Oscar Wilde I most admire have read the manuscript, or portions of it, and saved me from numerous blunders, both of omission and fact. I am especially grateful to Regenia Gagnier, Isobel Murray, E. H. Mikhail, and Peter Raby.

My colleagues at Miami University have been an unfailing source of help. Frank Jordan, Barry Chabot, Ann Ardis, and Peter C. Hall have read the manuscript at various stages and provided encouragement and good advice when I was most in need. William Wortman has been indispensable in helping to locate manuscripts and rare printed plays without which this book would have been impossible.

I also owe a major debt to many staff members at the British Library, the New York Public Library, the Mander and Mitchenson Collection, and the Theatre Museum, as well as Miami University libraries. I am grateful to *English Literature in Transition 1880–1920* for permission to use a chapter, ''Wilde and Ibsen,'' which appeared in a shorter and earlier version in that journal. Permission to use photographs from various theatrical productions of the 1890s has been kindly granted by the Mander and Mitchenson library, the Theatre Museum, London and the Victoria and Albert Museum. Much-needed time and financial support for this project were made available by the National Endowment for the Humanities, the faculty research committee at Miami University, and the college of arts and science and department of English at Miami. Trudi Nixon prepared the manuscript for publication with her usual expertise.

1

Rewriting the past

Remember, dans la littérature il faut toujours tuer son père.
                                    Oscar Wilde, to Will Rothenstein

The one duty we owe to history is to rewrite it.
                                    Wilde, in *The Critic as Artist*

Much of the theatrical landscape of Oscar Wilde's time, including some of its most imposing monuments, remains unmapped. Measured by the number of performances in their first run, the fifty most popular plays in major London theatres in the 1890s (excluding comic opera and pantomime) include only a handful which would be familiar even to most specialists in Victorian literature – *Charley's Aunt*, the longest-running play of the decade with 1,469 performances; Henry Arthur Jones's *The Liars*, 328 performances; Arthur Wing Pinero's *The Second Mrs. Tanqueray*, 223; Wilde's *Lady Windermere's Fan*, 197; and a revival of *Julius Caesar*, 161. Among Wilde's plays *Lady Windermere's Fan* enjoyed by far the longest run, but ranked only thirty-third with respect to dramas of the 1890s in general; *A Woman of No Importance* was seventy-second; *An Ideal Husband*, ninety-third.[1] Of the ten most popular plays of the decade, only *The Liars* has been published in standard book form; at least six were printed as acting chapbooks by the Samuel French company, and two never were published in any form – a farce by Seymour Hicks called *A Night Out* and Wilson Barrett's religious melodrama *The Sign of the Cross*.[2]

Perhaps the most successful dramatist of the 1890s was not Shaw or Ibsen in translation or even Wilde, Jones, or Pinero, but Sydney Grundy, nine of whose plays enjoyed runs of 100 performances or more – a generally recognized standard in the 1890s for a hit show. A number of these never appeared in print. R. C. Carton, pseudonym of the little-known dramatist Richard Claude Critchett, wrote six plays which ran a hundred nights or more in the 1890s, only two of which have been published even in acting editions. The melodramas of G. R. Sims, which typically enjoyed long engagements at the Adelphi, are almost entirely unpublished. The name of W. Lestocq, co-author of long-running and influential farces like *Jane* and *The Foundling*, is to be found today only in bibliographies of drama. Women dramatists who wrote hit plays – Mrs. H. Musgrave, Mrs. Hugh Bell, Mrs. C. L. Riley, Mrs. R. Pacheco – are, if possible, even more obscure. On the other hand the longevity of a play does not invariably provide an accurate measure of its popularity. The last performance of *Lady Windermere's Fan* played before a large audience, and actor-manager George Alexander apologized in a curtain speech for having to close the play prematurely "to tour several provincial towns" with his company.[3] The first engagement of *A Woman of No Importance* might have been considerably longer were it not for the fact that H. Beerbohm Tree closed it to honor a commitment to produce Jones's *The Tempter* at the Haymarket.[4] But generally the number of performances can be referred to now, as it was then, to provide some indication of the commercial success of a play.

The theatrical scene in which so many barely remembered authors played a vital part would have appeared extremely seductive to Wilde. The introduction of Ibsen on the London stage in 1889, along with the frequent appearances of Sarah Bernhardt beginning a decade earlier, lent the stage an intellectual and aesthetic excitement that was missing when Matthew Arnold, in "The French Play in London," bemoaned the torpid state of English drama.[5] Henry James, it is true, continued to insist that the art of writing drama was "a lost one," replaced by mere scenic effects such as the leaping flames and blue vapors of Henry Irving's production of *Faust* at the Lyceum.[6] Even James, however, could work up mild enthusiasm for Elizabeth Robins and Marion Lea's successful effort to bring *Hedda Gabler* to the London stage, finding that "Acted, it leads [one's intellectual sympathy] over the straightest of roads with all the exhilaration of a superior pace" (even if there was little else, for James, to "get from it").[7] The conditions were right for someone like Wilde, who self-consciously styled himself an artist, to undertake the writing of plays which made more than superficial claims upon his audience.

Wilde aspired to be the "English Ibsen"; but even such recognition would not, in itself, have been enough. Bitterly disappointed with his royalties from *The Picture of Dorian Gray*, published as a book in 1891, Wilde turned for at least partly financial reasons to the stage.[8] With him the need for cash was always urgent, and the theatre had become the likeliest place where an ambitious writer could make money. The *Era*, a theatrical trade newspaper containing a wealth of unindexed and unexplored information about the late Victorian theatre, observed in 1892 that successful playwrights no longer struggled with poverty as Dion Boucicault had done early in his career, or died in want like the popular farceur H. J. Byron only a few years earlier. Far from it – for by 1892, the *Era* noted, the standard arrangement provided the dramatist with "ten per cent on the gross" for each performance. "An ordinary West-end theatre holds £200 when quite full," the newspaper pointed out, so the author's fee for a single performance in a sold-out house would be £20. A long-running play, therefore, could bring the author a very considerable sum. G. R. Sims, the *Era* said, was paid £30,000 in fees for *The Lights o' London* alone.[9] "I am often asked," wrote the actress Madge Kendal in her memoirs published in 1890, "whether playwrights make large fortunes. There is no doubt about it, they do."[10]

Today the English theatre of the 1890s has been reduced to the plays of Wilde and Shaw, the influence of Ibsen, and – to a far lesser extent – certain works by Pinero and Jones. But for its patrons the *fin-de-siècle* drama bore scant resemblance to the highly selective recollection of it in the twentieth century. J. T. Grein, manager of the Independent Theatre and producer of plays by Ibsen and Shaw as well as several women playwrights, recorded his impressions of the English theatrical scene in a long-lost lecture of 1892, just as the so-called New Drama was coming to life. Grein rated Sydney Grundy as "the most talented of all our dramatists," just ahead of Haddon Chambers, Jerome K. Jerome, Louis N. Parker, and the author of *Lady Windermere's Fan*.[11] The year 1892 – which saw the London premiere not only of *Lady Windermere's Fan*, but *Widowers' Houses*, *Ghosts*, and *Hedda Gabler* – seemed to the *Era* "the worst theatrical year that most playgoers can remember."[12] *A Woman of No Importance*, seen now as the least of Wilde's comedies, was in 1895 "generally regarded as the most successful of Mr. Oscar Wilde's plays."[13] Wilde himself discounted the worth of *The Importance of Being Earnest* and estimated *An Ideal Husband*, infrequently performed in this century, as the best-written of his plays.[14] It may be that people in the 1890s took a view of their theatre so different from ours because they saw more of it. Most plays of the period, even prominent ones, disappeared utterly with the final performance. Canon formation, therefore, has been haphazard, influenced not only by critical but legal and financial concerns that worked against the publication of plays and removed most of them from consideration. "We have to talk in the air," complains a character in Henry James's dialogue "After the Play," regretting the failure of Victorian playwrights to publish their work; "I can refer to my Congreve, but I can't to my Pinero."[15]

Many of the most popular dramas which precede Wilde's own work lapsed into oblivion as soon as the footlights were extinguished, having never been published, or printed in cheap acting editions of which only a scattered remnant survives. It is this vanished but essential context of Wilde's theatrical career that needs to be recaptured, and to that end some "desperate raids on oblivion," to use a phrase of Max Beerbohm's, cannot be dispensed with. But this oblivion holds a fascination of its own, for some interesting work is buried there. From these largely forgotten plays Wilde's own writing derives, yet at its best surpasses. Sydney Grundy once wrote that Wilde ought to be "washed in Lethe and forgotten," his bones sprinkled with "chloride of lime."[16] But it is Grundy and Wilde's other rivals who have suffered that fate – unjustly, perhaps, in some cases.

Wilde's plays began as a collaborative enterprise which their author, even if he did not understand it fully himself, was anxious to conceal. "My works are dominated by myself," he declared, telling a reporter that no dramatist of the nineteenth century had influenced him even "in the smallest degree."[17] But the fact is that without the spur of influence he could scarcely write a play at all. Nevertheless Wilde forms a surprising contrast to the "strong poets" who, according to Harold Bloom, emerge triumphant from "wrestling with the greatest of the dead."[18] In his best plays Wilde contends not with the titanic dead, but with the living, and these often nameless enough – a W. Lestocq or Pierre Leclerq, although in the right mood he could challenge Henrik Ibsen with success. Plays such as *Lady Windermere's Fan* and *An Ideal Husband* grow out of once-popular theatrical types, yet in imitating resist them. The struggle can be prolonged and the outcome suspended in doubt until the final act, but when he succeeds Wilde overcomes the force of his predecessors and reverses in his own play the important tendencies of statement and character in theirs. What begins in cliché thus finishes in upset of expectation, in paradox, and Wilde's dramas take on a bold individuation. An observer almost feels, strangely enough, that the earlier plays by others are somehow feeble imitations of Wilde's later successes.

The relation of Wilde to so-called sources, despite his wounded denials of influence, has fascinated critics from his first theatrical reviewers to Harold Bloom, who introduces *The Anxiety of Influence* and the more recent *Oscar Wilde*, an anthology of criticism, with all-too-brief remarks upon Wilde as a writer whose "anxiety of influence" was too unformed for the "strong poet" who could prevail in the struggle with the literary past and achieve distinctive work of his own. From this perspective Wilde is like Dorian Gray, mesmerized by the influence of another and older, struggling for an autonomy beyond his reach and thus, for him, fatal.[19] To a large extent Bloom's suggestion of tension between Wilde and his predecessors, although less complimentary to Wilde, has much in common with what some other notable and recent critics have observed. The work of Isobel Murray, for example, exposes a central truth about Wilde – that the influence exerted upon him came from a wide variety of "sources," their very number protecting Wilde from "undue influence" by any single author or work.[20] The question of influence in Wilde's writing is further complicated by the fact that among the works most telling upon him at any particular stage of his career are those that he had already written himself.[21] For Wilde, moreover, his plays, like all literature in a Paterian world, were fundamentally self-expressive:

Those great figures of Greek or English drama that seem to us to possess an actual existence of their own, apart from the poets who shaped and fashioned them, are, in their ultimate analysis, simply the poets themselves, not as they thought they were, but as they thought they were not; and by such thinking came in strange manner, though but for a moment, really so to be. For out of ourselves we can never pass, nor can there be in creation what in the creator was not.[22]

But it would be a mistake to apply this account of the artist's radical subjectivity too literally to Wilde's own career as playwright. What has been termed his most original work, *The Importance of Being Earnest*, is perhaps the one most conditioned by literary precedent — but a precedent transfigured in its rewriting.

Although Wilde at his finest "misreads" many of the most popular dramas of the 1890s, this action is not generated – as it is in Bloom's "anxiety of influence" – by a love for the precursor which is complicated by the latecomer's need to clear his own poetic space.[23] It is not Browning's regard for Shelley, or Keats's for Milton, that attracts Wilde to Sydney Grundy, R. C. Carton, the anonymous farceurs of the *fin-de-siècle*, or even Arthur Wing Pinero and Henry Arthur Jones. Of his contemporaries in drama (Shaw and Ibsen excepted), Wilde usually speaks, when he speaks at all, with unmitigated disdain. To write for the popular stage was to risk the loss of artistic prestige, even at a time when theatres attracted increasingly fashionable audiences and held out to dramatists the prospect of wealth. Robert Buchanan, like Wilde a poet turned playwright, asked that his dramas appear under a pseudonym after Robert Browning sneered at him as "the man who writes plays with Sims at the Adelphi."[24] Buchanan reckoned "us poets" as a class distinctly apart from the melodramatists and farce writers of the day, and it was a difference that he meant, in his own interest, to respect. Wilde's method of keeping himself in the company of what Buchanan called "us poets" was to deny that his plays owed anything at all to other Victorian drama, being, as he said, "dominated by myself." At the end of his career he would describe himself as one who poeticized the drama, making it "as personal a mode of expression as the Lyric or the Sonnet" and enlarging its "artistic horizon."[25] Against this background it is easy to see why Wilde overestimated the merit of a "poetic" drama like *Salomé* and was so comparatively modest, even deprecatory, about *The Importance of Being Earnest*. Indeed he regarded *Earnest*'s lack of "serious interest" as the very quality to ensure its box-office appeal.[26] Even the authorship of a popular society comedy like *Lady Windermere's Fan* seems to have made Wilde uneasy. "In Paris," recalled his friend Will Rothenstein, "he had been rather apologetic about his first play; as though to write a comedy were rather beneath a poet."[27]

In spite of himself Wilde was energized by popular writing – he liked it when he scorned it, and found his own voice, when he found it at all, in answering the melodramatic clamors and boisterous humor of his rival

5

playwrights. What we sometimes assume to be Wilde's voice *par excellence* is really that of another, lost to memory, speaking through him. Wilde's real attitude toward the popular theatre of his day was thus something more complicated than disdain. Its vigorous currents overpower him, or threaten to, even in his best work – *especially* in his best, one is tempted to say. Thus in a forgotten, unpublished play called *The Foundling*, popular in the summer of 1894 when Wilde was setting to work on *The Importance of Being Earnest*, a 25-year-old orphan is regarded askance by the formidably conventional mother of the young woman he wants to marry. To satisfy her demand for "blood," Dick Pennell considers christening as a way out of his difficulty, like Algernon Moncrieff in a parallel situation in *Earnest*.[28] In both plays the young heroes desire to know, as they say, "who I am"; and each brings down the house with laughter when, with the cry of "Mother!", he embraces a maidenly woman of advanced age, thinking her his long-lost parent. The author of *Earnest* denied all influence, but the truth is that at times he was mesmerized by the humblest precursors in the most undistinguished literary modes of the age.

His denial of influence failed to keep Wilde from falling into embarrassing echoes of other playwrights, but it also resulted in a revenge upon the source. One frequently finds that the popular playwrights whom Wilde repeats are ultimately ambushed in some larger matter of substance or style. In *Earnest* Wilde often took the words directly from the mouths of other people's characters, but merged them into a stylistic texture – epigrammatic, literary, aristocratic – which was utterly divorced from the pedestrian language that usually characterized farce. In this respect going to see *Earnest*, as one reviewer observed, was like "drinking wine out of the wrong sort of glass."[29] In statement, however, as well as expression Wilde's play subverts the comedies which from another point of view it imitates. In popular Victorian farces the heroes typically begin with deceit and disguise, abrogating responsibility, but end by dutifully enjoining truth, constancy, work, and earnestness – the great verities of the world beyond the footlights. Wilde's play, however, refuses to deny the revolutionary fun from which its humor springs. For its characters there is no turning back from the life of masquerade and lie, no retreat to the stern embrace of authority. The last line of the play – Jack's defiant remark that "I've now realized for the first time in my life the vital Importance of Being Earnest" – is a parody of the contrite moral speeches offered up in the last act by the heroes of such plays as *The New Boy* (1894), *Charley's Aunt* (1892), and *The Foundling*. Jack's being "Earnest" is a victory won by defying "earnestness" and the army of Victorian virtues which held in check the disruptive tendencies of other late-century farces.

In *Salomé*, regarded by some critics as the author's most original play, Wilde falls captive to prior dramas in a way which he would escape in *Earnest*. He detached Salomé from her biblical incarnation as a marginal,

6

passive woman and gave her an eruptive nature, swerving between violence and listless yearning – made her, in short, a Sarah Bernhardt character in the mold of Fédora, Floria, and Théodora in the plays of Victorien Sardou. The clipped, hieratic style of Wilde's French, furthermore, was a perfect vehicle for the monotonous, one-note chanting which by the 1890s had become the trademark of Bernhardt's delivery. In this instance Wilde even abandoned English altogether to write in his predecessor's language. The very costume Bernhardt was to wear as Salomé had been borrowed from the wardrobe of Sardou's most recent showcase for *la grande Sarah*, an adaptation from Shakespeare called *Cléopâtre* (1890).

As usual, however, Wilde's play was generated from a variety of "sources," and the painter Will Rothenstein, who recognized one of them as Flaubert's *Hérodias*, understood that in *Salomé*, at least, Wilde had not experienced what Harold Bloom might characterize as a sufficiently intense "anxiety of influence":

When he gave me a copy on its first publication in its violet paper cover, he knew at once that it put me in mind of Flaubert. He admitted he had not been able to resist the theft. "Remember," he said with amusing unction, "Dans la littérature il faut toujours tuer son père." But I didn't think he had killed Flaubert; nor did he, I believe.[30]

Rothenstein acutely perceived that Wilde's achievement depended somehow upon an aggression against the past in which prior writers had to be "killed." Being unable to "resist" Flaubert – or any other who preceded him – thus signified failure. It is in this sense that Wilde's plays may be seen as struggles against literary and theatrical precedent, contests in which Wilde himself is sometimes overwhelmed.

Thus in *A Woman of No Importance* the cynical humor of Lord Illingworth and the feminist iconoclasm of Hester Worsley and, at times, Mrs. Arbuthnot introduce modern and original notes into a play in other respects dominated by the melodramatic forerunners which inspired it. But these individuating aspects of *A Woman of No Importance* engage in conflict with the dramatic formulas which organize it. In the end Wilde surrenders to tradition when he silences Lord Illingworth's wit and allows Mrs. Arbuthnot the old-fashioned satisfaction of striking her seducer in the face.

Lady Windermere's Fan, Wilde's first success in the theatre, derives from the strangely numerous plays, both French and English, in which disreputable mothers have abandoned their husbands and children. Like most before him, Wilde depicts the absconded mother insinuating herself, with belated maternal instincts, into the presence of the child she left long ago. In such plays as Sardou's *Odette* (1881), Pierre Leclerq's *Illusion* (1890), and the notorious *East Lynne* (played in many versions from the 1860s through the end of the century), the mother repents, cries bitterly over the deserted child, and finally pays dearly for her crime – typically with death or exile.

At first, indeed for much of the play, *Lady Windermere's Fan* is captive to its tradition, but finally Wilde's Mrs. Erlynne, although stirred by motherly feeling for her daughter, bluntly refuses to "weep on her neck and tell her who I am, and all that kind of thing."[31] The orgy of sentiment which repulses Mrs. Erlynne was actually the outcome which history had written for Wilde's play; in refusing it, she enables the author of *Lady Windermere's Fan* to make it his own in a sense in which *Odette*, for instance, does not really belong to Sardou.

Nevertheless the indecisive early acts of *Lady Windermere's Fan* transcribe the theatrical past as much as rewrite it. Something similar can be observed in *An Ideal Husband*, which combats but imitates a type of late nineteenth-century drama in which men are held to an impossible standard associated today almost entirely with Victorian demands made upon women. This fuss about "ideal" men and "perfect" husbands was not unrelated to the movement for equal rights for women, for it was an unlikely attempt to put an end to what Wilde once described as the insistence upon "separate sorts of virtues and separate ideals of duty" in the sexes.[32] Plays such as Ibsen's *Pillars of Society*, staged in England in 1889 (an adaptation appeared earlier), assaulted the double standard of conduct by domesticating the ruthless male rather than altering the standard of purity by which women were judged. The "ideal husband," feminized in this way, elected to forgo the liberty given men to violate official morality in sex, business, and politics. In a half-dozen plays being staged in London when Wilde's was introduced in early 1895, this sanitized man is a central figure, and in most of them, as in *Pillars of Society*, a revisionary masculinity is in some sense endorsed. For a nearly fatal interlude in the middle of *An Ideal Husband*, reminiscent of hesitations which nearly spoiled *Lady Windermere's Fan*, Wilde's play assigns speeches and situations to Sir Robert Chiltern and Lord Goring which are not genuinely their own, but belong to a host of other dramas. As in *Lady Windermere's Fan*, however, the last act separates it from plays which in other respects it overlaps. Sir Robert Chiltern discards – rather too suddenly, indeed – the mantle of "ideal husband," refuses to confess his crime, and evades punishment. The irreverent and paradoxical humor of Lord Goring and Mrs. Cheveley, moreover, has been the stylistic correlative of this overthrow of precedent, providing a foundation upon which the hard-won but flawed conclusion of Wilde's divided play can be laid.

The Picture of Dorian Gray (1890) had anticipated Wilde's plays in organizing itself as a countermeasure against certain literary clichés in much the same way that Lord Henry Wotton's aphorisms, with their whiplash of surprise, attack familiar wisdom. Wilde's novel takes its story and its imagery, even the names of its characters, from a popular subgenre of fiction, rife in the 1880s, which included tales such as *The Picture's Secret*, *The Portrait and the Ghost*, *The Veiled Picture* and *His Other Self*. These stories

of occult pictures and magical mirrors are almost invariably simple alle-
gories of good and evil, often ending with a painter or model destroying a
canvas whose evil influence must be purged before virtue can prevail. But
the *doppelgänger* motif so basic to this mode of fiction is given unique
expression in *The Picture of Dorian Gray* when the hero destroys himself as
the consequence of his very predictable attack on the "evil" portrait.
Wilde's didactic predecessors are answered with a supernatural picture
which becomes many things at once – diabolic yet good, loathsome but
beautiful – and as a result *Dorian Gray* avoids making the portrait simply
another unimaginative caricature of evil and attains a psychological truth
not found in other works of the kind.[33] But Dorian's frantic drive for
repentance does some damage to *Dorian Gray*, as the author himself seems
to have sensed – for the book's only "artistic error," Wilde said, was its
overdeveloped tendency to state a moral.[34] Even at his best Wilde does not
prevail in every phase of these contests with the source, but he survives
influence to pronounce the last word. He achieves his own voice – and this
is what one misses not only in much of his earlier work, but in a considerable amount of his dramatic writing in the 1890s. The verse Wilde
published in 1881, for example, belongs in a real sense to other and better
poets of the nineteenth century – including Swinburne, Keats, and Rossetti. Wilde's college at Oxford spurned a gift copy with the explanation
that these authors were already well represented in the library.

Like his poems, Wilde's early and virtually ignored plays, dating from
the early 1880s, are too much the passive receptors of influence. With its
story of a noblewoman, her treacherous husband and forbidden love, *The
Duchess of Padua* contains little not attempted earlier and with more success
by John Webster and Robert Browning. The passion which Wilde's
duchess feels for Guido Ferranti and her murderous gratification of it
suggest a fusion of *The Duchess of Malfi* and *The White Devil*, another play
with a duchess of Padua in it. Wilde's, written in 1882–3 but not staged
until 1891 in New York, is one of the last gasps of nineteenth-century
blank-verse drama, but its atmosphere is Jacobean and its imagery Webster's. The duchess is a "devil," and human nature gives rise to an extreme
type of mordant speculation:

> The world's a graveyard, and we each, like coffins,
> Within us bear a skeleton.[35]

This is the mode of Webster, united with something of Browning. The
aesthetic, ego-mad Duke of Padua in Wilde's play, like the Duke of Ferrara
in "My Last Duchess," resents his wife's generous good nature, her
popularity with the people, her regard for others than himself: "I will not
have you loved" (p. 50). His wife must be, says the duke, "mine own,"
and if not content as his possession must suffer the fate of the "last
duchess" of Browning's poem. In fact Wilde's duke cites his own last

duchess as a warning to the new one. "Madam," he says, when his wife asks by what right he restricts her behavior, "my second Duchess/Asked the same question once: her monument/Lies in the chapel of Bartholomew,/Wrought in red marble; very beautiful" (pp. 53–4). Wilde's aesthetic but brutal duke recognizes that a sculpted duchess might satisfy his taste and ego more than a living one, just as Browning's duke, for the same reasons, prefers the painted duchess to the actual women whose death he caused. The double suicide at the end of the play evokes memories of *Romeo and Juliet*, while the heroine who murders her partriarchal oppressor suggests Wilde may be working in the shadow of Shelley's *The Cenci*, a play he much admired. What is missing in this play is the author's own voice – the "personal" mode of expression which, in Wilde's view, was his distinctive gift as a playwright. A voice of his own would later salvage *Lady Windermere's Fan* from the melodramatic tradition behind it, as Robert Sherard discerned. Rising above the threadbare plot, as Sherard says, "his dialogue was wonderful because it was he himself talking all the time."[36]

For *Vera; or, the Nihilists*, Wilde's first play, no source is certain. It is tempting to imagine that *Fédora*, written by Victorien Sardou for Sarah Bernhardt, inspired Wilde with its story of a Russian "nihilist" heroine who vents murderous impulses before dying herself in the last act. But *Vera*, published in 1880 and staged unsuccessfully in 1883 in New York, evidently preceded Sardou's play, first acted in December 1882 in Paris while Wilde was concluding his American tour. Perhaps the Russian settings, the anarchist themes, and the bloody-minded heroines of both plays stem from popular literature which capitalized upon the same materials.[37] A letter by Wilde, unpublished until recently, shows he was well aware of one such work – a French novel by M. L. Gagneur, translated into English as *The Nihilist Princess*. Wilde's *Vera* had been withdrawn from its scheduled production in London in 1881, deemed politically too sensitive in the period following the assassination of Czar Alexander II. In America Wilde asked Clara Morris to take the role of the nihilist heroine Vera Sabouroff, but she knew of *The Nihilist Princess* and its heroine, who calls herself "Vera Perowsky," and told Wilde she was "afraid of it." The author of *Vera* sent word that "the novel *The Nihilist Princess* is a sham, and empty of all dramatic matter."[38] In reality, however, the book is breathlessly melodramatic, like *Vera* itself, and, in a manner suggestive of *Vera*, finds its basis in the idea of a conspiratorial heroine who dies a martyr to the cause. In Nikolai Chernyshevski's novel *What Is To Be Done?*, widely available in French when *Vera* was written, the heroine, called Vera, is converted to nihilism under circumstances similar to those in Wilde's play.[39] *Vera*, with its revolutionary heroine, discloses some interest in social reform and an enlarged conception of women's capabilities, yet its overriding and final impression is that of a woman who extravagantly sacrifices herself for her lover and her country. In this play, as in *The Duchess of Padua*, Wilde had drawn an assertive, unconventional woman without redeeming her from the melodramatic context in which he found her.

Strangely, however, these unimpressive early plays are in one sense more autonomous than *Lady Windermere's Fan* and *The Importance of Being Earnest*. Their stories of passionate women who plot to kill their lovers are written in the spirit of Webster, of Browning, of sensational popular literature – but in actual expression *Vera* and *The Duchess of Padua* seem mostly Wilde's own. The daring thefts of language and incident which characterize Wilde's best plays are, if anything, less apparent in his first efforts for the stage. One almost blushes at the echoes of other writers to be found, for instance, in *Lady Windermere's Fan*, but in that play Wilde is writing against the grain of his forerunners rather than merely absorbing influence. What seem at first shameless borrowings become, after a contest, the means to a surprising and individuated dramatic utterance. Paradoxically, therefore, it might be said that Wilde's early plays fail because they are not as dominated by influence as his later successes. The more intimate the embrace of the source, the more Wilde seems able to produce work really his own.

In *Vera* and *The Duchess of Padua*, furthermore, many of the elements of Wilde's successful plays of the 1890s can be seen in their germinal phase. Salomé's bloody passion, potentially more disturbing to Victorians than the unconventional behavior of Ibsen's women, is anticipated in the nihilist and the noblewoman whose love in the early plays turns deadly. The lost-parent motif which underlies all of Wilde's comedies except *An Ideal Husband* appears first in *The Duchess of Padua*, where it is the basis of Guido Ferranti's motivation and brings him into disastrous contact with the heroine. The odd, distinctively late Victorian notion of an immaculate man, the governing idea of *An Ideal Husband*, also makes its first appearance in *The Duchess of Padua* in the heroine's idolatry of Guido as "a thing unblemished, unassailed, untarnished" (p. 111). But these are pale versions of the brilliant and revisionary treatments of the same ideas in Wilde's mature comedies of the next decade. The amusing epigrams of Prince Paul in *Vera* and the duke in *The Duchess of Padua* look forward to the glittering dialogue of the society comedies, but in these first plays seem almost detachable from the conventional sentiments and melodramatic gestures which engulf them. In these clever speeches one is released briefly from the stylized manner which shapes the early plays as a whole, but although bearing Wilde's signature they are hopelessly alienated from the larger works that contain them.

This conflict between witty paradox and melodramatic tradition occurs in a far different way in a later drama such as *Lady Windermere's Fan*, where it becomes a struggle for the soul of the play, out of which a new voice emerges. Wilde may have felt his way to the world of his later plays in a fragmentary manuscript, edited by Rodney Shewan under the title *A Wife's Tragedy*.[40] It is difficult, as Shewan says, to be certain about the particulars of characterization and action in this dramatic fragment. But it is clear that by the end of the 1880s, when it was probably written, Wilde was exploring an alternative to the merely imitative, romantic melodrama that so far had claimed his activity as a playwright. With its modern characters and unconventional sentiments, this aborted drama of marital infidelity represents an advance in the direction of *Lady Windermere's Fan* – but as yet Wilde seems not to have discovered, or at least not employed, the dramatic form in which material of this kind could be expressed.

That form would be, to a large extent, a dialogue in which Wilde "answered" his dramatic predecessors. The oppressive presence of the source and Wilde's embattled resistance characterize his best plays, but the context in which mature works such as *Earnest* were produced has so faded that these operations have gone, for the most part, unrecognized. In important respects Wilde's dramas are enmeshed in the web of popular theatre of the 1890s, but our idea of the drama of the period is sketchy in the extreme – a result, at least in large part, of various factors which worked against the publication of plays. To publish a play – and so preserve it for posterity – meant until nearly the turn of the century that an English author forfeited stage rights in America, where the play entered the public domain. Enactment of the American Copyright Bill in 1891 eased this problem, but did not protect the author from what the *Era* called "unscrupulous managers" who would perform published plays "without payment of the just fees."[41] Furthermore an attitude existed among playwrights that drama was not literature, and a printed play an irrelevancy. "A play ought to be written to be acted," said Sydney Grundy. "To a real dramatist it matters no more how his drama reads than how a hen crows."[42] These conditions have rendered the bulk of dramatic writing in Wilde's day extinct, except for manuscripts which had to be submitted to the censor and now survive, for the most part, in the Lord Chamberlain's collection of the British Library.

Michael R. Booth has urged that an attempt be made to view nineteenth-century drama in its larger social, economic, and theatrical contexts; and with respect to Wilde in particular, Joseph W. Donohue Jr. has argued for an interpretation of the plays that reconstructs them against their original background – the theatrical marketplace as a whole.[43] Donohue and James Ellis's huge microfiche collection of nineteenth-century plays, although still omitting most of the numerous dramas never published, is an indispensable tool for such "reconstructive" study.[44] Some of the best recent criticism of Wilde's plays — for example, that of Rodney Shewan and Katharine Worth — has discovered the considerable impression made on them by Restoration comedy, Shakespearean drama, and Wilde's own prior writing, while offering a tantalizing glimpse of the complex relations between Wilde and his contemporary playwrights.[45] Regenia Gagnier has analyzed the plays from a Marxist point of view as critiques of Victorian society – of their audiences – in which Wilde the outsider takes upon himself "the reflective apparatus of the dominant group" in order to mock it. Conventional elements in the dramas thus, in effect, "distract" the audience sufficiently to create an opening for Wilde's criticisms.[46] John Stokes has pointed out in *Resistible Theatres* the effect upon Wilde of the "aesthetic" stage-manager E. W. Godwin, who persuaded him of the scenic value of costume in productions staged by a manager who could be both artist and archeologist.[47] Thus the significance of forces outside a particular play – the operations of influence in a variety of senses – is suggested by a good deal of later scholarship on Wilde and nineteenth-century theatre generally.

But "all influence is immoral," says Lord Henry Wotton, who dominates Dorian Gray, "because to influence a person is to give him one's own soul . . . He becomes an echo of someone else's music, an actor of a part that has not been written for him."[48] Wilde, despite his boast that no other playwright influenced him even slightly, is no less the precursor's victim than Dorian himself. The hero of Wilde's novel slashes the canvas of his own portrait in a frantic denial of what Harry's influence has wrought; but it is a suicidal attack, for Dorian, at that stage of his life, cannot be divided from the influence he would negate. Wilde, anxious to guard his own independence as man and artist, happily did not go so far. To purge himself of influence would have produced on Wilde the dramatist a result as suicidal as that of Dorian's assault on his portrait. His plays depended for life upon dozens of now obscure but once well-known forerunners in the late Victorian theatre. Yet to be dominated was intolerable. The struggle was begun in *Lady Windermere's Fan* and carried on until the last scene of *The Importance of Being Earnest*. It is that strife and its mixed results which this book is meant to illuminate.

2

Lady Windermere's Fan *and the unmotherly mother*

A mother does not abandon her children
From *The Cross of Honour* (1892), a play by Arthur Shirley and Maurice Gally

I

Not long after the American actor-manager Lawrence Barrett had given *The Duchess of Padua* its first production, in New York in 1891, Wilde failed to persuade Henry Irving to produce the play at the Lyceum. George Alexander, who had left Irving's company to enter management himself and just taken over the St. James's Theatre, read and liked *The Duchess of Padua* but believed that, with its elaborate scenery, it would be too expensive to produce. Instead, Alexander paid Wilde £50 in advance to write a play on a modern subject. After delaying several months and offering to give the money back, Wilde at last finished *Lady Windermere's Fan* and read it aloud to Alexander one day late in 1891. "It is simply wonderful," the young actor-manager declared, and audiences who saw the play during its first engagement at the St. James's agreed.[1]

Wilde's first hit play was seen immediately as the offspring of earlier dramas. "Half a dozen plays," wrote one reviewer of *Lady Windermere's Fan*, "have been made to pay toll in entrance to its plot."[2] He did not name them, but other critics suggested at least that many – from *The School for Scandal* to *L'Etrangère* to a far-fetched melodrama called *The Red Lamp*.[3] Meanwhile the popular dramatist Sydney Grundy, in a newspaper interview, claimed he could not stage a revival of his own play *The Glass of Fashion* (1883) "because Mr. Oscar Wilde did so, under the title of *Lady Windermere's Fan*."[4]

Critics since have continued to recognize that *Lady Windermere's Fan* both reflected and helped stimulate the theatrical and literary fashion of its day. Like *The Second Mrs. Tanqueray* and *Mrs. Warren's Profession*, as Wendell Stacy Johnson has pointed out, *Lady Windermere's Fan* is concerned with "fallen women" devoted to "gaining or regaining the love of a daughter."[5] In Ibsen's *Ghosts*, first performed in London in the same year as

Lady Windermere's Fan, Mrs. Alving conceals the truth about his disreputable father from Oswald, just as Lord Windermere shields his wife from knowledge of her mother's scandalous past. Both plays, Katharine Worth observes, are concerned with "the horrific image of the past repeating itself."[6] Alan Bird notes that the subtitle of Wilde's play – *A Good Woman* – emphasizes a redefinition of morality similar to Hardy's in *Tess of the D'Urbervilles* (1891), subtitled *A Pure Woman*.[7]

Lady Windermere's Fan ironically reflects – as Shaw's *Candida* (1895) would in a different way – the old-fashioned domestic comedies in which a dandy or poet of "honeyed words" and "showy graces" nearly seduces the heroine from the strong, silent husband whom she must learn again to appreciate and love.[8] Like Lord Darlington in Wilde's play, the male intruders function as critics of society – from their viewpoint, writes Tom Taylor in *Victims* (1857), "sin looks heroic, and duty despicable."[9] Like his predecessors, Darlington's appeal in Wilde's play stems largely from his daring speech and dandy appearance, while Lord Windermere, the endangered husband, finds his ultimate resource in silence, like Mildmay in Tom Taylor's *Still Waters Run Deep* (1855). Windermere's power over the situation is best measured by what he leaves, by choice, unspoken: the scandal of Lady Windermere's mother. This protective silence, and the patriarchal authority it upholds (Windermere, not unusually, calls his wife "child"), in the end expels Darlington from the Victorian hearth he would profane. But Lady Windermere comes through these experiences, despite childlike ignorance of her true circumstances, embracing a morality quite alien – and superior, from Wilde's point of view – to that of her doggedly conventional husband. Unlike the husband in Shaw's *Candida*, Windermere remains ignorant of his wife's near seduction by an aesthetic intruder, yet his limitations are laid bare in a way that anticipates Shaw's exposure of the Reverend James Mavor Morell in *Candida*. Whereas the abused husband was wholly vindicated by Tom Taylor, in Shaw's and Wilde's plays he wins back his wife without winning the larger point. The "honeyed words" of Darlington and Marchbanks – calling into question the most fundamental values of the age – prevail intellectually while falling short of their aim romantically.

Most recent discussion of the play has centered on formal matters – whether Lady Windermere is enlightened or deluded at the end of the fourth act, whether Mrs. Erlynne's unmotherly behavior is justified, and whether the flippant wit of Cecil Graham really belongs in a drama concerned with serious issues of conduct.[10] But critics often allude to long-established antecedents of Wilde's play – especially the screen scene in *The School for Scandal* and the familiar "woman with a past" who dominates such "well-made" French plays as *La Dame aux camélias* and *Le Mariage d'Olympe*.[11] More generally, the story of *Lady Windermere's Fan* has been called "immortal" and related to "the French tradition."[12] On occasion one finds a particularly suggestive insight like Alan Bird's linking of *Lady Windermere's Fan* with the work of Haddon Chambers, "a writer now lost in the mists of oblivion."[13]

Those mists have engulfed not only Haddon Chambers, but other dramatists of the 1880s and 1890s whose plays disclose – even more than Chambers's, in some cases – a strange consanguinity with *Lady Windermere's Fan*. Critics in 1892 had a better but still fragmentary view of Wilde's relation to other playwrights. Although few failed to name one or two plays of which *Lady Windermere's Fan* reminded them, no one seems to have remembered the short-lived drama of less than two years earlier that it perhaps most resembles. And no one saw that Wilde's play, far from being founded upon a "source" or two, actually drew from, yet resisted, a curiously increasing number of plays depicting derelict mothers who abandon their husbands and children.

Wayward *fathers* had long been familiar figures in nineteenth-century literature, from Hindley Earnshaw to old Goriot to Michael Henchard. Persecuting or neglecting their children, such men distinctly contrasted with the morally idealized fathers of an earlier time like Squire Allworthy and eccentric but warm-hearted Walter Shandy. Evocative of trust and security in certain contexts, the father figure could seem threatening in a period characterized by social upheaval and lost belief.[14] A less familiar but complementary character was the undutiful mother, particularly the woman who, like Lady Dedlock or Becky Sharp, abandoned her child to secure her own position in a corrupt society. Such women, particularly on stage, became familiar figures in literature by the 1890s. In one play after another, both French and English, they are seen deserting their families, following their lovers, but returning home full of repentance at last. Nothing, however, atones for their having transgressed the most basic precepts of a woman's duty. They may repent – and usually do – but justice demands they die, with or without medical cause, or enter a convent at least. The extremity of their case invited the kind of clear-cut and melo-dramatic division of right and wrong which was increasingly difficult in the modern world. By 1892 – the year of *Lady Windermere's Fan* – the absconded mother was a stock character who could be relied upon for a tearful curtain and a nostalgic invocation of settled values and undisturbed norms of conduct.

With very few exceptions, plays dealing with this subspecies of the woman with a past have been long forgotten. But Oscar Wilde knew the type well, and his irreverent, yet intensely traditional handling of her story is in itself the best explanation of what he meant by *Lady Windermere's Fan*.

II

When it was first produced in February 1892, Wilde's play seemed to some critics reminiscent of its recent predecessor at the St. James's Theatre – *TheIdler* by C. Haddon Chambers. They remembered that in Chambers's play, as in *Lady Windermere's Fan*, a young wife visits the rooms of a raffish man who wants her to run away with him.[15] In both plays the husband calls at the critical moment; the wife hides behind a curtain, but gives herself away by forgetting to take her fan with her.[16] *The Idler*, however, with its story of a politician harboring a secret guilt, was actually more a harbinger of the yet-to-be-written *An Ideal Husband* than of *Lady Windermere's Fan*. Similarly the screen scene in *The School for Scandal* constitutes its most obvious resemblance to Wilde's play, and the same can be said for other dramas – such as *Françillon* by Dumas *fils* – which make use of that device.[17] The concealment motif, like the significance given to stage properties (fans, gloves, bouquets), was used by playwrights whose work was otherwise quite divergent.

Even the hidden-wife episode is handled by Chambers in a fashion different from Wilde's. The woman who conceals herself behind the curtain in *The Idler*, unlike Lady Windermere, is discovered by her husband and turns out to be innocent of wrongdoing. Apparently only Sydney Grundy (and possibly Oscar Wilde) remembered an earlier screen scene, closer in detail to that of *Lady Windermere's Fan*, which had appeared in Grundy's own play *The Glass of Fashion* (1883), written with G. R. Sims. In that society drama the young wife, Nina Trevanion, hides behind a curtain in the studio of Prince Borowski when her husband unexpectedly enters. But she absent-mindedly leaves behind her glove, which the husband sees and recognizes – just as in Wilde's play Lord Windermere spots the fan his wife left lying in Lord Darlington's rooms. Windermere dashes for the curtain, as Colonel Trevanion does in Grundy's oldest play, but at this crisis both men are diverted by a second woman who emerges to distract attention from the guilty wife. In Wilde's play it is Mrs. Erlynne who saves Lady Windermere by stepping forward to make herself seem the guilty party. In *The Glass of Fashion* the heroine's sister Peg sacrifices herself in the same way, allowing Nina to slip out undetected.[18]

The Glass of Fashion, which by 1892 had not been performed in nearly a decade, was unsurprisingly absent from reviews of *Lady Windermere's Fan* while the less germane but more recent *Idler* was named frequently as an influence. A resentful Grundy accused Wilde of plagiarism, but his charge was buried deep in a long interview with the *Era*.[19] In any event, not only does *Lady Windermere's Fan* run parallel to Grundy's play in details of the screen scene, it shares with the older play a story which concerns the plight of a young married woman of rank who in infancy was abandoned by her mother. Colonel Trevanion in Grundy's drama, like Lord Windermere in Wilde's, spares no effort to conceal from his wife the shocking identity of her long-lost mother, believed by the daughter in both plays to be dead. His elaborate evasions of the truth, however, place Trevanion, like

17

Windermere, in awkward positions which ironically lead his wife to suspect him of betraying her.

Grundy was right in believing *Lady Windermere's Fan* resembled his own play, but wrong to charge that Wilde simply took over *The Glass of Fashion* under a new name. Both works belonged to a growing number – mostly dramas, but including one notable novel by a friend of Wilde – which were founded upon the vagrant mother and abandoned daughter motifs. Some of these, like the perennially successful dramatizations of *East Lynne* – staged at least half a dozen times in London in 1891 and 1892 – dealt primarily with the delinquent mother. Others, like *The Glass of Fashion*, dwelled mostly on the neglected child. In some plays the estranged mother and daughter were about equally prominent, as in *Lady Windermere's Fan* and two French plays of the 1880s which Wilde probably knew – Victorien Sardou's *Odette*, adapted into English at the Haymarket in 1882 and again at the Princess's in 1894, and Jules Lemaître's *Révoltée*, apparently never performed in London or translated into English.[20] A usual wrinkle in these dramas, long before *Lady Windermere's Fan*, was for the daughter to desert her own family as her mother had abandoned hers. Such assaults upon the most fundamental ideals of family and social order are shown in nearly all these plays to be a tragic mistake. Shooting herself or contracting a disease is sometimes the only expiation a repentant mother can make, although in some cases she is permitted to work out her shame as a nurse or in a convent or even to rejoin her family after a scene of self-abasement before the wronged husband and child.

Frequently such plays are launched with an attempted seduction – sometimes of the unmotherly mother herself, sometimes of the daughter tempted to reenact the parent's fall. The dandiacal seducer, like Rafael di Rivola in Arthur Shirley's *Saved; or, a Wife's Peril* (1885), typically relies on unusual powers of speech to overcome the defenses of another man's wife. He encourages her jealousy or (as with di Rivola) points out how her husband neglects her. His appeals to the woman may be perfectly sincere, as in the case of di Rivola and Wilde's Lord Darlington, dandies whose armor of wit and cynicism has been pierced by love. Wives cannot resist them. Mistakenly jealous of another woman, Lady Isabel in *East Lynne* leaves a note for her husband and runs away with Francis Levison after suffering the disgrace of receiving her rival in her own home. Similarly Lady Windermere in Wilde's play, enraged at having to entertain the woman she imagines is her husband's lover, leaves a letter of farewell before running away to Lord Darlington. Sometimes these letters reach their destination, sometimes not. The first act of *East Lynne* ends with Lady Isabel's husband sunk in his chair, *"overcome by deep grief"* after reading her letter of explanation. In *Saved; or, a Wife's Peril* the erring wife writes a letter which, when he reads it, leaves her husband crying "Gone! Beatrice gone! ... May Heaven forgive her" as *"he sinks on knees"* to provide a strong curtain for the first act in the manner of *East Lynne*.[21] But in Wilde's play and in Lemaître's *Révoltée* the wife's note never arrives. In the French play the heroine's mother, who years ago abandoned her, seizes the letter, declares her true identity, and cries "Je ne veux pas, je ne veux pas que tu passes par où j'ai passé." In *Lady Windermere's Fan* Mrs. Erlynne intercepts her daughter's incriminating letter, reveals herself as Lady Windermere's lost mother, and cries, "Life doesn't repeat its tragedies like that!"[22]

In some plays the abandoned daughter has constructed an illusory ideal from the memory of a mother she has been told, falsely, is dead. Thus for Lady Windermere, informed by her father that her mother died "a few months after I was born," the lost parent has undergone an apotheosis in her mind. "We all have ideals in life," she says. "Mine is my mother" (p. 83). Young Bérangère in Sardou's *Odette*, first performed in 1881, finds herself in a parallel situation. Told when a child that her mother "était au ciel," she has cultivated ever since an ideal conception of the parent who, like Mrs. Erlynne in Wilde's play, deserted her for a lover. "Elle était si aimante, si devouée, si tendre," she imagines.[23] Both Lady Windermere and Bérangère unwittingly expound their mistaken ideals to women who are their actual, disreputable mothers – Mrs. Erlynne and Odette. And both daughters keep by them a miniature portrait of the "dead" mother which, for them, emblemizes her fine qualities. Bérangère proudly shows hers to Odette. Lord Windermere wishes aloud that his wife might show Mrs. Erlynne "a miniature she kisses every night before she prays" (p. 79), believing that it would shame the shameless mother – just as it did Odette in Sardou's play a decade ago.

A mother's desertion of her child seems in another play so basic an abrogation of good order that it is actually inconceivable. "A mother does not abandon her child," asserts the Countess de Bellegarde in a drama of 1890 called *The Cross of Honour*, explaining that she left her own child only because she was duped into thinking him dead.[24] In most cases the mother consciously abandons her child, but the maternal instinct reasserts itself in due course and leads the wayward woman home again, often in disguise. Lady Isabel, for example, returns to East Lynne under the name Madame Vine to serve her own children as governess. In *Revoltée* Madame de Voves first makes a friend of the daughter she abandoned years ago, then discloses their real relationship. In *Frou-Frou* (1869) the heroine returns home, dying of a vague malady, to fall on her knees before the husband and son she deserted. In *Odette*, as in *Lady Windermere's Fan*, the lost mother returns to her child without declaring who she really is. Both Odette and Mrs. Erlynne, deeply moved, decide to withdraw when they learn how their absent daughters have idealized them. Just before she departs, Odette tells Bérangère: "Cette image de votre mère que vous avez là dans votre coeur, conservez-la toujours aussi belle, aussi pure! Elle sera la gardienne de votre vie!"[25] Lady Windermere means to do the same.

"Only once in my life I have forgotten my own mother – that was last night," she tells Mrs. Erlynne, referring to the near elopement with Darlington. "Oh, if I had remembered her I should not have been so foolish, so wicked" (pp. 85–6). Similarly, in Arthur Shirley's *Saved; or, a Wife's Peril*, Beatrice Fane attributes her desertion of husband and daughter to the temporary neglect of her dead mother's memory – "I had forgotten her! I had forgotten her!" (p. 19).

The stirrings of latent maternal feeling which the women in these plays experience are not enough to redeem their error. They may succeed in getting a glimpse of the abandoned child, may even make their mother-hood known, but cannot elude the severe punishment – often death or banishment – which suits their crime. Even the heroine of *The Awakening*, another play of 1892, feels she must give up everything although guilty of nothing more than flirting. Repentant, Helen Peyton tearfully asks her husband to cast her away as he ought and take charge of their daughter. "And perhaps someday," she adds, "you will be able to forget it all and forgive me and let me die at home with you. Turn me away – I have been unworthy, and I deserve it."[26] In Shirley's *Saved*, Beatrice Fane cries to her wronged husband, "Let me kneel to you and kiss your hand for the blessing it bestows" – but he turns away and *"sternly points off"* (p. 20). The mother in *East Lynne* experiences her son dying in her arms without knowing who she is, then falls ill and dies herself. In *Révoltée* Madame de Voves must watch her son dying of wounds suffered in a duel which arose out of the complications of her own guilty past. "Frou-Frou, pauvre Frou-Frou," cries the title character of Meilhac and Halévy's play just before she dies at the final curtain.[27] In a melodrama of 1890, *This Woman and That*, the runaway wife Lady Agnes Ingleside shoots herself after being refused forgiveness by her husband. "To forgive you would still further degrade me in my own eyes," explains Sir George Ingleside. "I cannot."[28] Nor can Sardou forgive Odette, who drowns offstage in the fourth act.

To these scourged women, however, Mrs. Erlynne at the end of *Lady Windermere's Fan* bears little resemblance. She too has known belated maternal feeling, but unlike the others she scorns remorse, telling Windermere that "repentance is quite out of date" (p. 81). It costs her some anguish to part from her daughter a second time, but she does so to spare Lady Windermere's motherly ideal and to spare herself the perform-ance of an awkward and painful role. In a speech to her son-in-law, in which the stage direction notes that *"for a moment she reveals herself,"* Lady Windermere explicitly rejects one of the set scenes of this genre:

Oh, don't imagine I am going to have a pathetic scene with her, weep on her neck and tell her who I am, and all that kind of thing. I have no ambition to play the part of a mother. Only once in my life have I known a mother's feelings . . . They were

20

terrible – they made me suffer – they made me suffer too much . . . I want to live childless still.

(p. 80)

Until the last act Wilde followed the long-established precedent of plays dealing with the undutiful mother and abandoned child. Then he swerved. "The fourth act," he wrote in a letter, "is to me the psychological act, the act that is newest, most true."[29] Torn by conflicting emotions, Mrs. Erlynne declines to repent her unmaternal past and, what's more, gets away with it. The play concludes with her brilliant engagement to Lord Augustus Lorton – not with her shooting herself, falling fatally ill, or drowning. Not only does Mrs. Erlynne escape retribution and prosper, but the last line of the play, spoken by her daughter, characterizes her, with force, as "a very good woman!" Thus did Wilde work through the melodramatic formula, only to upset everything at the end by repudiating the categorical assumptions about right and wrong, sin and punishment, upon which this curious dramatic type was founded.

III

Lady Windermere's Fan also resembles a novel called *Eden*, written by Wilde's American friend Edgar Saltus and published in 1888. If Wilde read the book, as he is known to have read other works by the American "aesthete," he found in it a story and characters which in some respects look like a blueprint for the play he would write a few years later.[30] He would have seen in *Eden*, named after its heroine, a young wife who has stitched the motto "Keep Yourself Pure" for display in her bedroom. The moral rigidity of this inexperienced, aristocratic woman – along with the dramatic situation in which she is placed – makes her a figure more like Lady Windermere than could be claimed for almost any other heroine of the type.

Like Lady Windermere, Eden in the story by Saltus protests being asked by her husband to receive the woman she misconstrues as his mistress. As in Wilde's play, a cynical dandy uses this domestic breach to ingratiate himself with the wife, scheming to elope with her. Dugald Maule, twirling his moustache, also exhibits some of the epigrammatic flair of Wilde's Lord Darlington ("No one has any reputation, nowadays," he retorts when Eden charges him with having a "deplorable" one).[31] Encouraged by Maule, as Lady Windermere is by Darlington, Eden decides to leave her actually blameless husband John Usselex. "It was just such a thing as this that marred your mother's life," Eden's father warns her, "let it not mar your own."[32] Eden thus learns a little more of the truth than does Lady Windermere, but both women begin to reenact the calamity that befell their long-absent, mistily idolized mothers. Both leave farewell notes which, happily, their husbands never read, and both see their error in time to rejoin the family circle in the end.

What is missing in *Eden*, however, is the very thing toward which Wilde's play strives – the relaxation of an ossified standard of morality. Saltus never really challenges the militant purity of his heroine, who has stood at the edge of the precipice herself but learned nothing from it – at least nothing to raise qualms about her motto "Keep Yourself Pure" or the traditional rectitude which underlies it. *Eden*, despite its close similarities to *Lady Windermere's Fan* in certain respects, is comfortably at home in a pious genre that Wilde takes up with a mocking smile.

But one play – quickly forgotten after its London production in July 1890 – shows a still more surprising correspondence to *Lady Windermere's Fan*. Tried out as a matinee at the Strand Theatre, the "new and original play in three acts" called *Illusion*, by Pierre Leclerq, was yet another variation upon the vagrant-mother theme. Matinees, according to the *Era*, offered a way to test promising plays and encourage "the struggling dramatist" – a category in which Leclerq, despite his distinguished family ties, certainly belonged. The *Era* added: "The house at a matinee production is usually filled by artists who come to see brother and sister artists act" and "by the friends of the matinee-giver."[33] Whether Wilde himself was there when *Illusion* was performed cannot be determined. If not, the detailed likenesses between Leclerq's play and *Lady Windermere's Fan* show that even the smallest details of action and character in Wilde's drama fell within the province of the bad-mother play by the beginning of the 1890s. But there is reason to think this particular matinee might have drawn Wilde's interest. *Illusion* was acted by a stellar cast, several of whom would play a part in Wilde's own emerging theatrical career. They included the playwright's sister Rose Leclerq, later to create the roles of Lady Bracknell in *The Importance of Being Earnest* and Lady Hunstanton in *A Woman of No Importance*; Lewis Waller, the original Sir Robert Chiltern in *An Ideal Husband*; and Ibsenite actress Marion Lea, who on at least one occasion – soon after *Illusion* was given – wrote a personal invitation for Wilde to attend a performance of hers.[34]

The critic for the *Stage* commented that in this, his second play, Leclerq "was not strong enough for the flight he set himself," yet had written a work of promise, one "applauded throughout the progress, and most emphatically stamped with the final approval of the audience upon the fall of the curtain." The reviewer noted that the story of *Illusion*, although marred in the telling, "has in it elementary features that a dramatist of *finesse* would know how to treat to advantage, expanding here, repressing there, and revising in a general way."[35] Oscar Wilde, who could have seen *Illusion* on stage only a few months before he began to write *Lady Windermere's Fan*, became that "dramatist of *finesse*" to whom the *Stage* prophetically referred. It is no exaggeration to say that Wilde's play holds more in common with Leclerq's *Illusion* than with any other play of the kind, including Grundy's, Shirley's, and Sardou's. But *Lady Windermere's*

Fan and *Illusion*, parallel as they are for the most part, work toward sharply divergent effects in their closing scenes.

Una Revellin in Leclerq's unpublished play, like Lady Windermere, keeps the image of her lost mother before her as a maternal presence and guide:

Remember I have never known a mother's love and care – and oh, how I have hungered for it – yet from my childhood (*looking up devoutly*) I have whispered to her spirit, and I have – felt her answer.[36]

But in *Illusion*, as in *Lady Windermere's Fan*, the father has misled the daughter into believing her "sainted mother" dead – "a myth," as Una's father says, "to quiet the questions of her childhood" (Act I, p. 13). In both plays the heroine becomes suspicious of her husband's association with an aging beauty of scandalous reputation who, in due course, is revealed as her own mother. And Una, like Lady Windermere, celebrates her birthday in Act I, receiving a gift from her husband (flowers rather than a fan) which is spoiled by her jealousy of the older woman.[37] Lady Windermere is enraged because the disreputable Mrs. Erlynne – actually her mother – has been asked to the birthday celebration, so much so that at the end of Act I she threatens to strike her with the fan. Una Revellin, by comparison, is seen at the end of Act I staring disconsolately at the flowers her husband gave her on her birthday – a gift spoiled by the knowledge that he also sent flowers to the infamous woman called La Faneuse (her own mother, unknown to Una). Neither heroine sees any alternative to breaking with her husband, thus ironically reenacting the error of her mother. "Our married life is at an end," cries Una Revellin to John (Act I, p. 17). "From this moment my life is separate from yours," declares Lady Windermere to Lord Windermere (p. 27).

After abandoning husband and infant daughter, both women – "horrid" Mrs. Erlynne and "vile" Faneuse – return to England many years later to vex the marriage of the child they never knew. Each proceeds to view the deserted child without disclosing who she is. At long last Mrs. Erlynne knows, as she says, "a mother's feelings" and discovers that she has a "heart" after all (p. 80). La Faneuse, in language more pathetic, belatedly discovers "a mother's feelings" too:

My child! Yes, I left her . . . but I feel her little fingers – on my bosom now, so plainly! I feel her tiny arms that I unwound from me – for ever – still clinging about me! Oh!

(Act III, p. 11)

Torn between this new affection for their daughters and the desire not to shame or disillusion them, Mrs. Erlynne and La Faneuse determine to keep the secret of their maternity and be content with small consolations. Mrs. Erlynne asks for a photograph of Lady Windermere; La Faneuse asks for pictures that her daughter Una has painted.

Both Blanche Faneuse and Margaret Erlynne are about forty years old. "She'll never see thirty-eight again, you know," says one of the men in *Illusion*, adding that La Faneuse claims to be "only thirty now!" (Act III, p. 3). Mrs. Erlynne in Wilde's play says she admits to being "thirty at the most. Twenty-nine when there are pink shades" (p. 80). The worldliness of these graying sirens is further developed in their wit, although in this respect Leclerq's lapsed mother is but a faint anticipation of Wilde's. "Oh! how you have been criticizing me, with the uncharitableness of all true Christians!" says La Faneuse, entering a room full of chattering guests at her home in St. John's Wood (Act III, p. 5). Mrs. Erlynne's verbal thrusts of this sort are somewhat bolder and brighter: "If a woman really repents, she has to go to a bad dressmaker, otherwise no one believes her. And nothing in the world would induce me to do that" (p. 81).

Thus Mrs. Erlynne and La Faneuse, like female Dorian Grays, present a front of youthful insouciance which conceals their real age and state of mind. Behind the mask lies a festering guilt. "Oh! I have been vile," cries La Faneuse, who in reality can find no excuse for her past, not even the fact that her husband had been "harsh, mercenary, cruel" (Act III, p. 10). Mrs. Erlynne adopts the same tone when she urges Lady Windermere not to leave her family for Lord Darlington:

Believe what you choose about me. I am not worth a moment's sorrow . . . Back to your house, Lady Windermere – your husband loves you! He has never swerved for a moment from the love he bears you. But even if he had a thousand loves, you must stay with your child. If he was harsh with you, you must stay with your child. If he ill-treated you, you must stay with your child. If he abandoned you, your place is with your child.

(pp. 57–8)

Here, in Act III of *Lady Windermere's Fan*, Wilde comes perilously close to letting his delinquent-mother character subside into mere imitation of Blanche Faneuse and others like her. In fact Mrs. Erlynne's homily is a maudlin compost of Leclerq and *East Lynne*, in which Lady Isabel rants:

Oh, lady, wife, mother! Whatever trials may be the lot of your married life . . . resolve to bear them . . . Bear them unto death, rather than forget your good name and your good conscience.[38]

Those in Wilde's audiences who had seen *East Lynne* or *Illusion* or other such plays must have feared by this point that Mrs. Erlynne would imitate her predecessors in the fourth act too – perhaps by expiring in the arms of a forgiving daughter, drowning in the sea, or seeking peace in a convent.

In *Illusion* Blanche Faneuse cries:

Una! I dare not raise my eyes to you – I am that wretched creature La Faneuse, I am your mother! God pity me! God pity me!

(Act III, p. 13)

There follows the scene which Mrs. Erlynne scorns in Wilde's play. After recovering from a swooning fit, Una folds her mother in her arms and forgives her, weeping. The errant mother rains tears on her daughter's neck and tells her, in Mrs. Erlynne's disdainful phrase, "who I am, and all that kind of thing." In her last scene La Faneuse appears in a severe black costume – the work, no doubt, of the "bad dressmaker" to whom repentant women must go in *Lady Windermere's Fan*:

My costume till I die! . . . Yes! I have disposed of all I possess to found a home for others who have been as I have been, who would be as I will be. I am penniless! Thank God! . . . My past is black! My future shall whiten it!

(Act III, pp. 18–19)

To stay with Una is out of the question, morally, but her mother vaguely hopes that they can meet again when she has suffered more.

Although Mrs. Erlynne qualifies for admission to the "home" which La Faneuse will found, she cannot be imagined going there. "Repentance," as she tells Windermere, "is quite out of date." And even though she knows at last "a mother's feelings," her aesthetic nature recoils from the "pathetic scene" in which she would weep over her daughter, "tell her who I am, and all that kind of thing." The speech in which *"for a moment she reveals herself"* shows a woman stricken with guilt but preferring to "live childless still" in spite of the love she has learned to feel for her long-lost daughter. Her complex state of mind is what justifies Wilde's own estimate that his fourth act "is to me the psychological act, the act that is newest, most true."

Perhaps *Illusion* was on his mind as an example of the "old" mode of writing such plays when he shaped a different outcome for Mrs. Erlynne. One key speech of hers, interestingly, uses the word *illusion* pointedly and echoes La Faneuse's ardent desire to keep her identity secret from her daughter:

No, as far as I am concerned, let your wife cherish the memory of this dead, stainless mother. Why should I interfere with her illusion? I find it hard enough to keep my own. I lost one illusion last night. I thought I had no heart. I find I have, and a heart doesn't suit me, Windermere. Somehow it doesn't go with modern dress. It makes one look old.

(p. 80)

Her feelings are not so callously uncomplicated as her speech makes them out to Windermere, who is filled "with horror – with absolute horror" by what she says. There is a measure of self-sacrifice in her behavior of which the son-in-law is unaware, and her plans to walk out of her daughter's life a second time are motivated by a concern for Lady Windermere as well as for herself.

But she explicitly rejects the finale of *Illusion* in which La Faneuse comes on in the black garb of a "nurse" with the intention of founding a conventual retreat for undutiful mothers:

I suppose, Windermere, you would like me to retire into a convent, or become a hospital nurse, or something of that kind, as people do in silly modern novels.

(pp. 80–1)

Early typescript versions of *Lady Windermere's Fan* add "and silly French plays" to the end of this sentence, as Ian Small points out in his edition of the play (p. 81). Perhaps Wilde had in mind Meilhac and Halévy's *Frou-Frou*, in which the repentant mother turns to nursing the sick and contemplates entering a convent – "il y a des couvents . . . Tenez . . . tout près d'ici," Gilberte muses remorsefully (p. 44).

Instead of applying to La Faneuse's "home" for bad mothers, Mrs. Erlynne turns her charms upon hapless Lord Augustus Lorton, who will make her his wife – rescuing her from motherhood and England with its "demmed clubs, demmed climate, demmed cooks, demmed everything" (p. 88).[39] Mrs. Erlynne thus passes from the stage with wealth and a title before her instead of seeking out a convent or house of refuge. Her career has so disturbed the familiar balance of right and wrong that the last line of the play pronounces her "a good woman." But it is spoken by Lady Windermere, whose estimate of Mrs. Erlynne as "good" is only marginally more informed than her earlier opinion that she was "bad." Actually Mrs. Erlynne is worse than she imagines now, just as she was better than she imagined then. In this fashion, Wilde's fourth act skewers the melodramatic morality upon which plays like *Illusion* were founded.

IV

From one point of view it is regrettable that Wilde gave in to those who urged him to inform the audience earlier than the fourth act that Mrs. Erlynne was really Lady Windermere's mother. He summed up the argument against doing so in a letter to George Alexander, manager of the St. James's Theatre and Lord Windermere in the first production, who had himself asked for such a change:

With regard to your . . . suggestion about the disclosure of the secret of the play in the second act, had I intended to let out the secret, which is the element of suspense and curiosity, a quality so essentially dramatic, I would have written the play on entirely different lines. I would have made Mrs. Erlynne a vulgar, horrid woman and struck out the incident of the fan. The audience must not know till the last act that the woman Lady Windermere proposed to strike with her fan was her own mother. The note would be too harsh, too horrible.[40]

Wilde thus wanted to disengage from the delinquent-mother myth its most melodramatic, exaggerated effects, preferring an approach in which the "harsh" and the "horrible" would be allayed in order to see the whole matter in a new light. But the press, like Alexander, wanted the cruder and more traditional arrangement in which the audience identifies the mother

26

before it has an opportunity to know and understand her. "Throughout the play the audience remain ignorant of the real position and antecedents of Mrs. Erlynne," complained the *Era*. "Had they been let into the secret at the commencement that this fast and cynical woman was the mother of the heroine, what a gain it would have been to the dramatic interest, and how greatly it would have enhanced the effect of the scenes between mother and daughter."[41] Wilde relented, and soon Mrs. Erlynne was speaking near the end of the second act in a way to make her maternal relation to Lady Windermere plain. History has portrayed Wilde as being satisfied with this alteration, but on at least one occasion Alexander was persuaded to try the play again as Wilde had written it – although the record of this experiment seems to have been overlooked. "The result," said the *Era* confidently in March 1892, "confirmed Mr. Alexander's original judgment: the play did not go down nearly so well."[42]

Perhaps the only other play of this kind in which the mother's identity is withheld until the last act is, oddly enough, Leclerq's *Illusion*. In this case, as in Wilde's, the critics were not impressed. The reviewer for the *Times* was "perplexed" by the first two-thirds of the play, and the *Era* reproved Leclerq for having kept "his audience too long in the dark as to the real condition of affairs."[43] This was precisely the criticism that the *Era* would make of *Lady Windermere's Fan* one year and a half later – without mentioning *Illusion* at all. But keeping the mother's secret from the audience served no real purpose in Leclerq's play, which works to a conclusion no less melodramatic, perhaps more so, than usual for this species of drama. Of all the surprising similarities between *Lady Windermere's Fan* and *Illusion*, however, it is withholding of the mother's identity that serves Wilde best – by softening the "harsh" and "horrible" elements which would deter his aim of showing how a conventionally "bad" woman is in some sense (as the play's original title put it) "a good woman" after all. All this provides at least some basis for printing the play in accordance with early drafts rather than submitting – as Wilde reluctantly did for the stage production and the first edition of 1893 – to the argument that dramatic effect requires early disclosure of the secret.

Despite its pervading similarities with *Illusion*, however, *Lady Windermere's Fan* can be traced to no single source at all. In the most general way it derives, as Morse Peckham has pointed out, from the "well-made plays" of the period and their women with a past – women like Marguerite Gautier and Olympe Taverny, who struggle to "get back," as Mrs. Erlynne puts it, and leave a scandalous past behind them.[44] But Wilde's play more accurately belongs to a tributary of this type of drama, the mostly unknown, reactionary pieces which found in the vagrant mother and abandoned child an opportunity to affirm, in a time of unsettling changes, certain basic precepts about social order and sexual behavior. *Lady Windermere's Fan* is outfitted with a veritable lexicon of characters, situations and motifs pertaining to such plays – the young wife who suspects her husband of having an affair with another woman (sometimes her own mother), the dandified and epigrammatic seducer who nearly succeeds in winning her from her family to reenact her mother's sin, and the returning and repentant mother herself, who may (as in *Illusion*) or may not (as in *Odette*) make herself known to the daughter. Wilde's play shares with others the daughter's dreamy idealizing of her vanished mother, her penning a farewell letter to the husband, her puritanical standards of conduct. Even features of *Lady Windermere's Fan* which might seem unrelated to the lost-mother myth turn out to have precedent in these plays – the allusions to photographs, flowers, and pictures; the daughter's birthday celebration; the fan itself; even Mrs. Erlynne's pretense of being thirty when she is really forty. The difference is that Wilde uses more of these devices than most authors, and he uses them, after a period of indecision which nearly sinks the play, to a radically different end.

In its final act *Lady Windermere's Fan* is subtle, dramatic, and (just as Wilde claimed) psychologically "new," or at least up-to-date. At the end it is the worthy companion of two theatrical successes of the period which, like Wilde's first comedy, took up the errant-mother motif only to explode the conventional morality which it usually bolstered. In *A Doll's House* Ibsen had scandalized London theatregoers with a story which ended where most plays about child-abandoning mothers began. Nora Helmer, observing that she has "duties towards myself," refuses to be a "doll-wife" any longer and leaves Torvald and her children to fend for themselves.[45] It is not Nora's leaving her family which makes *A Doll's House* so interesting a departure from the past; rather, it is her leaving husband and children without melodramatic self-accusation and retribution, in service of an ideal which leaves traditional notions of womanly duty in the dust. In *Mrs. Warren's Profession*, which George Bernard Shaw wrote two years after *Lady Windermere's Fan* played at the St. James's, the undutiful mother is a prostitute and brothel-keeper who left her daughter to be reared by other hands. Her fault, however, is not her "profession" – for a poor woman in an exploitative society, "it's far better than any other employment."[46] Her real failing is that beneath her idol-shattering corruption she is a conventional woman after all.

Most plays about unconventional mothers were written by men, and with notable exceptions – Shaw's, Ibsen's, and to a degree Wilde's – they use the genre to shore up prevailing notions of woman's place; namely, that her destiny is inseparable from the roles of wife and mother. When such plays were written by women, however, they sometimes adopted an entirely different perspective on the issue of female duty. In women's plays, mothers abandon, even slay, their offspring for good cause – because their children deserve it, or because such apparent harshness is really best for both mother and child. In Mrs. Crackanthorpe's unpublished and unstaged *The Turn of the Wheel* (1901), banned by the censor, a mother abandons her illegitimate infant son without remorse. In response to pleas that she visit or at least take an interest in "it," Isabel Broadwood, the heroine, is unmoved. She replies, in words impossible to be spoken on an English stage of the time:

> Talk to me of *it* – the child you mean I suppose? Why how ignorant you are. How conventional – I care nothing for the child – I don't even care enough for it to hate it. Let it live, let it die, what does it signify to me? It's not me – it's not part of me I tell you – I've done with it. I'm myself again, and I'm never going to be reminded by you or by anyone else of what is not me – *is not me,* do you hear?[47]

The child grows up years later into a dissolute, unpleasant youth who makes jokes about his "long lost mother." Despite a somewhat conventional ending, *The Turn of the Wheel* leaves an unmistakable impression that motherhood is by no means worth the price it exacts. The militant tone is not far removed from that of a radical feminist like Mona Caird, whom no censor could forbid to write in the novel *The Daughters of Danaus* (1894): "A woman with a child in her arms is, to me, that symbol of an abasement, an indignity, more complete, more disfiguring and terrible, than any form of humiliation that the world has ever seen."[48]

In the unpublished *Mrs. Daintree's Daughter*, licensed in 1894 and written by actress Janet Achurch – the first Nora in an English production of *A Doll's House* – the adventuress and businesswoman Leila Daintree has grown wealthy in operating a gambling den that, although she denies it, looks suspiciously like a house of prostitution as well. Like Mrs. Warren in Shaw's play, this entrepreneur has spent her labor to make an easy life for the daughter (named Violet in Achurch's play, Vivie in Shaw's) whom she has had reared in protective seclusion at a great distance from herself. But this "daughter of Arcadia" is an entirely worthless person, lacking most of the vital qualities of Shaw's Vivie Warren except ruthless ambition. Achurch's Violet is not only subjected to the machinations of her mother's sinister business partner, but, unlike Vivie in Shaw's play, willingly cooperates by going wholeheartedly into the business herself. Violet, like Vivie, rejects an established scene of the genre when she declines to kiss her long-absent mother – instead, the stage direction reads, *"VIOLET pauses – shrugs her shoulders and goes out."*[49] Her last action in the play is to poison her mother with an overdose of morphia – convincing evidence that Mrs. Daintree was not so much mistaken in having left the child as in returning to her fourteen years later. In plays by women, then, the rejection of motherhood is often made to seem a necessary and even desirable step. Thus Elizabeth Robins and Mrs. Hugh Bell, in *Alan's Wife*, produced by the Independent Theatre in 1893, create a woman who kills her deformed child as an act of kindness and strength.[50]

At times, perhaps most of the time, *Lady Windermere's Fan* belongs in the company of plays by women and by Ibsen and Shaw that give the story of the unconventional, "undutiful" mother a new telling. At the same time, however, the play never completely transcends predecessors like *Saved; or, a Wife's Peril* and *East Lynne*. Mrs. Erlynne's advice to her daughter to bear patiently whatever domestic misery befalls her is an echo not only of *East Lynne*, but Victorian conduct books like Mrs. Ellis's *The Daughters of England* (1845), which counsels unhappy wives "to suffer and be still."[51] Lady Windermere is what Martha Vicinus has termed the "perfect lady" of Victorian times, combining "sexual innocence, conspicuous consumption, and the worship of the family hearth."[52] She must have seemed extremely old-fashioned even to the play's original audience, for by the 1890s, as Vicinus has shown, women – single as well as married – were breaking free of the stereotype which had made them "perfect" Victorian ladies. Women had become leaders in philanthropic and other social endeavors; they attended universities, if in small numbers; and the literature written for them, and often by them, forthrightly discussed free love, frigidity, and venereal disease.[53] Clearly Lady Windermere belongs to the reactionary band who opposed what Margaret Oliphant scornfully referred to as the "anti-marriage" tendencies in such writers as Thomas Hardy and Grant Allen – tendencies that cast over the Victorian drawing room itself an unwholesome atmosphere: "Things are discussed freely and easily which it would a few years ago have been a shame to mention or think of."[54] Lord Darlington – a refugee in spirit from Restoration comedy, a Dorimant who lives for wit and pleasure – must finally be suspect for having loved Lady Windermere at all, as Rodney Shewan has pointed out.[55] Yet such a play as *Lady Windermere's Fan* required just such a character – the Victorian stage villain, like Rafael di Rivola in Shirley's *Saved*, whose dandy exterior is punctured by love. He was the Victorian stage villain, and his type was everywhere. "He wears a clean collar and smokes a cigarette," explains Jerome K. Jerome in *Stage-Land* (1890), and his love for the heroine is "sublime in its steadfastness."[56]

Mrs. Erlynne also belongs to a distinct type – in company with women like La Faneuse of *Illusion*. Jerome, in his mocking survey of late Victorian stage fashion, calls her the "adventuress." Such women are likely to come from, or be associated with, a foreign land ("they do not make bad women in England"). They are businesslike, dress magnificently, and speak with witty sarcasm. The adventuress is "alive," Jerome concedes. "She can do something to help herself besides calling for 'George.' " Furthermore, "She has not got a Stage child – if she ever had one, she has left it on somebody else's doorstep."[57] Yet this is the woman who, at a critical moment in Wilde's play, urges the unhappy wife (as Mrs. Ellis said) "to suffer and be still." This ambivalence in Wilde's conception of the character, of the play itself, perhaps accounts for the markedly different assessments that critics have offered of Mrs. Erlynne. For Christopher Nassaar, being bad is for Mrs. Erlynne "far more comfortable than being good."[58] Yet Epifanio San Juan Jr. finds that Mrs. Erlynne proves herself "a genuine mother in feeling" in sacrificing herself for her daughter's happiness.[59] There is truth on both sides. Showing the "bad" mother to be a "good" mother at heart was an effect deeply rooted in the genre Wilde had taken up. It was this complex mixture to which *East Lynne* itself owed something of its powerful appeal – audiences wept, after all, when the errant Lady Isabel died.[60]

The weakness of *Lady Windermere's Fan* – and here it suffers by comparison with Ibsen's and Shaw's plays – is that for the first three acts it is very nearly drawn into the vortex of the fallen-mother myth it subverts. For a time Mrs. Erlynne seems little better than a reincarnation of Lady Isabel in *East Lynne*, damning herself by the inflexible moral rule which in the end she has the nerve to defy. Indeed Mrs. Erlynne's name itself may be an echo of the older play – without the "r" it would be spelled "E lynne." In an early draft, as Ian Small points out in his edition of *Lady Windermere's Fan*, the mother-character's name is "Mrs. Alwynne" (pp. xxix–xxx). Wilde changed her name to "Erlynne" in later drafts as the play evolved thematically into a direct challenge of "good" and "bad" women as inscribed in a host of plays in the tradition of *East Lynne*.

In the early acts, nevertheless, Wilde seems on his way to the kind of ending composed for *East Lynne* and *Illusion*, awash in tears, self-imprecation, and renunciation. At that point the main anchor against such a fatal drift is a part of the play often denounced as irrelevant – the rich epigrammatic wit issuing from such characters as Darlington and the Duchess of Berwick. "There are lots of people who say I have never really done anything wrong in the whole course of my life," says Darlington. "Of course they only say it behind my back" (p. 13). Such remarks, with their ambush of conventional wisdom, pave the way for the "new" material of the fourth act and the upsetting of deeply rooted notions in a different way. The language of Darlington and Cecil Graham functions as "a relief," says Reginia Gagnier, "in a society in which serious language inevitably entails deceit, self-deception, or hypocrisy."[61] Perhaps, though, from Wilde's point of view, the dandies could not have it all their own way if *Lady Windermere's Fan* was to succeed with its audience. Wilde has something new to say, but "getting away with it" would mean extravagant and even (where the play was concerned) damaging concessions to sentiment, self-sacrifice, and all the other mangled values of a society that worshipped at the shrine of Victorian motherhood.[62]

In a sense *Lady Windermere's Fan*, like many of Wilde's works, is an epigram writ large, whose force and wit derive from the antithesis of expectation. But epigrams are incompatible with sentiment and convention, and intrusions of that sort give Wilde's first comedy an ambivalence which in the final analysis injures it – but not mortally. Its final act completes a clever, but hesitating reversal of a retrograde theatrical genre. Wilde thereby fleshes out, from the dry bones of forgotten plays like *Illusion* and *The Glass of Fashion*, a work that is, in a strangely limited sense, his own.

3

Salomé, *the censor, and the divine Sarah*

Why in French?

Graham Robertson, when Oscar Wilde began to read from his new play

There is much, I think, in it that is beautiful, much lovely writing – I almost wonder Oscar doesn't dramatize it.

Max Beerbohm, on *Salomé*

I

Modern criticism has made *Salomé* one of the most copiously annotated of all Oscar Wilde's works and accorded it a respect which at first it was rarely paid. It has been called Wilde's second-greatest achievement in drama,[1] and "the one unquestionable masterpiece of the English decadence."[2] Yet the discussion of *Salomé* has not yielded final or even satisfying answers to some of the most obvious and pertinent questions which its strange career suggests. Why did Wilde write the play in French? How could he have gone into the third week of rehearsal when the subject matter appeared certain to arouse the censor and make performance impossible? Is *Salomé* a triumph of Wilde's dramatic art or, as one French critic has abruptly put it, "one of the most famous and one of the worst of his works"?[3]

Complicating any verdict on *Salomé* is the fact that few in the English-speaking world have seen it performed, the one-act piece having been banned by the Lord Chamberlain until 1931 and staged infrequently since. At a time when religious drama as mild as *Everyman* could not be produced, Edward F. S. Pigott, the Examiner of Plays, wondered aloud that Wilde had submitted for licensing a drama "half Biblical, half pornographic."[4] Everyone knew of the rule forbidding the dramatization of Scripture, even the quoting of it on stage, although in the Age of Ibsen some disagreed with it. Henry Arthur Jones, in an article of 1895 called "The Bible on Stage," regretted bitterly that scriptural stories "such as those of Saul, David, Joseph and his brethren," and the like could not be staged, no matter how reverently, thanks to the "virtuous dwellers in Peckham and Camberwell" and the circumspect censor.[5] William Archer knew – as soon as he learned in mid-June 1892 that *Salomé* was scheduled as part of Sarah Bernhardt's London season – that the suppression of the play was "inevitable."[6] Yet Wilde appeared astonished when *Salomé* – not only an adaptation from the Bible, but hardly reverent – was refused a license. Noting that "costumes, scenery, and everything has been prepared," that rehearsals were far advanced, he told interviewers the censor's action was "a great disappointment" which would make it impossible for him to tarry longer in England. He would go to Paris, "that vivid centre of art, where religious dramas are often performed."[7]

The biblical background of the play, in itself, might have passed the censor in a decade in which, in *The Notorious Mrs. Ebbsmith*, Pinero got away with having a Bible thrown into the fire. But the presentation of sexual matters in *Salomé* was a complicating factor. The heroine not only shatters Victorian conceptions of womanhood, she actually pursues "sex for sex's sake, without purpose or production," and in so doing "subverts the laws and authority of the Tetrarch and the Kingdom."[8] In her unrelenting insistence upon controlling her own sexuality, Salomé attacks the very foundation of patriarchal culture with murderous female energy – an attack, it has been suggested, with which Wilde sympathizes even as he recoils from it as artist and male (as its victim, that is).[9] Perhaps, also, there is something in Wilde's characterization of Salomé which reflects what Karen Horney has called the "dread of woman" – an "energetically repressed," yet integral part of masculine existence and behavior.[10] Salomé belongs as well in the company of those demon-women whom Nina Auerbach finds so pervasive in Victorian culture, the other face, as it were, of the "angel in the house," whose powers constituted an implicit challenge to the patriarchal family and state, as well as to God the Father.[11] These subversive characteristics of *Salomé* probably had their share in producing the censor's flabbergasted reaction to it.

Perhaps unconsciously, Wilde scripted his own victimization by authority in the *Salomé* matter – just as he would in bringing the catastrophic libel action against the Marquess of Queensberry four years later. There were measures – obvious ones in 1892 – that he might have taken to secure the right of performance for *Salomé*, but these, so far as can be told, Wilde never attempted. In testimony before a parliamentary committee in late May 1892, just days before he anathematized *Salomé*, Pigott emphasized that he welcomed "personal intercourse" with managers and authors "to avoid unnecessary friction" and remove obstacles which stood in the way of licensing. His successor, George Alexander Redford, who invoked with respect the traditions he learned under Pigott, allowed Richard Strauss's operatic version of *Salomé* to be produced in 1910 with only cosmetic editing. Conflicts of this sort were routinely negotiated, Pigott said, in "private correspondence and private interviews" in which he "talked the thing over with the authors."[12] Instead of negotiating, Wilde publicly denounced the Examiner as an inept and "commonplace" official, thus destroying, in all probability, any chance of producing the play in England.

Pigott's testimony on this issue, buried in old newspaper columns, has gone largely unopened. Beyond doubt, however, Wilde was aware of an alternative course, although one with less opportunity for posturing as the victim of officialdom. Only two months earlier he was involved in a three-sided negotiation with the Examiner of Plays and Charles H. E. Brookfield and James E. Glover – authors of *The Poet and the Puppets*, a travesty on Wilde himself. Hearing that he was mentioned by name in Brookfield and Glover's musical parody, Wilde took his grievance directly to Pigott, complaining of objectionable references to himself. Glover, co-author of *The Poet and the Puppets*, recalled that Wilde "appealed to E. S. Pigott [*sic*], the licenser of plays, and insisted on our reading him the libretto." Word was passed to the authors, who accordingly read their play to Wilde, who all the while puffed on a cigar and reacted with good humor while making clear that some changes would be insisted upon. "What Wilde really objected to was the inclusion of his own name," Glover recollected, and so "to please the Licenser of Plays" it was deleted from the script."[13] *The Poet and the Puppets*, blue-pencilled through Wilde's connivance with the censor, was being performed at the Comedy Theatre at the very time Pigott received the manuscript of *Salomé* for licensing. If Wilde knew the ways of the Lord Chamberlain's office well enough to force censorship upon other authors, it is difficult to accept the persistent notions that he held deep convictions against censorship or that he was naive about the standards by which the Examiner of Plays awarded licenses.

Against this background the question of the play's having been written in a foreign language takes on new interest. "How came you to write *Salomé* in French?" inquired one of the reporters to whom the author spoke during the stir caused by the censor's ban. Wilde immediately fell into the lacquered elegance he used when being less than candid, whether in the courtroom or in conversation. He wrote in the French language, he responded, because "I wanted once to touch this new instrument to see whether I could make any beautiful thing out of it."[14] But there were better reasons – at least more urgently practical ones – for not writing *Salomé* in English. Wilde, like everyone else in the theatre of the 1890s, knew that the Examiner of Plays permitted works in French to get away with more – much more – than plays written in English. There was the added, and by no means trivial, consideration that Sarah Bernhardt did not speak English.

II

Wilde was not the only one surprised by the censor's banning of *Salomé*. The *Era* offered the sardonic reflection that the ruling "raises an entirely new point in the ethics of licensing. It has hitherto been held that the drama in England was free to deal with every conceivable subject – on the one trifling condition that it dealt with it in French."[15] Almost a year later the *Era* was still shaking its head over the Lord Chamberlain's decision. Under the headline "Oscar Wilde's Curtain-Raiser" it ran a leader, prompted by book publication of *Salomé*, asking what the censor was thinking of when he banned a religious play written in French:

After reading *Salomé*, which has just been published by the Librairie de l'Art Indépendant, Paris, we cannot exactly understand upon what principle the piece was prohibited . . . If Mr. Wilde or anyone else can find interesting and dramatic material in such an incident as John the Baptist's death – an incident which has been over and over again the subject of pictures and poems – we see no reason why – especially if veiled in the decent obscurity of a foreign language – an interesting experiment like the performance of *Salomé* should not have been allowed to be tried.[16]

The *Era* might have added, although it did not, that *Salomé* scarcely would have been the first religious drama to be staged in London "in the decent obscurity of a foreign language." Covent Garden had been "filled from floor to ceiling," the *Times* reported, for a performance of Giacomo Meyerbeer's opera *Le Prophète*, staged at Covent Garden in 1890 and again in late June 1892, the very time when the Examiner of Plays was sitting in judgment on *Salomé*.[17] Sarah Bernhardt herself, who would have played Salomé at the Royal English Opera House, had just appeared in the role of the saint in Jules Barbier's *Jeanne d'Arc*, listening, said the *Times*, with a "rapt and ecstatic air" to voices from Heaven.[18]

Not only in matters religious, but sexual as well, the censor applied a double standard to plays written in English and those in French. The *Era* reflected splenetically on this state of affairs two years after the banning of *Salomé*, in June 1894, pointing out that a current production at Daly's Theatre, starring Eleonora Duse in a comedy by Sardou, would not have been tolerated in English:

It is doubtful whether anything has ever been done on any modern stage as indecent as this last act of *Divorçons*; and we very much wonder whether, had an original English piece of equal piquancy with the very much modified version used by Signora Duse at Daly's been submitted to Mr. Pigott, he would have thought for a moment of licensing it. The French author may steal a horse while the English playwright is hanged for looking over the hedge.[19]

Thus an adaptation of a French play might be forbidden by the strict standards regulating plays in English – as happened with Sydney Grundy and Joseph Mackay's *A Novel Reader* – while the censor would grant routinely a license for "one of the most openly indecent of modern French comedies." *Divorçons* only had to be acted in a foreign language to win the exemption – or be adapted into watered-down English versions such as

Charles H. E. Brookfield's *To-day* (1892) and Herman C. Merivale's *The Queen's Proctor* (1896).

The *Era's* accusations were grounded in obvious fact, not inference, for the Examiner of Plays made no secret of the unequal justice by which licenses were awarded to dramas in French and English. Pigott, in testimony before a select committee of the House of Commons in 1892, shortly before he banned *Salomé*, frankly acknowledged that a double standard existed. He justified it in terms of the expectations of theatrical audiences:

With regard to French plays, my principle has always been to extend to them an extra-territorial privilege. People who go to see French plays, played by French companies and written for French purposes, know what they are going to see. The plays are always submitted to me, and I am extremely indulgent in regard to them.[20]

The censor's testimony, strangely enough, came just a few weeks before his refusal to license *Salomé* – a French play to have been acted by a French company. If *Salomé* was "half pornographic" as well as "half Biblical," its being written in French should have excused both offenses. Wilde was too canny to submit such a play to the Lord Chamberlain's office in the English language, for the signs of the time made its rejection certain. But written in French, *Salomé's* suppression was perhaps not nearly as "inevitable" as Archer had imagined. The reporter who asked Wilde "How came you to write *Salomé* in French?" was never really answered, but the obscure details of the censor's methods in 1892 suggest that Wilde was availing himself of a well-known loophole. Although not the only comical aspect of the play, *Salomé's* being written in French was from the first, or at some point became, an elaborate joke on the censorship of the stage and a practical response to the difficulties it presented to a playwright concerned with forbidden subjects. Unfortunately, and against reasonable expectation, it misfired.

If French was to cloak *Salomé* in the "decent obscurity" which would get it past the censor, a similar use might have been conceived for the texture of Wilde's language – "akin to music but not of it."[21] William Archer, when he read *Salomé* in 1893, became perhaps the first of many critics to find in its elaborate repetitions and chanted measures a quality "borrowed from music."[22] Wilde himself spoke of "the refrains whose recurring *motifs* make *Salomé* so like a piece of music and bind it together as a ballad."[23] Richard Strauss, who saw *Salomé* in Max Reinhardt's production at the Kleines Theater in Berlin in 1901, used an abridged German translation of Wilde's text as the libretto of an opera more famous than the play which inspired it. First performed in Dresden in 1905 to a reported thirty-eight curtain calls, Strauss's violent score was the outcome of his realization that Wilde's play "was simply calling for music."[24] The production of Wilde's

Salomé by Tairov at the Kamerny Theatre in Moscow, after the Bolshevik revolution, employed settings designed to produce "harmonies of colour" rather than illustrate locale. Tairov also "orchestrated" the actors' voices so that Salomé was characterized as an oboe, Iokanaan as sounding brass, the Young Syrian as a flute, and the soldiers as double basses.[25]

This musical aura of Wilde's *Salomé*, like its French text, might have been expected to stimulate the "extreme indulgence" which the censor allowed dramas comfortably remote from plain English reality. The opera by Strauss with Wilde's dialogue as libretto played Covent Garden in 1910, licensed and performed before enthusiastic houses at a time when Wilde's drama was still banned.[26] (Iokanaan became merely "the Prophet" in the Covent Garden production, but Salomé, Hérode, and Hérodias were allowed to retain their proper names.) Another opera on the story of Salomé and John the Baptist, the *Hérodiade* of Jules Massenet, had been performed in French at Covent Garden in 1904 with all the characters identified by Gallicized versions of their biblical names. And in 1909, a year before Strauss's opera arrived in London, an English opera, with music by Robert Hilton and Granville Bantock and a libretto in English evidently based on Wilde's play, ran for a brief engagement at the Aldwych Theatre.[27]

A few years earlier A. W. Pinero had gotten by the censor with *Dandy Dick*, although the play contained comic allusions to the Salomé legend which now furnished Wilde his subject. One of the heroines of Pinero's farce – a girl named Salome Jedd – is to dance harmlessly at a provincial masquerade, and her love imperils her suitor, Major Tarver, only because of his weak liver.[28] Wilde's play, professedly a tragedy, tempts comic reactions in its own way, and to that extent is transplanted to a safer distance from the biblical source and the censor's displeasure. Not only are there obvious comic elements such as Hérodias's nagging reproaches of her husband the king, but, for example, the scene of savage gratification in which the heroine addresses the severed head of Iokanaan rests uneasily on the edge of caricature. Aubrey Beardsley, whose illustrations of *Salomé* make fun of Wilde and his characters alike, represents the scene as one of such ghastly and exaggerated passion that a grimace or a laugh seems an equally plausible response. The humorous potential of that climactic moment in the play was felt by Max Beerbohm, who saw it dramatized in an unlicensed production in 1905 in Bayswater. "In the Bijou Theatre," he wrote tongue-in-cheek, "Salomé brought the head briskly down to the footlights, and in that glare delivered to it all her words and desires."[29] Were the actress Sarah Bernhardt, sighed Beerbohm, "all might almost be well" – but of that, with his sense of the play as unmixed tragedy, he could not be certain. The effects of the scene lay somewhere between disgust and comedy. Others, however, assumed the possibilities for laughter in *Salomé* to be intentional. When early in 1892 Wilde read from his new play to

MISS MAUD ALLAN AS SALÓME, WITH THE DUMMY HEAD OF JOHN THE BAPTIST
TO WHICH OBJECTION HAS BEEN TAKEN.

Plate 1   Maud Allan dancing in 1908 as Salomé in a music hall performance not subject to
the censor's ban (from *The Sketch*, 25 March 1908)

artist and costume designer Graham Robertson, his listener hesitated at first, then decided the dialogue was meant to be funny and gave forth what he meant as a "complimentary chuckle" – a reaction which seemed, however, both unwelcome to the author and unexpected.[30]

It is difficult to imagine what more, beyond a personal appeal (a curious and important omission), could have been done to gain Pigott's approval of this "half pornographic" scriptural piece. Not only had Wilde submitted a French text and secured a French troupe to perform *Salomé*, but he, whether intentionally or not, had also imbued his play with suggestions of the operatic and comic, as if to moderate, in artificial lighting, his audacious raid upon the Bible. By design or intuition he appealed to the prejudices of the Examiner of Plays in just the manner most likely to relax his guard and make him feel "extremely indulgent." Today we have lost sight of the very reasonable case *Salomé* presented to the censor, and of a factor which may partly explain the stillborn death of the Royal English Opera House production of Wilde's play. In May 1892 Edward Pigott had testified before a select committee of the House of Commons inquiring into whether the censorship of drama served any good purpose. Many persons in theatrical life joined the Examiner of Plays in defending state control of the stage, and hearings which could have endangered Pigott's livelihood and authority turned out to have the opposite effect. The committee held its final meeting on 2 June 1892, issuing a report which concluded that the censorship "has worked satisfactorily" – far from being abolished or left to local authorities, it should be extended "as far as practicable to the performances in music halls."[31] It was a strengthened, and probably emboldened, Edward F. S. Pigott who only a few days later looked into the French manuscript of *Salomé* and declared it unfit for performance on an English stage.

III

To elude the censor, however, was not the only reason Wilde had to write *Salomé* in French instead of English. Sarah Bernhardt, who was to star in the play at the end of her London season of 1892, did not know English – despite having had lessons, hoping to act Shakespeare in his own language – and performed, like the rest of her ensemble, entirely in French. When the London *Times* remarked that the play was "written for Madame Sarah Bernhardt, for performance in this country," an angry Wilde fired off a letter to the editor:

My play was in no sense of the words written for this great actress. I have never written a play for any actor or actress, nor shall I ever do so. Such work is for the artisan in literature, not for the artist.[32]

Wilde, however, had just finished writing *A Woman of No Importance* for H.

Beerbohm Tree, the role of Lord Illingworth resembling that of the Duke of Guisebury in which the Haymarket actor-manager had just scored a momentous success. Before he began writing the fourth act Wilde offered the play to Tree, who unsurprisingly leapt to the bait and became directly involved in at least the revision of the play.[33] On the first leaf of the manuscript of *The Duchess of Padua*, furthermore, appear these words in Wilde's hand: "written for Mary Anderson."[34] In these dramas – *Salomé* included – Wilde behaved with characteristic shrewdness in creating roles tailored to popular actors of the day. His letter to the *Times* and his other denials that he ever wrote "for any actor or actress" cannot be taken seriously, except to reveal the nervousness with which he concealed the truth from the public and perhaps from himself.

Impostures of originality were not unusual with Wilde, who portrayed himself as an artist set apart, one for whom it was unthinkable to be influenced by another dramatist or the requirements of a fashionable actor. The truth is that the author of *Salomé* could not write at all, or write well, without the organizing inspiration of some kind of recipe. But Wilde himself was a convincing actor, as his courtroom performances would soon show, and the pretense that he wrote *Salomé* without a thought of Sarah Bernhardt has never been seriously challenged. In 1908 Robert Ross attached a brief preface to *Salomé* in his edition of Wilde's works to deny flatly that the play was intended for the French actress, and more recent critics have made similar assurances. Others have passed over Wilde's vehement denials, noting, in the manner of the *Times*, that *Salomé* was "written for" the great Bernhardt.[35] Whether the banned drama was another in a series of "Sarah Bernhardt plays" is a question unresolved, but one that can lead to explanation of some curious features of *Salomé* and provide a basis for judgment of a play that has sometimes been regarded as one of Wilde's most impressive achievements.

We cannot be sure that Wilde began *Salomé* with the conscious intent of writing a play for Sarah Bernhardt, or that he ever knowingly adopted such an aim. Wilde's "anxiety of influence" required that his dramas be seen, by himself and by others, as the products of an autonomous genius, impervious to tradition in both performance and play writing. The details surrounding the composition of *Salomé* are more obscure than usual for Wilde's plays, thus compounding the difficulty of knowing the author's conception of it as he wrote. Apparently, however, *Salomé* was begun, or at least substantially written, during Wilde's stay in Paris in late 1891. Wilfrid Blunt recorded in his diary for 27 October 1891 that Wilde had told some friends at breakfast in Paris that he was writing a play in French.[36] Vincent O'Sullivan relates that "one day, when he was in Paris," Wilde improvised the Salomé story for a group of young writers at lunch, then returned to his lodgings in the Boulevard des Capucines where he wrote the entire play later the same day and night.[37] All the surviving drafts of *Salomé* in Wilde's hand are in French, indicating that from the beginning the play was framed in that language rather than English.[38] But not until he showed *Salomé* to Sarah Bernhardt several months after he wrote it, with the aim of persuading her to act it in her London season of 1892, is there any record of Wilde himself linking his play with the French actress.

When Wilde read *Salomé* to Sarah Bernhardt at the home of Sir Henry Irving, probably in May 1892, he was exposing a work modelled upon her most spectacular successes of late and her inimitable acting style – and a work which, being in French, none of the English actresses he knew and admired could have performed. A "mania" for Bernhardt had infected the London theatre since her first English tour in 1879, and this was not the first occasion on which Wilde had sought to immerse himself in the glow which her meteoric visits occasioned.[39] Indeed Wilde helped to ignite the Bernhardt craze when as a young man he was conspicuous among the crowd at Folkestone to welcome her to England in 1879. He threw an armful of lilies on the ground in front of the actress and cried "Vive Sarah Bernhardt!" – the first time, the actress recalled in later years, she ever heard that exclamation.[40] Wilde later would give supper parties in honor of Bernhardt, who wrote her name on the walls of his "white room" along with the signatures of other celebrities of the time. He observed with good humor in his last days that she was one of three women – the others were Queen Victoria and Lillie Langtry – whom he could have married "with pleasure."[41]

To the author of *Salomé* Bernhardt was "the greatest artist on any stage," and hers "the most splendid acting I ever saw."[42] He told an interviewer after the ban on *Salomé* that hearing, in rehearsal, "my own words spoken by the most beautiful voice in the world has been the greatest artistic joy that it is possible to experience."[43] Bernhardt never performed *Salomé* in Paris – although she promised to produce it at her own theatre, the Porte St. Martin, and had taken the play to Paris with her – and when Wilde languished in prison she turned a deaf ear to his plea for assistance. She told Robert Sherard, commissioned by Wilde to work out financial arrangements, that "under existing circumstances it would be impossible to produce *Salomé*." She even reneged on her promise to convey a loan to "the poor man," as she now called Wilde, evading Sherard on several occasions by leaving word she was "out."[44] Wilde wrote from prison to his emissary: "Sarah, of course, did not keep her appointment – she never does," referring perhaps to a still greater disappointment she inflicted – failing to carry out the plan to act *Salomé* in Paris after the play was banned in London.[45] But Wilde, ever good-natured, seems to have made a point of seeing Bernhardt in *La Tosca* after his release from prison, and of meeting her for an emotional reunion after the performance. At this distance from the exciting events of 1892 he could acknowledge, at least in a private letter, the real relation of his banned play to the famous actress. "The only person in the world who could act Salomé," he wrote, "is Sarah Bernhardt."[46]

Galvanized by celebrity, athirst with ambition, fluent in French – how could Wilde have resisted breathing the charmed atmosphere of the Parisian actress who moved Londoners to tears with her performances in a foreign tongue? At premium prices, year after year, theatregoers crammed the Royal English Opera House, Her Majesty's, and other West End theatres to experience the thrilling effects described by Arthur Symons in a retrospective essay. When Bernhardt performed, he wrote –

There was an excitement in going to the theatre; one's pulses beat feverishly before the curtain had risen; there was almost a kind of obscure sensation of peril, such as one feels when the lioness leaps into the cage, on the other side of the bars. And the acting was like a passionate declaration, offered to someone unknown; it was as if the whole nervous force of the audience were sucked out of it and flung back, intensified, upon itself, as if it encountered the single, insatiable, indomitable nervous force of the woman.[47]

Such acting brought down the house in her English tours from the beginning. Appearing before a London audience for the first time at the Gaiety in 1879, as Phèdre in Racine's play, Bernhardt was recalled with thunderous cries at the final curtain. It was an ovation, wrote John Murray in the *Gaulois*, "which I think is unique in the annals of the theatre in England." Wrote William Archer: "It is not in the least necessary to understand the words she utters. She is an incarnate harmony, who speaks intelligibly to the nerves, if not to the brain, of all mankind."[48]

A century later it seems obvious that the theatrical season of 1892 was a vintage one for the London theatre – the year of *Lady Windermere's Fan*, the banned *Salomé*, *Widowers' Houses*, and *Ghosts*, the first notable harvest of a New Drama which repudiated the bland conventions of its Victorian inheritance. But in 1892 the season appeared to some observers a failure theatrically – the *Era* called it "disastrous," a year "unrivalled in its badness," and welcomed Bernhardt's advent in May, which concluded a world tour begun in 1891, for the excitement it provided. She performed, as usual, a variety of roles, from Phèdre to Cléopâtre in Sardou's adaptation of Shakespeare, but her *Tosca* most powerfully affected the crowds who filled the Royal English Opera House (soon to become the Palace Theatre). "It is possible," said the *Era* of her savage performance as Floria Tosca on 13 June, "that the great actress was on this night absolutely and literally at her greatest," stimulating the audience to a "frenzy" of applause – "a demonstration almost unparalleled in England."[49] During the torture scene women spectators emitted muffled screams, men fidgeted nervously, and some in the audience "arose and departed" their expensive 15-shilling seats.

It came as no surprise that Bernhardt chose to repeat *La Tosca* for her farewell performance at the end of July – *Salomé* had been laid aside several weeks ago – and if anything the sensation it provoked was greater still.

The effect was electrical. Bouquets and wreaths were handed over the footlights; "Sarah" was called and recalled, amidst cheers and cries of "Brava!" and it seemed as if the audience would stay and summon her till midnight . . . and finally the house was emptied at an hour considerably later than that at which carriages are usually called.[50]

Graham Robertson, who designed the sets and costumes for the ill-fated *Salomé*, pronounced the general opinion when he called Bernhardt, beyond dispute, "the greatest actress of our time."[51] Such was the glamor and acclaim in which Wilde sought to baptize his play.

Some believed Bernhardt degraded her unique talent by her choice of roles, performing, for example, a French adaptation of *Antony and Cleopatra* instead of a translation of the original. "The actress who plays Sardou by choice, instead of Shakespeare," the *Era* commented, "sits in judgment on herself."[52] By the 1890s she had become "universally associated" with the stagey melodramas of the popular French playwright, who had created a *persona* for Bernhardt that continued much the same in play after play, calling for performance in the passionate vein in which she excelled.[53] Although she continued to reprise earlier successes in *Phèdre* and *Adrienne Lecouvreur*, her name in the 1890s was inseparable from Victorien Sardou's – they were the fabled "two S's" whose collaborations inspired the byword "There is but one Sarah and Sardou is her prophet."[54] Beginning with *Fédora* (1882), the playwright unashamedly wrote parts tailored to Bernhardt's unique style and talent, then read the plays aloud for her approval – the same strategy Wilde adopted with *Salomé*.

Whether as Fédora or Théodora, Floria or Cléopâtre, the great actress appeared in Sardou's plays as a woman of passionate extremes, childishly jealous on one hand, primitive on the other – "an alternation of the spoilt child and the *bête féroce*."[55] By the mid-1890s, at least, her manner was in some ways quite predictable. "The grinding out of the words through the teeth, and the torrent of passion, followed by a violent wagging of the towzled head, never fails to bring down the house," said a reviewer of a play called *Izeyl*, written by Armand Sylvestre and Eugène Morand just as Wilde wrote *Salomé*, to the proven formula of the "two S's."[56] Oddly matched with this savagery of emotion, however, was a languid and melodic quality which seemed as alien to France as England, remote from the modern world – the *voix d'or*, the dream-like face of "the divine Sarah." She awakened visions of a violent and seductive Salomé in some critics – in Jean Lorrain and Jules Lemaître, as well as the English reviewer A. B. Walkley – years before Wilde conceived the idea of his one-act drama. Of the impression Bernhardt made in *Théodora*, Lemaître wrote:

In the first act, lying on a bed, a mitre on her head and a big lily in her hand, she resembles the fantastic queens of Gustave Moreau, those dream figures, in turn hieratical and serpentine, possessing a mystical and sensuous attraction.[57]

Most suggestive of Moreau's painted Salomés in a pageant like *Théodora*, the actress yet brought the same exotic quality to all her performances. "Even in modern parts," Lemaître observed, "she keeps this strangeness which is given her by elegant thinness and her Oriental, Jewish type." And it was the opinion of Lemaître which Wilde, languishing in Reading Gaol, wanted to know when in 1896 *Salomé* was given its first production, at the Théâtre de l'Oeuvre in Paris.[58]

IV

To regard *Salomé* as partly the product of extraliterary influence – the acting style of Bernhardt, the state of dramatic censorship in the 1890s – is not to deny, but qualify, the play's relation to literary texts, including Wilde's own. Hérodias, it has been pointed out, resembles the "tart dowagers" in *Lady Windermere's Fan*, and from one point of view the play develops and perfects a motif first tried out in *The Duchess of Padua* – the rejected woman as passionate murderer.[59] Mario Praz sketched the place of the play in relation to other nineteenth-century treatments of the Salomé story and discovered little that could be termed Wilde's own.[60] Indeed many critics noted the Salomés of Flaubert in *Hérodias*, of Huysmans in *A Rebours*, and of Heine in *Atta Troll* as being influential upon Wilde's portrayal of the dancing girl as a character of beauty, lassitude, and cruelty. The peculiar style of *Salomé* has been traced to the jeweled language of Gautier and the choppy, phrase-book sentences of Maeterlinck.[61] "*Salomé* is a mosaic," wrote the critic for the *Pall Mall Gazette* – "a library in itself." Wilde's heroine is "the daughter of too many fathers," he added, naming Gautier, Maeterlinck, and Flaubert; "she is a victim of heredity. Her bones want strength, her flesh wants vitality, her blood is polluted."[62]

Richard Ellmann struck out on a new approach, suggesting that Wilde dramatized himself as Hérode suspended indecisively between the influence of Ruskin and Pater.[63] Viewed in this light *Salomé*, as Rodney Shewan says, deserves to be taken seriously "as the most intensely self-expressive of Wilde's plays."[64] Salomé herself is one of those exceptional personalities whose intensity, Wilde believed, was "created out of sin."[65] In realizing her individualism she moves irresistibly to crime and revolt, for "Most personalities have been obliged to be rebels," Wilde had written in "The Soul of Man Under Socialism" (1891).[66] Such a role was an appropriate vehicle for Sarah Bernhardt, who by 1892 selected parts which made her the dominant presence on stage – parts in which neither Albert

Darmont (who would have been Hérode in London) nor anyone else seriously challenged her for the limelight.

The plays that Sardou wrote for Bernhardt were all what the *Era* called "star plays." The press observed during the London season of 1892 that after the first week or two she gave eight performances a week of plays "which might almost be called monologues" and wondered that she could endure "this constant overwork."[67] If not literally monologues, her plays were "duologues, in which one other actor was deputed to talk while the 'star' recovered her breath."[68] Thus Sardou's adaptation emptied, by necessity, the rich gallery of characters in Shakespeare's *Antony and Cleopatra*, banishing some and subordinating others to a woman whose explosions of passion illuminate herself but leave the remainder in darkness. Except for Antony, who in Sardou is slave to the dominant heroine, the other characters are, as the *Times* pointed out, "names and nothing more."[69] So it was that Sardou rewrote Shakespeare to the unique demands of a "two S's" play, and Wilde accommodated himself to the same plan when in *Salomé* he rewrote the Bible. The Salomé of the gospels and even of Flaubert is a marginal character, unimpassioned, moving at the bidding of others, and to that extent inconceivable as a role for *la grande Sarah*. In his play Wilde moves Salomé to the foreground and makes her passionate recoil from thwarted desire the center of interest, causing both Hérode and Hérodias to recede in importance by comparison with their precursors. In *Salomé* the blood lust is the dancer's, not her mother's; the murder of the prophet is her own idea; and her eruptive nature veers between listless yearning and implacable fury. Wilde knew what he was doing when he named his drama *Salomé*, for in his heroine the vital forces of the narrative unite – in her he adjusted the Salomé legend to the precise measurements of a Sarah Bernhardt *persona*.

Although he insisted upon his own uniqueness, Wilde would rather have been the English Maeterlinck than the English Sardou – an artisan who sacrificed art upon the altar of melodrama and gorgeous costumery. In fact two years before *Salomé* he had contracted to bring out an English edition of the avant-garde Belgian's play *La Princesse Maleine*, a drama which resembles *Salomé* in style and in its story of an aging king whose desire for a "pale" young princess is complicated by a nagging, bloodthirsty queen. Although Wilde's edition of Maeterlinck's play never appeared, *La Princesse Maleine* may have been of use to the English playwright in other ways. It offered a model for the strangely abrupt yet rhythmic sentences of *Salomé*, and in its odd concerns with developments in the weather and the sky *La Princesse Maleine* established itself on an ironic scaffolding which Wilde would use as his own. Further, Maeterlinck the Belgian provided an example of a playwright writing in a language not really his own – precisely Wilde's task in *Salomé*.

Wilde's and Maeterlinck's dialogue is often so similarly textured that, were it not labelled, one could hardly know which author to hold responsible. The characters in Maeterlinck's play observe bloody portents and stars falling in the heavens:

> *Stephano*: Encore la comète de l'autre nuit!
> *Vanox*: Elle est énorme!
> *Stephano*: Elle a l'air de verser du sang sur le château!
> *Vanox*: Les étoiles tombent sur le château! Voyez! voyez! voyez!
> *Stephano*: Je n'ai jamais vu pareille pluie d'étoiles! On dirait que le ciel pleure sur ces fiançailles!
> *Vanox*: On dit que tout ceci présage de grands malheurs![70]

And characters in *Salomé* do likewise, in the same blunt accents:

> *Hérode*: Ah! regardez la lune! Elle est devenue rouge. Elle est devenue rouge comme du sang. Ah! le prophète l'a bien prédit. Il a prédit que la lune deviendrait rouge comme du sang. N'est-ce pas qu'il a prédit cela? Vous l'avez tous entendu. La lune est devenue rouge comme du sang. Ne le voyez-vous pas?
> *Hérodias*: Je le vois bien, et les étoiles tombent comme des figues vertes, n'est-ce pas? Et le soleil devient noir comme un sac de poil . . .[71]

Some time in 1892 Wilde turned up at Graham Robertson's and began to read, in French, from the new play he was writing. "Comme la princesse Salomé est belle ce soir!" he intoned, chanting his borrowed measure. "Vous la regardez toujours. Vous la regardez trop."[72] Confused, the costume designer interrupted with the observation that "it's exactly like . . . like Maeterlinck." Wilde stopped reading and scowled. "Didn't you mean it to be?" Robertson asked.[73]

Although Sarah Bernhardt never had performed in a play by Maeterlinck, apparently Wilde recognized the suitability of her acting to the literary style of the new dramatist from Belgium. By the 1890s Bernhardt's captivating voice had taken on an artificial, musical quality, an eerie intonation upon which everyone commented. This priestly chanting – perhaps adopted originally to protect the *voix céleste* from overwork – had become her artistic signature, a bewitching if monotonous music which she used to express the full range of emotions. The *Times*, for example, pointed out in a review of her performance as Jeanne d'Arc in 1890 that "what she has to say is pitched throughout in a single key, relieved only by a single declamatory passage."[74] Of her performance as Sardou's Cléopâtre in 1892 the *Times* noted again "the monotonous chant whereby Cléopâtre expresses her love as she hangs upon Antony's neck, and in which, almost without a change of key, she bewails his absence."[75] For such speech as this the incantatory, clipped rhythms of *Salomé* are a perfect match:

> Ah! j'ai baisé ta bouche, Iokanaan, j'ai baisé ta bouche. Il y avait une âcre saveur sur tes lèvres. Etait-ce la saveur du sang?[76]

Here was dialogue tailor-made to what the *Era* described as the "half-monotonous inflections" of the divine Sarah.[77] Hers was a voice, wrote Symons, which spoke "chantingly," with a "throbbing, monotonous music, which breaks deliciously, which pauses suspended, and then resolves itself in a perfect chord."[78] With the curate, Graham Robertson observed, the chant is a "singsong and dull monotony" – with Bernhardt "it was the cooing of doves, the running of streams, the falling of soft spring rain."[79] So exaggerated is the ritualistic style of *Salomé*, in fact, that its language comes dangerously near to a travesty of the speech which was the hallmark of the actress Wilde most admired.

Just as she pitched nearly all her speeches in a one-note, chanting inflection, so Bernhardt in the 1890s seemed to enact the same part again and again under different names and in a variety of costumes. Of her June 1892 performance as Cléopâtre the *Era* observed testily that this new role varied little from others the actress had played in "two S's" dramas. "Call her Fédora, La Tosca, what you will," the reviewer pointed out, "she would answer just as readily to the name. Théodora, indeed, had far more of Cléopâtre in her."[80] Salomé was to have been another such role – so much so that neither Bernhardt nor her stage designer saw any urgent reason why the characters in Wilde's play should not appear in costumes left over from one of Sardou's pieces. Bernhardt's London season was short, and *Salomé* had been scheduled at the last minute, so in any event there was nothing else to do. "We must contrive it all somehow out of the 'Cléopâtre' costumes," Graham Robertson quoted her as saying. "We can arrange and alter and get quite a good effect, I'm sure." Had the play been performed, Bernhardt's gold-fringed robe and jeweled breastplate from *Cléopâtre* might have seemed strangely familiar to some in the audience. But the costume designer was satisfied, and so apparently was the star. "The Cléopâtre dresses proved very useful," Robertson recollected later, describing rehearsals, and "all was going well" – until Edward Pigott intervened.[81]

More, however, than the costume of Salomé was interchangeable with the roles Sardou had written for Bernhardt. These dramas, some never translated to English, always cast the actress as a queen or princess – Fédora, Théodora, Cléopâtre – or a Tosca who moves in imperial scenes. Like Wilde's Princess Salomé, Sardou's women of purple conceive a desperate passion for an outlaw-figure or outsider whose challenge to authority both complicates and intensifies the situation. The woman's radical passion is matched and even deepened by the extremes which converge in her romantic pairing – the Judean princess and the rabble-rousing prophet in *Salomé*, the Byzantine queen and the rebel Andréas in *Théodora*, the Russian princess and the suspected nihilist in *Fédora*. Personalities and emotions *in extremis* erupt violently in all these Bernhardt plays. "She seems to come into her splendid self only when she murders or when she dies," observed Jules Lemaître.[82] Thus when *Gismonda* made its London premiere in 1894, reviewers fastened on the climactic scene in which Bernhardt seized an ax and struck a man dead. This brutal role, one critic noted, "re-embodies all her previous triumphs."[83]

The tigerish passion of Salomé exceeds, if possible, that of the roles written by Sardou for Bernhardt. It is Salomé reborn as a Sarah Bernhardt character who chants malignantly to the severed head of Iokanaan:

Ah! tu n'as pas voulu me laisser baiser ta bouche, Iokanaan. Eh bien! je la baiserai maintenant. Je la mordrai avec mes dents comme on mord un fruit mûr. Oui, je baiserai ta bouche, Iokanaan. Je te l'ai dit, n'est-ce pas? je te l'ai dit. Eh bien! je la baiserai maintenant . . .[84]

In ways that count most, in fact, Salomé has less in common with her scriptural precursor than with the terrifying heroine of Sardou who slays Zaccaria with an ax. She belongs with the violent Gismonda, and with Fédora, who lays aside her femininity to pursue a bloody revenge:

Ce n'est pas de mon sexe . . . ce n'est pas chrétien, ce n'est pas humain! C'est barbare, cruel, sauvage, tout ce qu'il vous plaira. Mais c'est ainsi. Je suis ce que je suis.[85]

Théodora stabs Marcellus in the heart with a gold hairpin to save her lover from being betrayed to the authorities. Cléopâtre, in a scene which Sardou did not find in Shakespeare, orders her slave to drink poison as a means of placating a jealous Antony. Tosca, plunging a knife into Scarpia, taunts her dying victim:

Regarde-moi bien, bandit! . . . me repaître de ton agonie, et meurs de la main d'une femme . . . lâche! Meurs, bête féroce, meurs désespéré, enragé! . . . Meurs! . . . Meurs! . . . Meurs! . . .[86]

Had he seen Bernhardt as Salomé, it is doubtful Bernard Shaw would have witnessed anything to alter his view of her. To him she was as much lion-tamer as artist, indeed an "ex-artist" who simply made money by going round the world "pretending to kill people with hatchets and hairpins."[87]

When Hérode cries "Tuez cette femme!" and his soldiers crush Salomé beneath their shields, Wilde's play conforms itself to the obligatory curtain in which Bernhardt becomes the victim of a spectacular or excruciatingly slow death. Fédora is strangled by her lover – "la mort est là!" she cries in an agony too long to be believed. "Je n'ai pas cinq minutes à vivre!"[88] To the fanfare of trumpets and cheers of soldiers, a noose is tightened around the neck of Théodora as the curtain slowly descends. Floria Tosca hurls herself from a parapet, and poisoned Cléopâtre *meurt, en souriant* in her last scene. Sardou set the pattern, and other dramatists (not only Wilde) understood the necessity of the big death scene in ending a Sarah Bernhardt play of the 1880s and 1890s. In *Jeanne d'Arc*, which Barbier wrote for Bernhardt, fagots are lit beneath the heroine to conclude the last act. In

Léna (1889), written for her by Paul Berton, the star takes poison and waits silently on death for what was termed an unprecedented amount of time.[89] In *Izeyl*, the Bernhardt play by Silvestre and Morand, the heroine has her eyes plucked out and is left in a lonely glen where she dies, as usual, just as the curtain drops.

"Is it necessary," asked A. B. Walkley in an astute review of 1889, "to point out that *Fédora*, *Théodora*, and *La Tosca* (leaving rubbish like *Léna* entirely out of the account) are not works of art, but pieces of mechanism?"[90] These Sarah Bernhardt plays were "constructed to pattern," Walkley observed, tailored to the specifications of one actress, voluble, chimeric, and egotistic. Within a year of her first English season Bernhardt had broken with the Comédie Française and launched an independent career built upon spectacular roles in bad plays written especially for her. The French actress had degenerated, Walkley feared, into a "burlesque" of herself. She needed a "larger, saner, more varied repertory" than Sardou and his imitators were providing. She needed the Comédie Française, its wider range of plays, its proud tradition, "its discipline, its equality, its subordination of player to play."[91] And yet, Walkley conceded, Bernhardt in this self-indulgent phase of her career had given the stage a "new type . . . which one would not willingly have missed." She embodied an Oriental exoticism which reminded him of women in Baudelaire, Swinburne, and Pater. She reminded him – two years or more before Wilde's play – of such idol-women as "Gustave Moreau's Salomé."[92]

A. B. Walkley pointed out in his percipient review of 1889 that the plays Sardou and his imitators were turning out for Bernhardt were simply "vehicles for one and the same personality, mere strings of situations conditioned by that personality." They were, he concluded, *"not real plays."*[93] Not only Walkley, but many reviewers of the time showed an implicit reluctance to consider these Sarah Bernhardt plays as drama at all. They were seen as "monologues" or at best "duologues" in which another actor spoke while the star inhaled. Her narcissistic performances failed to provide the intersections of character and action which were assumed needful where dramatic literature was concerned. In *Salomé* Hérode is a major character with numerous speeches, but to most of his remarks the heroine is sublimely inattentive. The gilded language in which he proposes various rewards for the Dance of Seven Veils goes unheard by the dancer so self-sufficient in her passion that she can make love to a corpse. "Donnez-moi la tête d'Iokanaan," she chants repeatedly, as if Hérode had not spoken at all.[94] To actual conversation with the Tetrarch – or with anyone – she never descends. This lack of dramatic exchange ranked high among the attributes which contemporary critics noted in "two S's" plays, and it was a similar quality that Beerbohm cited in his clever summation of *Salomé* – "I almost wonder Oscar doesn't dramatize it."[95]

That Salomé's most impassioned speech should be addressed to a dead

Plate 2   Sarah Bernhardt as Izeyl

man is a delicious parody of the self-regarding Sarah Bernhardt persona as everyone knew it in 1892. His head struck off, Iokanaan is even less likely than other characters in Bernhardt plays to interrupt the star or challenge her for the limelight in the climactic final scenes. Her remarks to the bloody head – "j'ai soif de ta beauté. J'ai faim de ton corps," and the like – can thus proceed unimpeded through some 100 lines, nearly four pages in the Ross edition, making it by far the longest speech in the play as well as the most emotionally intense (pp. 76–80).[96] Nothing quite like this macabre monologue appears in any versions of the Salomé story named as models for Wilde, but in a play designed for Sarah Bernhardt it was exquisitely appropriate. *Too* appropriate, perhaps – for its extravagance draws such attention to the egocentrism of what had come to be the Bernhardt style that laughter seems a distinctly possible response.

Although Bernhardt could make Wilde's fame as a dramatist by performing *Salomé*, she also made any dramatist, and the words of his creation, matters of secondary interest. "It is not in the least necessary," as Archer said, "to understand the words she utters." Shaw also knew the extent to which Bernhardt simply appropriated the playwright's script to her own uses:

The dress, the title of the play, the order of the words may vary; but the woman is always the same. She does not enter into the leading character: she substitutes herself for it.

The susceptibilities of the audience were jogged, Shaw believed, not by anything the playwright wrote, but by Bernhardt's own "elaborate Monna Lisa smile, with the conscious droop of the eyelashes and the long carmined lips coyly disclosing the brilliant row of teeth."[97] Rather than giving expression to an author's words, it was in her own "incarnate harmony," as Archer characterized it, that Bernhardt's appeal lay – what she could communicate by the sound of her voice and the attitudes of her body. John Stokes points out that as late as age seventy-six the actress (likened even before Wilde's play to painted Salomés) was being described in terms of statuary and painting.[98] Thus what has recently been called the "visual" or "pictorial" quality of Victorian theatre was exemplified in a remarkable way by this actress who electrified London with performances in a language that most of her audience could not understand.[99] For one of Bernhardt's self-absorption, marginalizing both play and playwright, Salomé seems a perfectly complementary role. But the egotism of Wilde's princess is both morbid and exaggerated; and Beerbohm, reviewing the first English performance of the "tragedy," wondered whether even Bernhardt could have acted it without looking ridiculous.

In *Salomé*, therefore, Wilde comes perilously close to writing a Sarah Bernhardt role in which the star would perform a travesty upon herself – one way, but one of many, in which the play expresses a half-realized comic potential of which the author claimed to have been unaware. In its excesses of style and content, furthermore, the play at times has as much in common with popular dramatic parodies of the 1890s as with tragedy – parodies of Ibsen (as in *Ibsen's Ghost*), of Jones (*The Duke of Disguiseberry*), of Wilde himself (*The Poet and the Puppets*). *Salomé*, that is, invites a mocking smile at Maeterlinck as well as Sardou and Bernhardt, although this was hardly Wilde's announced or perhaps even conscious intention. So Beerbohm found himself on the edge of laughter at the unlicensed performance of 1903, and critics, at least since Mario Praz, have detected in the atmosphere of *Salomé* a quality redolent of comedy. Thus when Wilde dropped by to read from his new play, some time before Bernhardt was exposed to it at Irving's, Graham Robertson was uncertain how he was supposed to react to the French dialogue which Wilde chanted "with great satisfaction."

Certainly Wilde took *Salomé* seriously and acknowledged nothing comic about it – he speaks of it as a sombre work of art, fit vehicle for "the greatest tragic actress now living," and in wounded tones denies the influence of any other author or actor. Whether Wilde was lying or merely unaware of his own processes is not so important as the apprehension which gave birth to these protests: he could not admit that his work was dominated by any external agency. So he subsequently devoted much energy and conscious effort to denying it, but perhaps too little in the actual composition of *Salomé* to the struggle of overcoming it. The rich comic element in *Salomé* is a loaded gun pointed at Sardou and Sarah Bernhardt and Maeterlinck, but its existence Wilde seems unaware of, or determined to ignore. Comic irony was the weapon he would use successfully to tame the precursor in his best plays – dramas such as *Lady Windermere's Fan*, in which the predictable Victorian motif of the delinquent mother is redeemed by comic and surprising permutations. Incipiently *Salomé* resembles Wilde's best dramatic work, including *The Importance of Being Earnest*, in combining the thoughtful and funny in an uneasy alliance which, although it threatens at moments to disorganize the plays, makes them an expression of Wilde more than his sources. But the comic element in *Salomé* remains mostly latent. The play is poised awkwardly between conscious tragedy and possibly unpremeditated humor, as Beerbohm and Robertson instinctively felt, with the result that Wilde never exorcizes the French playwright and performer who animate *Salomé*.

"Why in French?" asked Robertson when he heard *Salomé* read. "Because," Wilde replied, "a play ought to be in French."[100] The flippant answer conceals an unwillingness – or was it an inability? – to confront what Robertson's obvious yet fundamental question would disclose. We cannot be sure now whether Wilde deceived himself as well as others by his insistence upon the autonomy of his own work, serenely resistant to the influence of other writing and performance. But we can be certain that in *Salomé*, whatever his conscious intent, he somehow wrote a play that fit perfectly the repertoire of the world's most famous actress. Wilde wrote the play in French, he read it to Robertson in French, Sarah Bernhardt would have acted it in French – she knew no other language. It was indispensable that *Salomé* be written in French, for by no other route could it elude the vigilant censorship of Edward Pigott or find expression in the musical chanting of *la grande Sarah*. In conception as well as execution it was a French drama, and out of this linguistic circumstance arise both the uniqueness and the failure of *Salomé*.

4

Unimportant women and men with a past

Qui est mon père?

                           Young Daniel, in *Le Fils de Coralie*

The woman with a past seems to have a peculiar fascination for
present day dramatists.

            The *Era*, 28 July 1894, from a review of *The Puritan*

I

Of Wilde's best-known dramas, *A Woman of No Importance* has been – by a
considerable margin – the least successful on stage and with critics. Its
original engagement at the Haymarket extended to only 113 performances,
far short of the "three or four hundred nights" which Henry Arthur Jones
cited as the run of a very successful play, "according to the standard of
popular amusement."[1] Revivals of *A Woman of No Importance* have been far
fewer than those of any other major play by Wilde.[2] Although it continues
to be regarded as one of Wilde's best plays, indeed one of the significant
dramas of the nineteenth century, comparatively little has been written on
A Woman of No Importance. Perhaps the best commentary on this neglected
play is now almost a hundred years old – William Archer's clearsighted
review of the original production in 1893.

In one sense Wilde rewrites himself in his second comedy. In *A Woman of
No Importance*, as Donald Eriksen comments, Wilde can be seen "reworking and intensifying the basic conflict of *Lady Windermere's Fan*" – that
between the values of puritan and dandy.[3] *A Woman of No Importance*
returns as well, as George Woodcock remarks, to the "general atmosphere
of social protest" which imbues *Lady Windermere's Fan*, especially protest
at the inequality of men and women.[4] The play is concerned, like *Lady
Windermere's Fan*, with a woman's secret; but instead of leaving it concealed, as Philip K. Cohen points out, Wilde in *A Woman of No Importance*
gives at least some of his characters an ability to "accept and forgive the
truth."[5]

A Woman of No Importance further resembles *Lady Windermere's Fan* in
the extravagant debt it owes to other authors, but Wilde's second comedy

never really establishes mastery over the well-traveled ground where it trespasses. It does not break free of the domination of earlier dramas to find its own voice or even to harmonize the babble of its many influences. The disintegrative force which endangered *Lady Windermere's Fan* and would harm *An Ideal Husband* is the same, therefore, which more seriously damages *A Woman of No Importance*. A victim of influence, it represents the failure of Wilde's method as a playwright, just as *Earnest* embodies its greatest success.

Those who have written on *A Woman of No Importance* have by no means ignored its shortcomings. Archer acclaimed Wilde as the most talented dramatist of his age, but was disturbed by the melodramatics in the play – especially the thrilling tableau at the end of Act III in which Gerald Arbuthnot, threatening to kill Lord Illingworth, is restrained by his mother with the pathetic cry, "Stop, Gerald, stop! He is your own father!"[6] More recent critics acknowledge the hysterical excesses of *A Woman of No Importance*, but argue that the play still resounds with a significance which transcends its stock characterization of the fallen woman, abandoned child, and wicked aristocrat.[7] Donald Eriksen, however, states the consensus in terming *A Woman of No Importance* "the least successful of Wilde's comedies."[8] The dramatic situation of the play – an illegitimate son who as a young man meets his father for the first time and learns the truth about his mother – was identified by Kelver Hartley, years ago, as coming from *Le Fils naturel* by Alexandre Dumas *fils*.[9] Others since have made the connection with Dumas, but oddly enough no one, including Hartley, has more than mentioned it in passing. Yet Wilde's play fails precisely because of its intriguing relation to the theatrical environment – not just *Le Fils naturel*, but large tendencies in both French and English drama.

II

The play by Dumas is but one of the notable French dramas of the day which revolve around a youth made aware of his own dubious birth and the fact that his mother is a woman with a past. Others, in fact, were being performed in Parisian theatres at just the time Wilde was writing, or preparing to write, *A Woman of No Importance*. In May 1892 the Gymnase was the scene of a revival of Albert Delpit's *Le Fils de Coralie* in which the hero learns that his mother was, in former times, a notorious courtesan. Some four months later, at the Odéon, *Monsieur de Réboval* by Eugène Brieux was played for the first time. Its hero, like Delpit's and Wilde's, finds that his illegitimacy complicates the affection he feels for a respectable and wealthy young woman. And in all these plays – including Wilde's – a point of psychological interest is the tolerance with which the son, abandoned by his father, regards his mother's shame. As Daniel tells his mother Coralie when he finds out the truth:

Je ne peux pas te maudire, puisque je suis ton fils . . . Tu n'es pas une femme pour moi, tu es la mère, l'être sacré qui a pris soin de mon enfance, qui m'a élevé, qui m'a aimé, moi qui étais seul au monde. Que d'autres te méprisent; moi, je te pardonne. Que d'autres te méprisent; moi, je te respecte.[10]

So spectacular was the popularity of *Le Fils de Coralie* that at the time Wilde's play was staged it had gone through twenty-five editions as a novel, also by Delpit, in addition to a successful career on stage.

A classic of the genre, Edouard Plouvier's *Madame Aubert* (1865), is compounded of much the same elements. Young Georges, "un pauvre enfant abandonné," loves wealthy Jeanne Bertin. The reputation of his mother, a former courtesan known as Flora, is the chief obstacle to their union. Georges behaves toward his mother, however, with the same affection that typifies most young men in these plays:

Vous êtes ma mère! c'est tout ce que je sais, tout ce que je vois, tout ce que je veux; vous êtes ma mère.[11]

Like other theatrical mothers and sons in this situation, Georges and Flora – who now calls herself Madame Aubert and dwells in virtuous obscurity – decide that "nous demeurerons ensemble . . . l'un près de l'autre."[12] Similarly Gerald and Mrs. Arbuthnot in Wilde's play cling to each other, prepared to form their own little society in defiance of a social system which makes no allowance for the woman with a past and her unhappy offspring.

One of the most striking resemblances between *A Woman of No Importance* and *Madame Aubert* is to be found at the end of Act III in both dramas. Le Marquis de Saint-Géry, the Lord Illingworth of Plouvier's play, vents his anger against young Georges in violent remarks to Madame Aubert, his mistress in the days when she was called Flora:

Le Marquis: Je le tuerais, ce Georges!
Madame Aubert: Vous!!! (*Prenant la main au marquis* . . .) Entrez donc là, pro-
          voquez-le donc! tuez-le donc! C'est votre fils.
Le Marquis: Lui! lui! Georges![13]

In Plouvier's play, therefore, the father threatens to slay the son he does not know. Wilde wrote the scene in reverse, Gerald crying "I will kill you!" as he attacks the man whom his mother will identify in the next instant as "your own father!"

In *Le Fils naturel* (1858) the familiar situation is presented in a manner closer still to that of Wilde's play. The drama by Dumas *fils* was probably seen for the first time by Wilde on 4 June 1879, when Sarah Bernhardt acted in it at the Gaiety in her triumphant first tour of England. Charles Sternay is the self-serving aristocrat this time, and Clara Vignot the inconsequential woman who bears him a son out of wedlock. Like Rachel Arbuthnot in Wilde's play, she has lived for years in quiet obscurity as a seamstress and brought up her son, now a young man, to believe his father dead.[14] When Jacques, the son, learns Sternay is his father, the first thing that occurs to him – as to Gerald in Wilde's drama – is the desirability of his parents' marriage. "Alors, monsieur," he demands of Sternay, "pourquoi n'avez vous pas épousé ma mère? pourquoi ne m'avez vous pas donné votre nom?"[15] Jacques's injured honor prompts him to threaten his father, but the anxious mother, like Mrs. Arbuthnot in *A Woman of No Importance*, intervenes just in time.

Dumas may have influenced the title as well as the treatment of Wilde's play. In Act IV of *Le Fils naturel* the name of Clara Vignot, Jacques's mother, is said to be "of no importance" in the legal acknowledgment of his natural son which Sternay has ordered drawn up. "Dans les actes," the father remarks off-handedly, "cela ne fait pas grand'chose."[16] But, as in Wilde's play, the father ironically becomes a *man* "of no importance" when his wealth and power turn out to be irrelevant to the advancement of his son. Dumas brings about this reversal by having Jacques achieve distinction on his own as a diplomat. In Wilde's play Illingworth intends to embrace Gerald as his son and sponsor a career for him – in diplomacy – but Gerald requires no career once he becomes the fiancé of American heiress Hester Worsley. Thus in both plays the indignant hero, after rejecting his father, overcomes a disadvantage of birth to win the young woman of means whom he loves – called Hester by Wilde, Hermine by Dumas. And in both *Le Fils naturel* and *A Woman of No Importance* the young couple join with the hero's mother to form a new family – one excluding the delinquent father. "Ma fille!" cries Clara at the end of Dumas's play, embracing Hermine.[17] In Wilde's fourth act, similarly, Hester and Rachel hug one another, resolving to live together with Gerald as a family unto themselves. Says the younger woman: "You'll let me be your daughter?" (p. 120).

Obvious differences exist between the two plays – Wilde's Mrs. Arbuthnot and Hester, for instance, are much more forceful characters than their counterparts in *Le Fils naturel*. Essentially, however, *A Woman of No Importance* imports a specialized type of French drama, refurbishing it with an English atmosphere and characters, while repeating what Dumas and others had already done. Wilde's own account of the matter was predictably quite different:

People love a wicked aristocrat who seduces a virtuous maiden, and they love a virtuous maiden for being seduced by a wicked aristocrat. I have given them what they like, so that they may learn to appreciate what I like to give them.[18]

To call Wilde's play an adaptation would be unfair, but there can be no doubt that *A Woman of No Importance* is overwhelmed by its French sources. Wilde allows them to escape the critical scrutiny and even mockery which enabled *Lady Windermere's Fan* to develop a voice of its own, although not without a struggle. In conception as well as execution, moreover, Wilde's second comedy was perhaps too much an alien affair. Illegitimacy was far less a concern in England than in France, where complicated legal and social considerations lent it special urgency. Although Wilde never carried out his threat to become a French citizen after the Lord Chamberlain suppressed *Salomé*, he did in effect the next best thing. He wrote another French play – this time, however, in English.

III

Just as a character's name in *Lady Windermere's Fan* pays an intended or unconscious tribute to the tradition behind the play (Mrs. "E[r]lynne"), so the names of Wilde's characters in his second comedy evoke literary and dramatic precursors of their own. Lord Illingworth's name bears a provocative – perhaps a taunting – resemblance to Chillingworth's in *The Scarlet Letter*, and Hester Worsley shares her Christian name with the more famous puritan of Hawthorne's novel. Wilde calls the illegitimate child Gerald, but to his mother the son is a "pearl" of great price, recalling the illegitimate Pearl in *The Scarlet Letter* (p. 106). Mrs. Arbuthnot, like Hester in Hawthorne's book, tends the sick and makes her living with her needle as a consequence of her "fall." ("Why Arbuthnot?" asks Illingworth of the woman he seduced years ago [p. 65]. "One name is as good as another, when one has no right to any name," she responds. But can it be fortuitous that this sign of her shame begins with an "A"?)[19]

It has been said that Wilde thought to invest *A Woman of No Importance* with a "serious purpose" by arming it with so many allusions to Hawthorne's book.[20] There may be truth in this suggestion, yet Wilde's play also engages in debate with Hawthorne's version of the story. In this context one should not forget Lord Illingworth's witty definition equating "American dry goods" and American novels (p. 24), or that Mrs. Arbuthnot is only a very reluctant Hester Prynne. She puts up with suffering and self-sacrifice because she must, and at the end, not without inconsistency, she resembles Ibsen's Nora as much as Hawthorne's puritan. Far from being a distant reflection of the woman who wore the scarlet letter, Mrs. Arbuthnot represents, from a Wildean perspective, an attempt to rewrite her.

Wilde was not the first English playwright to appropriate *The Scarlet Letter*. The other revisions of Hawthorne were outright adaptations, apparently the first and most successful being Joseph Hatton's *The Scarlet Letter; or, Hester Prynne* (1876). The focus on the pathetic situation of the heroine, reflected in the subtitle of Hatton's drama, is common to these latter-day dramatic versions – Wilde's included. Hatton's play ends with Hester bending over the dying Dimmesdale, who has welcomed his "agonies" as the agent of salvation.[21] But an adaptation of more than a decade later, in 1888, was played at the Royalty Theatre with a crucial difference. In this unpublished dramatization of *The Scarlet Letter*, the fallen preacher is spared exposure, and the ending – here it resembles Wilde's play – is made happy. The *Times* noted, with some surprise, that "the condonation of Hester's crime is a measure with which the house has the fullest sympathy."[22] Written by Stephen Coleridge and Norman Forbes, the play was competing in June 1888 with yet another version of *The Scarlet Letter* at the Olympic Theatre, written by Edward Aveling, the socialist and an early Ibsenite. In Aveling's adaptation the part of Hester was played by Janet Achurch, soon to win notoriety as the first Nora in an English production of *A Doll's House*. Within this context Wilde's use of *The Scarlet Letter*, in his attempt to reassess prevailing ideas of woman's duty, seems timely to say the least. He awards his heroine the happy exile that Hawthorne withholds in *The Scarlet Letter* and lets off the seducer with a slap in the face – melodramatic enough, but a penalty far less severe than the burning torments of Dimmesdale. Indeed, both Illingworth and Mrs. Arbuthnot reject out of hand the syndrome of guilt and repentance that Hawthorne's characters allow to wreck their lives. Sō much for "American novels" and their puritan morality.

Viewed in this light, *A Woman of No Importance* achieves what Harold Bloom would call an "anxiety of influence" powerful enough to form an effective resistance to the prior work. But also grafted onto the tradition of Dumas and Delpit is a strain of English melodrama. Like Wilde's French models, the English ones seem especially unpromising as the inspiration for a playwright who advertised himself as a serious and original artist. They concern themselves not with the Gallic issue of illegitimacy, but primarily with a fallen woman and, typically, the depraved aristocrat who led her astray. Sodden with penitent tears and swooning fits, these dramas usually exact stern penalties of both the seducer and his unhappy victim.

Of these English plays the most influential on Wilde was probably a melodrama by Henry Arthur Jones called *The Dancing Girl*. H. Beerbohm Tree, who commissioned Wilde's play, enjoyed one of his most successful roles as the evil-minded aristocrat in Jones's play. It opened its long run on 15 January 1891 at the Haymarket, where Tree was actor-manager. Fred Terry, later to act the part of Gerald Arbuthnot at the same theatre, was the *jeune premier* in *The Dancing Girl* as well. In both plays Julia Neilson was a puritan girl on whom the lecherous nobleman, called the Duke of Guisebury in Jones's play, practices his wiles. The role of the fallen Quaker in *The Dancing Girl* was the first important role in the career of Neilson, who would later be the morally inflexible Gertrude Chiltern in *An Ideal Husband*. Rose Leclerq, brilliantly witty as Lady Hunstanton in the original production of *A Woman of No Importance*, acted a similar but paler part as Lady Bawtry in *The Dancing Girl*. For Tree's Haymarket company, Jones's play was the more successful by far – it ran 266 performances over a full year, while Wilde's lasted but 113 and closed less than four months after its premiere. Tree, overshadowed only by Henry Irving as a stage manager, created a sensation in the role of the seductive Guisebury and found himself "in danger of becoming a matinee idol" as well.[23]

Although Wilde pretended that writing for a particular actor was beneath him, work for the artisan rather than artist, he fashioned for Tree a role as melodramatic, aristocratic "heavy" which reprised in many particulars the actor's smashing success as Guisebury. Shaw, who frankly confessed writing *Caesar and Cleopatra* for Forbes Robertson, believed every play was formed with a view to presentation and therefore to those who would act it. But Wilde did more than this in *A Woman of No Importance*, which ranks alongside *Salomé* as his most imitative drama, although his indebtedness to Jones was concealed beneath a mask of scorn. "I know and admire Pinero's work," he wrote with sly irony to George Alexander, "but *who is Jones*?"[24] On another occasion, venturing three rules for writing plays, Wilde remarked: "The first rule is not to write like Henry Arthur Jones, the second and third rules are the same."[25] Before he had written the third act, however, Wilde sent word to Tree, with whom he already had spoken about the play, offering him the English rights and proposing to read him the completed script "somewhere about the end of this month."[26] At least the disastrous second half of *A Woman of No Importance* therefore was written with Tree specifically in mind, and it is that portion of the drama which most emphatically invites comparison with Jones's play. Russell Jackson and Ian Small, furthermore, have drawn on newly discovered typescript drafts of the play to point out that Tree further imposed his own stamp on it by adding extensive stage directions to Wilde's text. These additions seem substantive enough to suggest the play is, in some limited sense, a "collaboration" – one in which Tree supplies the "theatrical sense" by giving Mrs. Allonby a cigarette to smoke (thus giving the audience a visual clue to her character) or allowing Mrs. Arbuthnot a melodramatic swoon onto the sofa to end Act III.[27] Some of the more extreme additions by Tree, Jackson and Small observe, were deleted when the text of the play was prepared for book publication – a fact suggesting that Wilde may have felt surer of himself, less vulnerable to influence, on the printed page.

Certainly Tree's influence seems to have awakened little anxiety in Wilde – "a most delightful man to work with, a most charming, courteous man," the actor recollected in an interview with the *New York Times* in 1916. Wilde, he said, would "write off a new scene" to order while observing a rehearsal; "he did not mind having suggestions made about his work." And, he recalled, " 'A Woman of No Importance' was written for me. Wilde had the idea of the character of Lord Illingworth for me and he came to me with it. I was playing in Belfast when he wrote the play, and he came there so that I could help him . . . I remember sitting up night after night in our rooms at the hotel, drinking porter and eating roast beef, while

Plate 3   Beerbohm Tree in *A Woman of No Importance*

the play was in process of formation."[28] Among the results of these consultations between Tree and Wilde were the cutting of a long diatribe against puritanism in Act III.[29]

If, as seems likely, Tree negotiated with Wilde for something in the manner of *The Dancing Girl*, he could not have been disappointed when *A Woman of No Importance* was completed less than a year after the last performance of Jones's play. Even some peripheral features of the later drama are anticipated by *The Dancing Girl*, such as the clever banter on the subject of "ideal" men in Wilde's second act. In Jones's play the idea of a faultless man receives an ironic turn that might be called Wildean, except that Wilde's play was yet unwritten. "A perfect man!" exclaims the title character of *The Dancing Girl*. "I could love him – all a summer afternoon."[30] And Tree's character, the Duke of Guisebury, comments on his own less than ideal reputation with a flippancy like Lord Illingworth's. Told he has a name for wickedness, Illingworth declares:

It is perfectly monstrous the way people go about, nowadays, saying things against one behind one's back that are absolutely and entirely true.

(p. 23)

The situation in Jones's play is exactly counterpoint to Wilde's. When the duke in *The Dancing Girl* hears from a friend that "you pretend to be a great deal worse than you are," he responds:

Most people pretend to be a great deal better than they are, so somebody must restore the moral balance.[31]

Both these patrician dandies, however, undergo a conversion of sorts in later scenes, after which their talk becomes, unhappily, more earnest than amusing.

Jones and Wilde both wrote parts for Tree which cast him as the despoiler of staunchly religious young women. In *The Dancing Girl* much is made of Drusilla Ives's Quaker upbringing, and in *A Woman of No Importance* the strict morality of Hester and Mrs. Arbuthnot is scorned as puritanism by Illingworth. After a change of heart, both Guisebury and Illingworth propose marriage to the women they ruined – and both are astonished to be turned down. This outcome was thoroughly consistent with the standard recipe for Victorian melodrama. Decadent aristocrats might seduce virgins, but they could not be allowed to leave the stage without experiencing a reciprocal loss of their own.

Women's loss, however, was not restricted to what was termed their purity. Other thunderbolts struck them, often in the form of exile or abrupt illness or some violent catastrophe deemed proportionate to their sin. In Jones's play, for example, the death of Drusilla Ives from an unnamed ailment is announced by a Sister of Mercy in Act IV. By that time Drusilla has sunk to a state lower than Wilde's heroine ever plumbs, having achieved fame as a professional "dancing girl." Cursed by her family, she

Plate 4   Beerbohm Tree as the Duke of Guisebury in *The Dancing Girl*

dies in America after dancing, of all days, on a Sunday – news which causes her Quaker father to utter *"a great cry of pain"* before he swoons into unconsciousness.[32] In an earlier play by Jones, *Saints and Sinners* (1884), a clergyman's daughter is seduced by an army officer with equally fatal consequences. After "worse than death" has occurred, Letty Fletcher is discovered in the last act on her deathbed, complaining of nothing more definite than being "so tired."[33] The fallen woman in a play by D. C. Murray called *The Puritan* (1894) escapes these maladies, but is scourged for her past in another way – she loses her fortune in an effort to save the business firm of the pious husband who renounces her.[34] In Sydney Grundy's *A Fool's Paradise* (1892) an unfaithful and unrepentant wife drinks poison in the last act, then throws the glass down behind her and curtseys defiantly before her husband. "This woman is my wife!" gasps Philip Selwyn. "But not for long," says a reassuring friend. "And she is better dead!"[35]

The woman with a past cannot avoid punishment even when the author is a "modern," or a woman, who sympathizes with her plight. Mary Elizabeth Braddon encouraged sympathy for her bigamist heroine, as feminist critics argue, but at the end of the sensationalized stage adaptation of *Lady Audley's Secret* (1863) she clutches her head and laughs deliriously before falling dead on the floor at the final curtain.[36] The woman's suffering, indeed, is sometimes most melodramatic when left to friendly writers to administer. Thus Thomas Hardy in his novel of 1892 makes Tess of the D'Urbervilles lie down symbolically upon a sacrificial stone before he finishes her off with hanging. *The Second Mrs. Tanqueray* (1893) was thought shockingly advanced, but Paula is trapped by her scandalous past no less than the heroines of Henry Arthur Jones. "The future is only the past again, entered through another gate," she complains before going into another room to kill herself.[37] Likewise, Wilde, although on the side of the sinner in *A Woman of No Importance*, does not spare Mrs. Arbuthnot the ritual afflictions which fall like rain on her sisters. She certainly gets off more leniently than Pinero or Hardy would allow, but since her son was born has endured a long exile from society, as she complains bitterly to Gerald:

You made many friends and went into their houses and were glad with them, and I, knowing my secret, did not dare to follow, but stayed at home and closed the door, shut out the sun and sat in darkness. What should I have done in honest households? My past was ever with me . . . And you thought I didn't care for the pleasant things of life. I tell you I longed for them, but did not dare to touch them, feeling I had no right. You thought I was happier working amongst the poor. That was my mission, you imagined. It was not, but where else was I to go?

(p. 107)

By the final curtain it is clear she will abide happily with her son and share in Hester's wealth, but not without having to turn her back on England – like Little Em'ly in *David Copperfield* – to find peace on foreign shores.

Wilde thus was ambushed by theatrical precedent in much the same manner as Pinero, whose most famous play began its long run at the St. James's – 223 performances – only a few days after *A Woman of No Importance* opened at the Haymarket. Both dramatists create women with a past who command more strength, and engage more sympathy, than was ordinarily the case, but neither successfully disentangles his heroine from the melodramatic web spun by the likes of Jones. Mrs. Arbuthnot and Mrs. Tanqueray are, in part, refugees from earlier plays, undergoing bitter experiences and making remorseful speeches which in a sense are not their own.

As some of their titles suggest – *Justice*, for example, and *A Woman's Revenge* – these formulaic melodramas are not content to punish only the woman. The lecherous duke in *The Dancing Girl*, although repentant at the end, is broken in fortune, rejected in love, and unsuccessful even in suicide. Bob Fenwick in *An M.P.'s Wife* (1895) kills himself with a pistol, and in *The Puritan* Sir John Sanderson, after thinking over what he has done, goes off to the desert to live among Arabs. Illingworth and Guisebury are humiliated by being turned down in marriage proposals to their victims, but the decadent aristocrat of *Justice* (1892) is compelled by law to marry his. "The punishment has so far exceeded the crime!" he complains with unintended humor. "Some day, perhaps, I may be less full of bitterness, but now – ."[38] It is with this stylized revenge of the wronged woman that Wilde concludes his own play, just as the recipe called for, but without the comic excesses often attending it. Mrs. Arbuthnot strikes her seducer across the face with a glove, then claims the last word with her humbling reference to Illingworth as "a man of no importance" (p. 120). It was threadbare material of this sort which reassured the critic for the *Theatre* that unlike so much of Wilde's writing, this play was morally innocuous. "The climax," he wrote, "reaches a high level of rightness – ethical and dramatic."[39]

IV

Others, however, were not so sure. "Mr. Wilde's piece," said an incisive review in the *Era*, "commences with epigrams and concludes with Ibsenism."[40] The critic picked up the scent of the controversial Norwegian primarily in Wilde's characterization of women. Hester Worsley, he observed, is an "advanced" young person – a New Woman with democratic opinions who seeks equality of the sexes where moral questions apply. "You are unjust to women in England," says this sexual revolutionary from America. "And till you count what is a shame in a woman to be an infamy in a man, you will always be unjust" (pp. 53–4). Like Hester,

Mrs. Arbuthnot revolts against the ideal of womanhood which the nineteenth century enforced, one which demanded she marry the man whose son she gave birth to. The conventional Gerald, however, insists it is "right" and "proper" – his mother's "duty" – to marry Illingworth even if she detests him (p. 104). "What mother," he asks, "has ever refused to marry the father of her own child? None" (p. 105). Gerald exaggerates, but in the theatre, as probably in life, very few refusals of that kind were witnessed. Mrs. Arbuthnot turns down Illingworth anyway:

> Let me be the first, then. I will not do it.
>
> (p. 105)

The *Era* was right; in her rebellion against customary ideals, Rachel Arbuthnot behaves more as a character in Ibsen than an English drama of the pink-lampshade variety.

The small group of critics who express a high opinion of *A Woman of No Importance* have been alert to that considerable part of the play which divides it from the conventional sentiments and emotional overindulgence of Victorian melodrama. Pronouncing the almost unique view (in the late twentieth century, at least) that *A Woman of No Importance* is "one of Wilde's most original and interesting achievements," Katharine Worth emphasizes the modernity of the play's form as well as content. She finds in the uneventful first act, with its almost exclusive emphasis on conversation, a premonition of Shaw's discussion plays and the theatre of Samuel Beckett, in which stasis creates a dramatic tension of its own.[41] Moreover, Worth points out, the aura of "secret pleasure and mockery" in the conversations among women provides an ironic commentary on the traditional idea of woman's place in society as formulated by the idealistic politician, Mr. Kelvil, who insists that "women are always on the side of morality, public and private" (p. 22). Women like Mrs. Allonby and Lady Stutfield show clearly enough in their witty private discussion that Kelvil is mistaken, and the history of Mrs. Arbuthnot, when we finally learn it, provides a more tangible rebuttal. In this play, as in *Lady Windermere's Fan*, Wilde invites comparison with other writers – novelists as well as dramatists, women as well as men – who in the early 1890s challenged the predominant sexual ideology.

One of the targets of Wilde's protest is the unequal division of suffering between men and women who exist in the relation of Lord Illingworth and Mrs. Arbuthnot. Like Hadria, the heroine of Mona Caird's feminist novel *The Daughters of Danaus* (1894), Mrs. Arbuthnot rebels against a system which lacerates the fallen woman "while it leaves the man for whose sake she risked all this, in peace and the odor of sanctity."[42] In a conventional melodrama Mrs. Arbuthnot would suffer excruciatingly and repent, following belatedly Mr. Kelvil's prescription that women be "always on the side of morality, public and private." But Mrs. Arbuthnot will not repent, nor will she submit to Gerald's insistence that mothers *must* marry the fathers of their children. The institution of motherhood is thus the weapon by which men (son and lover, in this case) subjugate women, or seek to do so. Wilde's language is less strident, but his analysis of the situation is essentially the same as that of the militant Hadria in *The Daughters of Danaus*:

Throughout history, she reflected, children had been the unfailing means of bringing women into line with tradition. Who could stand against them? They had been able to force the most rebellious to their knees. An appeal to the maternal instinct had quenched the hardiest spirit of revolt.

(p. 187)

Even her own children "represent to me the insult of society – my own private and particular insult, the tribute exacted of my womanhood. It is through them that I am able to be subdued and humbled" (p. 190).

A Doll's House had alarmed London in 1889 with its sympathetic portrayal of a woman who deserts husband and children to satisfy her own unorthodox idea of what is right. English plays, however, sacrificed everything to the ideal of wholesome domesticity if children as well as women were involved. The most popular drama of the late 1880s in London was not *A Doll's House*, but Pinero's fabulously successful *Sweet Lavender*, which logged nearly 700 performances while treating these matters from a conventional point of view – the point of view of Gerald in *A Woman of No Importance*. In Pinero's play Ruth Rolt is the familiar wronged woman who has lived in obscurity, passing as a "widow" and rearing the illegitimate child of her youth, since grown to womanhood. When the inevitable meeting with her old lover occurs, however, he receives no slap on the face or ironic denunciation. Instead there is a scene of tender *rapprochement*, with the prospect of marriage to follow, while plans are laid for the wedding of Ruth's daughter and the adopted son of the man who "betrayed" her.[43] A sentimental reunion of the former lovers and the child was not uncommon in English plays of this type. In Sydney Grundy's *Sowing the Wind*, which opened at the Comedy a few months after the debut of Wilde's play, the final act is marked by the father's recognition of the child he never knew. Whereas Illingworth is threatened with death by his unacknowledged son, Brabazon is embraced and welcomed tearfully as "Father!" by the abandoned child of Grundy's piece.[44] Plays like *Sweet Lavender* and *Sowing the Wind* thus solve the dilemma by reaffirming, with melodramatic excess, the Victorian insistence upon family solidarity. Traditional ties between father and mother, parent and child, triumph over the sternest challenge and bring families together at the final curtain.

But being modern "is the only thing worth being nowadays," Illingworth quips (p. 75) – and when Mrs. Arbuthnot transgresses the old-fashioned domestic ideal, refusing to marry her child's father, she brings a modern atmosphere into the creaking plot of *A Woman of No Importance*. The note of sexual equality sounded by Hester, and even the irresponsible wit of the early acts ("Nothing succeeds like excess," and so on), contribute in their separate ways to Wilde's attack on the most hallowed shrines of Victorian morality. Wilde was not the first, however, to give a "modern" treatment to the antique theatrical materials of illegitimate child, delinquent father, and betrayed mother. In September 1892, just when Wilde was writing the last half of his play, Brieux brought out *Monsieur de Réboval* in Paris at the Odéon. Regarded as a French disciple of Ibsen, Brieux had written a play about a politician who, like Consul Bernick in Ibsen's *Pillars of Society*, is esteemed as an ideal statesman and husband, a man with "une conscience élevée et incorruptible."[45] Behind the mask of the ideal, however, Réboval dishonors his wife and is the father of an illegitimate son. Yet instead of exploiting the melodramatic potential of this situation – the woman's outrage, the child's hysterical vengeance – Brieux prefers a slow dissection of Réboval to expose the hollow core of his traditional ideals and official morality.

While Brieux was staging a New Drama from old materials, Wilde was employing similar ingredients with a more uncertain focus in writing *A Woman of No Importance*. Gerald Arbuthnot, for example, is not authentically a character of Oscar Wilde; he is the familiar hero of Victorian melodrama who demands traditional justice for the woman betrayed. He tells his mother:

The wrong that has been done you must be repaired. Atonement must be made. Justice may be slow, mother, but it comes in the end. In a few days you shall be Lord Illingworth's lawful wife.

(p. 103)

Such lines were not so much written as merely unloaded from earlier plays in which indignant virtue speaks. Of course Mrs. Arbuthnot refuses Gerald's conventional justice, and does not regret her fall:

How could I repent of my sin when you, my love, were its fruit! . . . I cannot repent. I do not. You are more to me than innocence. I would rather be your mother – oh! much rather! – than have been always pure.

(p. 107)

She is a defiant and unconventional woman, but there are moments – critical ones – in which Mrs. Arbuthnot seems as if suddenly possessed by one of the queens of melodrama who preceded her. Her independent views on marriage and maidenhood are incompatible, for instance, with the swooning fit at the end of Act III when, Wilde writes, *"She sinks slowly on the ground in shame"* (p. 96). And if her sin has been the glory, not the ruin, of her life, does it make sense to strike her "betrayer" across the face with a glove?

In her modern phase Mrs. Arbuthnot's speech is fresh and spare, something of her own, as in the terse but electrical announcement to her son that "I cannot repent. I do not." But is this the same woman who moments later describes her youthful seduction as "my disgrace" – the same words Ruth Rolt used in *Sweet Lavender* – and as "my dishonour" and "shame" (p. 107)? Mrs. Arbuthnot is a marionette, not the individualist who resists her son's appeal to custom and authority, when with the voice of a thousand fallen women she refers theatrically to "the mire of my life" and to herself as "a tainted thing" (pp. 105–6). Indeed her third-person account of herself as the fallen woman is as numbingly conventional and sentimental as even the slow-witted Gerald could desire:

She is a woman who drags a chain like a guilty thing. She is a woman who wears a mask, like a thing that is a leper. The fire cannot purify her. The waters cannot quench her anguish. Nothing can heal her! no anodyne can give her sleep! no poppies forgetfulness! She is lost! She is a lost soul!

(p. 94)

This ranting speech, like a great deal she says, is in hopeless conflict with the independent nature which Mrs. Arbuthnot displays at other times. It belongs in a play like Jones's *Saints and Sinners*, in which "worse than death" befalls a heroine who reproaches herself bitterly as she dwindles to the grave. Mrs. Arbuthnot may be a character of Wilde's conception – at least in part – but her lips are moved too often by other authors with a result almost nonsensical.

Not only Mrs. Arbuthnot, but all the major characters exhibit contradictory and unpredictable behavior which damages in particular the crucial last act. Hester, for example, is presented as a reformer on the same model as Rhoda Nunn in George Gissing's novel *The Odd Women*, with an "ascetic ideal" applying equally to male and female as a means to achieve women's emancipation.[46] The fanatical puritanism of Gissing's character is not easily shaken – nor should it be, given her fervor and intelligence – but Wilde's Hester abandons her own passionate radicalism in the few moments it takes to overhear a conversation between Mrs. Arbuthnot and Gerald. "I was wrong," Hester suddenly remarks. "God's law is only love" (p. 110). This abrupt change in Hester's opinions is incredible, and her plans for the future – as proposed to Mrs. Arbuthnot – entirely out of harmony with her past:

There are other countries than England . . . Oh! other countries over sea, better, wiser, and less unjust lands. The world is very wide and very big . . . We shall somewhere find green valleys and fresh waters, and if we weep, well, we shall weep together.

(p. 108)

Their oratorical flavor betrays the falseness of these comments. This is no longer the speech of the stubborn agitator Hester had been shortly before, but the lament of the whimpering female in plays and novels about women with a past, defeated by circumstance, creeping into exile. It is the language, for instance, of Wilkie Collins in *The New Magdalen* (1873), which ends with the Rev. Julian Gray and Mercy Merrick, the rehabilitated prostitute, bound for "a home among new people, in a new world."[47] Wilde's ending is not only imitation, but sheerest fantasy – for Victorian melodrama generally, as Martha Vicinus has said, resolves the burden of the oppressed with the wish-fulfilment of dreams, not by entertaining real change in an exploitative social system.[48]

Whatever may be thought of Lord Illingworth, he is at least a plausible rascal in the early acts, disarmingly witty in his scorn for sincerity and earnestness, for "taking sides" in anything. But he becomes quite a different person in Act IV, an ardent father who cannot bear being separated from Gerald. "I want my son," he declares to Mrs. Arbuthnot. "I love my son" (pp. 115–16). But the basis of his change of heart is never dramatized. Illingworth and Gerald have almost nothing to say to one another apart from a short dialogue beginning the third act, and it is hard to imagine why anyone – especially a man like Illingworth – would desire young Arbuthnot for a son. Without enough warning, if any could be adequate, Illingworth becomes more like the penitent Duke of Guisebury in *The Dancing Girl* than Wilde's original conception of him in *A Woman of No Importance*. The repentant father who has deserted or failed to acknowledge his child was a familiar figure on the English as well as the French stage. "Our nateral feelings get the best of us, and we return like the Prodigal to the home of our offspring," as the disreputable cockney Saunders says in Dion Boucicault's *Formosa; or the Railroad to Ruin* (1869), revived in 1891 at the Drury Lane.[49] Boucicault makes Saunders become so devoted a father to his abandoned daughter Nelly that he tries to sacrifice his life for her – a change of heart almost as sudden and unbelievable as Illingworth's toward Gerald in *A Woman of No Importance*. (It was left to Shaw, in *Pygmalion*, to deal with the prodigal father in the light of cold common sense. Alfred Doolittle is an unsentimental portrait of Boucicault's Saunders.) Although Illingworth pays for his libertine behavior, his most grievous wounds, as Rodney Shewan has argued, are self-inflicted. He betrays the integrity of his own character when, in the second half of the play, he abandons without warning the dandy's point of view, the life of wit and pleasure, to become a sentimental stage father.[50]

Wilde had saved *Lady Windermere's Fan* from its sources with a fourth act which was fundamentally new and psychologically acute. He tried the same last-minute heroics with *A Woman of No Importance*, but the play was by that point too far out of control for such a rescue to succeed. For three acts it had developed partly as a typical French drama of the illegitimate son, partly as a standard English tearjerker of the wronged woman and wicked aristocrat. In the last act Wilde sought a sudden reversal through Mrs. Arbuthnot, who on moral grounds refuses to marry the father of her child. But this revolutionary development cannot find adequate expression in the old-fashioned, tintype rhetoric of Mrs. Arbuthnot and of the other characters, which continues largely unabated to the end. Wilde's boast that he had given theatregoers "what they like, so that they may learn to appreciate what I like to give them" is little more than wishful thinking. It is the failure of *A Woman of No Importance* to overcome its many sources that is the most important fact about Wilde's second society drama.

The play is marked, however, by the inhibitions that feminist critics have identified in the works of certain women writers – inhibitions resulting, Mary Poovey argues, from an independent spirit in conflict with "historical oppression."[51] Even the writer's hesitations and compromises can thus be seen as a form of resistance to custom. Was Wilde confusing the verbal signs to give his play a chance of success at "the smartest theatre in London," where the playgoers – aristocrats, politicians, lawyers – were as glittering and conservative as the dramas they were accustomed to see?[52] Or, as Shirley Foster argues was the case with many women writers, had Wilde himself not entirely escaped the dominant interpretation of womanhood as finding supreme fulfilment only in being wife and mother?[53] Is *A Woman of No Importance*, like *Salomé*, in part an unresolved struggle between the author's own fragmented personality – socialist and socialite, husband and homosexual, father and feminist, Paterian and puritan? The answers, could we know them, would perhaps explain more than redeem the numerous contradictions of Wilde's second comedy.

The Ibsenite conclusion, therefore, is not assimilated to the design of the play as a whole, if a play of so many undigested influences can be said to have a design. The same is true of the appealing wit of Lord Illingworth and Mrs. Allonby, and of the fresh, farcical passages in which Archdeacon Daubeny assures everyone that his wife is quite satisfied with the collapsed state of her health. In this overheated drama they have no proper place. *A Woman of No Importance* fails because it never frees itself of such uninspiring ancestors as *The Dancing Girl* and *Madame Aubert*. Its good moments are freakish appendages, not saving graces.

5

Wilde and Ibsen

Wilde shows no point of contact with Ibsen as a dramatic artist;
indeed, they are opposite poles in the drama of the time.

Archibald Henderson, Arena, 1907

I

Wilde always insisted that his plays, despite their popularity, were misunderstood and undervalued. He bristled when he was labeled "the English Sardou" by critics who saw his comedies mainly in terms of their likeness to *Dora* or *L'Ami des Femmes* – and his resentment, although exaggerated, was not unjustified. In fact when *Punch* caricatured Wilde leaning on a pedestal stacked high with volumes of French "well-made plays," it anticipated much of what criticism would have to say about his drama.

For himself, however, Wilde certainly made claims to a stature much greater than an "English Sardou." With respect to contemporary dramatists, for example, he felt less akin to Sardou than to Ibsen, viewing himself not as an imitator but an equal, working with the Norwegian playwright on a level above the popular dramatists who gave London one adaptation from the French after another. Although Wilde hinted on occasion, his critics never flattered him with the epithet "the English Ibsen." In fact where Ibsen figures at all in discussions of Wilde's plays, it has usually been to provide the sharpest possible contrast to Wilde's aims and methods as a dramatist.

Certainly the differences between the two playwrights are both obvious and fundamental. Ibsen wrote mainly tragedy; Wilde, comedy. Ibsen's plays are populated by middle-class people, Wilde's by aristocrats. Among Ibsen's humorless characters, prey to hereditary disease and madness, it is impossible to find any counterpart for Wilde's wits and dandies. The tense earnestness of *Ghosts* and *Rosmersholm* has no echo in the flippant and funny dialogue of Wilde's productions. Upon Wilde, wrote his youthful admirer Vincent O'Sullivan, there is "not the slightest sign" of Ibsen's influence; "his interest in foreign literature was practically confined to France."[1] And the critic St. John Hankin remarked, several years after

Wilde's death: "In the age of Ibsen and of Hauptmann, of Strindberg and Brieux, he was content to construct like Sardou and think like Dumas *fils*."[2]

One simply cannot accept Wilde's claim that neither Sardou nor any other nineteenth-century dramatist "has ever in the smallest degree influenced me."[3] E. H. Mikhail, in his study of Wilde's debt to French playwrights of the period, has shown how fraudulent that boast was.[4] Wilde's comedies follow the tradition of the *pièce bien faite* in providing a "seesaw of suspense and peripeteia" which is typically set in motion by various stage properties – fans, letters, jewelry. More than that, Wilde relies on French writers very frequently to suggest his characters and plot situations. The shadow of Marguerite Gautier is discernible upon such women with a past as Wilde's Mrs. Erlynne and Mrs. Cheveley. The central situation of *A Woman of No Importance* – the father confronted with a bastard son who spurns his offer of legitimacy – is anticipated in detail by Dumas's *Le Fils naturel*. The exposure of an adventuress by means of her jewelry had occurred in Emile Augier's *Le Mariage d'Olympe* before it was used by Wilde in *An Ideal Husband*. And the mislaid and misdirected letters so important to the plots of Scribe and Sardou take on a similar function in Wilde's plays. Whatever Ibsenite dimension Wilde's plays contain, it is not plausible to deny – as the author did – their important debt to French writers. In fact Ibsen himself was touched more than lightly by the tradition of Scribe and Sardou, as exemplified, among other things, by his tight, suspenseful plots and the emphasis he sometimes gives stage properties (the manuscript, for example, in *Hedda Gabler*).

But the relation of Wilde to Ibsen has little to do with their common reliance on the devices of the well-made play. It grew in an atmosphere suffused with Ibsen. *A Doll's House* and *Pillars of Society* were first performed in London in 1889 (the latter had been adapted nine years earlier by William Archer and performed under the title *Quicksands*, an undertaking he later renounced). The first performance of *A Doll's House* was without question, as Harley Granville-Barker recalled, "the most important dramatic event of the decade."[5] Within two years came *Hedda Gabler*, *The Lady from the Sea*, *Rosmersholm*, and *Ghosts*, and in 1893 *The Master Builder* and *An Enemy of the People*. Translations by William Archer and others appeared throughout the 1880s and 1890s, but the chic thing – as the popular novelist "Rita" noted with scorn – was to learn Norwegian in order to read Ibsen's works in their original language.[6] Wilde's friend More Adey translated *Brand*, and his protégée Elizabeth Robins played Martha Bernick when *Pillars of Society* became the second Ibsen play staged in England. Just when Wilde was launching his own theatrical career, Ibsen's plays were creating a sensation with what seemed shocking depictions of a mother deserting her husband and children, and of a young man, afflicted with syphilis, directing his mother to kill him. "That gloomy writer" could not survive in English soil, Beerbohm Tree declared in an address to the Play-goers' Club in 1891, except as "an admirable manure for the future, a dunghill from which many a fair flower of the drama may bloom."[7] On the one hand Ibsen's plays were hailed for the modernity of their social comment, and on the other damned as "crapulous stuff," as "a loathsome sore unbandaged," as "garbage and offal."[8] But whether praised or assailed, wrote William Archer after *A Doll's House* made its debut, "if we may measure fame by mileage of newspaper comment, Henrik Ibsen has for the past month been the most famous man in the English literary world."[9]

Ibsen thus became a polarizing force in the English theatre. Finding adherents like Archer and Shaw, he also attracted powerful enemies such as Clement Scott, Henry Irving, and Ellen Terry. There was no room in the repertoire for Ibsen (or Shaw or Wilde, for that matter) at the fashionable Lyceum, where Irving staged Shakespearean plays, historical pageants, and old melodramas. Ellen Terry, his leading lady and an icon of Victorian femininity, had no interest in playing what she called Ibsen's "silly ladies."[10] But the influence of Ibsen, if it could not penetrate the Lyceum, reached well beyond the coterie of the Independent Theatre. It is surprising, for instance, to find Louis N. Parker, a writer of traditional melodrama, declaring in his memoirs that "*Ghosts* overwhelmed me" and that *Rosmersholm* (of which he was an early and unheralded translator) "was, I now realize, the only useful lesson in playwriting I ever had."[11] Wilde himself was not counted among the Ibsenites or their detractors, yet to a significant degree measured his work as a playwright against the example that Ibsen set.

It is revealing that Archer, the foremost champion of Ibsen in England, judged Wilde to be London's best playwright even before he had written *The Importance of Being Earnest* and won at least the grudging praise of most critics. Wilde's work, Archer wrote, "stands alone" on "the highest plane of modern English drama."[12] J. T. Grein, founder of the Independent Theatre, which presented many of Ibsen's plays, recalled in an article published just after Wilde's death in 1900:

It flattered him that Archer placed him on a different plane from all other English dramatic authors . . . but even that could not satisfy him. He made it clear to me one day that he considered himself the peer of Ibsen, and when, after the production of *Lady Windermere's Fan*, I described him as an English Sardou, he said contemptuously, "The founder of the English Théâtre Libre calls *me* an English Sardou!" – thereby indicating that henceforth his confidence in me was radically shaken; while never again did he honour the Independent Theatre with his patronage or presence.[13]

Partly Wilde aspired to be what Ibsen had become – "the most famous man in the English literary world" – and partly he felt a keen interest in Ibsen's plays, although his friends and critics usually failed to see it. When in 1891 Wilde saw *Hedda Gabler*, perhaps the Ibsen play he liked best, he wrote a friend that "I felt pity and terror, as though the play had been Greek."[14] Shaw's *The Quintessence of Ibsenism*, which appeared at about the same time, seems to have fascinated Wilde. The book, he wrote Shaw, "is such a delight to me that I constantly take it up, and always find it stimulating and refreshing."[15] Years later, about to be released from Reading Gaol, Wilde told his friend Robert Ross that he had a "horror" of "going out into a world without a single book of my own," and asked him to provide not French plays, but translations of two recent works by Ibsen – *Little Eyolf* and *John Gabriel Borkman*.[16]

II

The Ibsen phenomenon was thus so potent in the early to middle 1890s that many London playwrights – Wilde among them – could be observed reacting to the Norwegian in a variety of ways. Shaw brought out *The Quintessence of Ibsenism* and, placing husband rather than wife in a nursery of false ideals in *Candida*, slyly wrote *A Doll's House* backwards.[17] Mrs. Hugh Bell rewrote *The Master Builder* tongue-in-cheek as *Jerry-Builder Solness* (1893), whose hero is a builder of suburban homes, one of which collapses upon him to end the play. J. M. Barrie's *Ibsen's Ghost* (1891) makes sport of the confusion between manuscript and child in *Hedda Gabler*. "Oh it breaks my heart," says Barrie's version of Hedda, burning old love letters, "for I look upon each of them as a little child, George's children and mine. There are a hundred & twenty-seven."[18] The forgotten Austin Fryers wrote a tragedy to show how Ibsen's dramatic instincts failed him in *Rosmersholm* by leaving out the events leading to the suicide of Rosmer's wife. Already dead when Ibsen's play begins, she is the central character in Fryers's *Beata*, which survives only in manuscript. Fryers brings Beata on stage as the long-suffering wife victimized by the "other woman," Rebecca West. As for Rosmer, no unchaste thought of Rebecca enters his mind. "Never has my regard for you involved a moment's thought of wrong to Beata," he tells a surprised Rebecca.[19] The absurd ending has a blameless Rosmer killing himself in the mill-race while Rebecca watches safely from a distance. Rewriting *Rosmersholm* in terms of axiomatic morality, Fryers deprives it of all mystery and symbolic resonance, as well as most of its shock value. "Ibsen drowned three people," the *Era* summed up in its review of *Beata*. "Mr. Fryers is content with drowning only two." The audience, it observed, was "puzzled and bored."[20]

It would have been strange, at a time when adaptation and parody were habitual with English playwrights, if there had not been considerable tampering with Ibsen's texts. Archer himself began that way, turning *Pillars of Society* into a work called *Quicksands* in 1880, and Henry Arthur Jones collaborated soon after on an adaptation of *A Doll's House*, staged as

Breaking a Butterfly. "Mr. Jones has been much happier when inspired by Ibsen than when he has translated him," wrote Augustus Filon in *The English Stage* (1897); indeed Jones and Henry Herman's version of *A Doll's House* is not a translation, but a shameless adaptation that butchers Ibsen's text.[21] Calling the heroine Flora rather than Nora, the authors reconcile her to her husband (not Torvald, but an understanding Englishman named Humphrey) with lines like these: "I have been no wife for a man like you. You are a thousand times too good for me . . . I'm not worth your caring for."[22]

Like Shaw, Barrie, Jones, Fryers, and the rest, Wilde yielded to the epidemic temptation to rewrite Ibsen. With Wilde there was no question of doing adaptations, but he could not resist, any more than Shaw, performing his own turns on characters and themes which the Norwegian had set moving. Sometimes Wilde merely takes over a dramatic situation in Ibsen, but more often adds something distinctive of his own – a comic twist or, like Austin Fryers, a transformation of Ibsen's text to make an effect and a point that is uniquely his. At times one suspects Wilde of travestying Ibsen in the mode of Barrie, Mrs. Bell and F. Anstey, whose *Mr. Punch's Pocket Ibsen* (1893) included comic revisions of several Ibsen plays. In Anstey's *Nora; or, The Bird-Cage* the little lark-wife one night abandons Torvald and the "eggs," only to return when she discovers she has "only threepence-halfpenny in my purse, and the Norwegian Theatres are all closed at this hour."[23]

While *Lady Windermere's Fan* is most obviously related to traditions of melodrama in both England and France, Wilde's first successful play also exposes, in a manner reminiscent of Ibsen, the hollowness of reigning domestic ideology. Wilde makes his heroine cherish the memory of her lost mother as an "ideal," an illusion which Mrs. Erlynne decides to shatter with the painful truth before she pulls back at the last moment, recognizing that to lose the "ideal" of the parent would mean the loss of everything to the child. In *Ghosts* – first produced in London while Wilde was writing his play – the child's "ideal" conception of his dead parent is treated in a similar way, although it is the ideal the son holds of the father. Ibsen's Oswald and Wilde's Lady Windermere cling to the image of the lost parent as the sole surviving "ideal," an ordering force amid the wreckage of adult disillusionment.[24] But in both dramas the "ideal" parents are actually sexual desperadoes whose real behavior, were it known, would not only disgrace their children, but undermine the bourgeois values which imbue their lives with significance, however illusory. To prevent that from happening, Wilde's Lord Windermere and Ibsen's Manders try to persuade the child's mother not to reveal the bitter facts about the idealized parent.

It is not necessary to deny the obvious differences between Wilde and Ibsen to see what is at work in the common ground of the two playwrights. In *Lady Windermere's Fan* and elsewhere, Wilde often lays hold of particular motifs from Ibsen's plays and in some way stitches them into the fabric of his own productions. For instance, in *The Importance of Being Earnest* Algernon's ungovernable lust for muffins and cucumber sandwiches is traceable in only a general way to the farceur's stock slapstick treatment of food and drink – the sort of thing Brandon Thomas does with tea in *Charley's Aunt*. Algernon's fetish for snacks is certainly funny, but colored by something more: his persistent snacking, as Jack says, is "perfectly heartless" – carried out in relentless pursuit of self-gratification, whatever the cost to others. It suggests the individual's revolt against repression by society, and the guilt, real or imaginary, that accompanies such individuated behavior. An eccentric appetite thus becomes revolutionary in its disregard for propriety and defiance of authority – Algy eats unfazed through high crises, and consumes all the cucumber sandwiches before his tyrannical Aunt Augusta even arrives. Similarly, in *A Doll's House* Nora Helmer can satisfy her craving for macaroons only by defying her authoritarian husband. Her surreptitious munching, comic as it may seem, is the first eruption of a revolt that will shake her and her family to their foundations. Like Ibsen, Wilde uses a farcical obsession with food to dramatize the individual's rejection of custom and authority, although Wilde transposes this gustatory business into a lighter key and produces an effect funnier and less didactic than Ibsen's.

Although *Hedda Gabler* and *The Importance of Being Earnest* may seem as unlike as any two plays could be, they exhibit another curious similarity in their depicting a lost literary work as a vanished child. Having dropped his manuscript in the gutter on a drunken debauch, Lövborg considers that he has lost the "little child" which was the fruit of his work with Thea Elvsted. The metaphor is picked up by Thea and later used by Hedda herself. In *Earnest* Wilde follows the example of Barrie in *Ibsen's Ghost* when he brilliantly burlesques this odd mixup of manuscript and infant in Miss Prism's anguished tale of her own negligence with a manuscript – the "three-volume novel" she wrote "in earlier days." But Prism's grief-stricken confession, unlike Lövborg's, makes a factual rather than figurative equation of baby and ms. From this striking reversal comes the hilarity of Wilde's scene. Absentmindedly depositing her manuscript in a bassinette and the baby Ernest in a handbag, Prism manages somehow to lose both of them "in a moment of mental abstraction, for which I never can forgive myself." But like Lövborg's, Prism's real grief is for a missing literary work, not for baby Ernest. And while Lövborg lost his "child" in a long night of alcoholic excess, Prism mislaid hers in a handbag with a "stain on the lining caused by the explosion of a temperance beverage."[25]

The drama by Wilde which seems most remote from the middle-class drawing rooms of Ibsen is the romantic, exotic *Salomé*. There was practically no precedent on the contemporary English stage for Wilde's portrayal of a morbid, sexually frustrated woman of borderline sanity whose only satisfaction comes from causing the death of the man she vainly craves. Perhaps it was this idol-shattering characterization of woman, in addition to the fact that Wilde was representing biblical characters, which moved the censor to forbid the play in London. After all, audiences there had seen, even in plays adapted from the French, few women more alarming than a watered-down Marguerite Gautier, the courtesan with a repentant heart. It was Ibsen, mainly, who before *Salomé* had dared confront them with stronger stuff – a woman who deserts her husband and children, another who silently contemplates killing her diseased son, and another of whom critic Clement Scott complained that "a woman more morally repulsive has seldom been seen on the stage." Elizabeth Robins, Wilde's friend who played that "morally repulsive" part with electrifying power, "has glorified an unwomanly woman," wrote Scott, the influential critic of the *Daily Telegraph.* "She has made a heroine out of a sublimated sinner. She has fascinated us with a savage."[26] Wilde saw Robins's performance at about the time he set out to create what was, in one sense, the same kind of role for Sarah Bernhardt in *Salomé.* But only the supreme advocate of Ibsen in England, William Archer, seems to have noticed the common bloodline of Wilde and Ibsen's heroines. "Salomé," he wrote, "is an oriental Hedda Gabler."[27]

Put away the masquerade extravagance of Wilde's style and setting, and the basis for Archer's remark becomes clear. Hedda and Salomé – nervous women whose desire turns murderous – represent a total contradiction of the serene purity with which the Victorian male endowed his feminine ideal. Critics wondered, blindly to be sure, why women seemed less shocked than men by Ibsen's characterizations of the female sex. "Many a man's face was expressive of disgust," cried one reviewer after *Ghosts* was given by the Independent Theatre, "but, I regret to say, that I did not mark such an expression upon any woman's countenance."[28] This critic's solution – "Where is the Lord Chamberlain?" – was a popular one in 1891. Editorial comment in the *Daily Telegraph* urged the suppression of *Ghosts,* while some critics suggested that, as one put it, "now surely the Lord Chamberlain must logically allow anything that has the excuse of art, however morally hideous."[29] As James Woodfield has pointed out, however, *Ghosts* was staged at the Royalty Theatre as a private, nominally free performance, and no license was sought or granted. Grein (whose nomadic Independent Theatre had no home of its own, but rented other theatres for its productions) had been told by E. F. S. Pigott, the Examiner of Plays, that *Ghosts* could never be approved by the Lord Chamberlain's office.[30] Oscar Wilde's *Salomé*, being written at just this time, came forward at an opportune moment. It enabled the Lord Chamberlain to show that, Ibsen notwithstanding, not "anything that has the excuse of art" could pass his review after all.

For Ibsenites, however, *Salomé* had much allure. Several years after

Archer acknowledged Wilde's princess as a woman with the stamp of Hedda Gabler, Wilde's play was performed for the first time by Lugné-Poë and his Théâtre de l'Oeuvre in Paris, a theatre associated, perhaps more than the Independent Theatre in England, with the works of Ibsen. Lugné-Poë, who played Hérode, had already produced many of Ibsen's plays, and his company had enacted *Rosmersholm* before Ibsen himself in 1894 with the manager playing the lead. From prison Wilde wrote Robert Ross to say "how gratified" he was by the Lugné-Poë production of 1896 – "it is something that at a time of disgrace and shame I should be still regarded as an artist."[31] J. T. Grein, founder of the Independent Theatre, seems to have been fascinated by *Salomé* over a long period of time and made an unsuccessful attempt to produce it privately in London in 1903 with Gordon Craig as stage director. In 1918, however, he revived the moribund Independent Theatre for a private performance of *Salomé* – an event that cost him his job as drama critic for the *Sunday Times* and precipitated a sensational libel trial over the supposed immorality of the play.[32] None of his productions of Ibsen, not even *Ghosts*, ever exacted such a heavy toll of the manager of the Independent Theatre.

By the time *Salomé* was banned in 1892, or soon after, Wilde had read Shaw's *The Quintessence of Ibsenism*, which he found so interesting "that I constantly take it up." If he looked into the *Quintessence* as often as he claimed, Wilde surely found much that he could use later – including at least four instances of the phrase "ideal husband" which he would employ in 1895 as the title of his most Ibsenite play. Shaw summarizes the action of Ibsen's dramas and invokes the phrase "ideal husband" repeatedly in analyzing *A Doll's House* as a trenchant criticism of "the sweet home, the womanly woman, the happy family life of the idealist's dream." Nora, writes Shaw, "is happy in the belief that she has attained a valid realization of all these illusions: that she is an ideal wife and mother, and that Helmer is an ideal husband."[33] Finally, however, when Nora recognizes Torvald as nothing like the "ideal husband" she imagined, she walks out on father and children "and goes out into the real world to find out its reality for herself, and to gain some position not fundamentally false." Her sense of duty, Shaw explains, undergoes drastic redefinition once she realizes that she and Torvald have only been "playing at ideal husband and father, wife and mother." Not only did Wilde find the phrase "ideal husband" in the *Quintessence*, but also what Shaw particularly stresses in his discussion of *A Doll's House* – the wife's measurement of her husband by an impossible, "ideal" standard, the situation forming the basis of *An Ideal Husband*.[34]

Ibsen of course had put more emphasis on doll's-house ideals as applied to the *wife*, but Shaw was soon to write a play which would turn on the husband's naive idealism. In *An Ideal Husband*, which like *Candida* was written in 1894 and first performed in 1895, Wilde builds on the "model husband" idea which Shaw specially emphasizes in the *Quintessence*. These two Anglo-Irish playwrights had before them, however, among Ibsen's plays already staged in London, numerous examples of "ideal husbands" in one sense or another. Some of these must also have been instructive for Wilde as he set out to create the perfect-seeming husband and unsoiled politician in Sir Robert Chiltern – men, for example, like Rosmer and Solness whose painted masks belie the canker inside them. But the play which, along with *A Doll's House*, left the strongest impact upon *An Ideal Husband* was not one of Ibsen's better-known. Nevertheless, Wilde's friend Elizabeth Robins performed her first Ibsenite role in it, and Shaw had discussed it and summarized the plot in *The Quintessence of Ibsenism*.

III

Pillars of Society, first performed in an English theatre in 1889 (although adapted by Archer earlier in the decade as *Quicksands*), was practically forgotten amid the uproar over *Ghosts* and *Hedda Gabler*. The play, acted at the Opera Comique, would not get another professional staging in London until the twentieth century, and remains today, as it was in the 1890s, one of Ibsen's lesser-known realistic dramas. Even William Archer, who translated it, had nothing to say of it in relation to *An Ideal Husband* when he wrote his review in January 1895 of Wilde's new comedy at the Haymarket. Yet the similarities between *Pillars of Society* and Wilde's play are as significant as they are surprising, bearing more on the substance of the play than anything Wilde appropriated from the French.

But the opinion put forward by Clement Scott in his own review – that "the similarity between Mr. Oscar Wilde's *Ideal Husband* and Sardou's *Dora* is too marked not to be noticed" – has become one of the maxims of Wilde criticism.[35] Wilde himself expressed surprise at the comparison with *Dora* – although as usual in matters of this kind, he was not being quite candid.[36] Mrs. Cheveley closely resembles the blackmailing adventuress Zicka in the French work, but in most other details, and certainly in its philosophical stance, *An Ideal Husband* owes very little to *Dora*. That the comparison occurred to Scott at all may be explained by his having written with B. C. Stephenson an adaptation of Sardou's play, under the title *Diplomacy* (1878), revived in 1893 at the Garrick Theatre. Well-positioned to spot any likeness between *Dora* and *An Ideal Husband*, Scott succeeded in establishing one of the benchmarks for critical discussion of Wilde's play for the next century.

In his third comedy – perhaps his best, besides *Earnest* – Wilde takes up the favorite Ibsenite device of the idealized man with a sordid history, giving but secondary notice to the *woman* with a past, of whom Sardou's Zicka was one among a throng in the annals of the *pièce bien faite*. But while Wilde's hero, Sir Robert Chiltern, can be compared at least generally to whited sepulchres like Solness or Alving or Werle, his case matches in much closer detail the circumstances of Karsten Bernick, the central figure of *Pillars of Society*. Chiltern, an M.P. with his eye on a Cabinet post, wears like Consul Bernick the appearance of "a pillar of society" – or as Shaw put it, "a model husband . . . and citizen." In a public tribute to Bernick, the most powerful official in his community, his friend Dr. Rörlund acclaims him as "the ideal citizen – the model of all the civic virtues." He seems a perfect husband and father, too, his family ties arranged according to "the ethical ideal." Even his disappointed former lover concedes him that "your home is a model, your life is a model." And Wilde's hero-politician is spoken of in the same terms, as an "upright nature" who achieves perfection in his official as well as private life. "You have never let the world soil you," Lady Chiltern tells her husband. "To the world, as to myself, you have been an ideal always . . . something apart from common life, a thing pure, noble, honest, without stain."[37]

The heroes of *An Ideal Husband* and *Pillars of Society* are both public men – Sir Robert Chiltern an undersecretary for foreign affairs in the British government, Karsten Bernick a consul in the Norwegian seaport where he lives. Both owe their power and wealth to corrupt acts for which they plead the excuse of necessity. Eighteen years before Chiltern sold a Cabinet secret to a stock-exchange speculator, and fifteen years before Bernick remained silent, to improve his position in business, when a scandal he knew was false ruined his friend Johan Tönnesen. Speaking when he should have been silent was, says Chiltern, "the origin of my fortune . . . the basis of my career" (p. 177). Falling silent when he should have spoken, Bernick points out, "made me the man I am" (p. 338). Both men conceal their guilt under a reputation for the "ideal," thus living a bold "lie" (both words are used repeatedly in Wilde's play and in Archer's translation of *Pillars of Society*). And in the case of both Chiltern and Bernick, the hero risks everything on a corrupt act – what he styles metaphorically as a desperate toss of the dice. "I have staked all I possess upon the throw," says Bernick (p. 343), while Chiltern refers to himself as one who ventured "to stake all" in life, "to risk everything on one throw" (p. 181).

Both Bernick and Chiltern hide a crime in their past, and both seem prepared to commit a fresh outrage in the near future. To serve his own interest, Wilde's hero decides to drop his long-time opposition to a scheme for a canal in Argentina. In Ibsen's play the hero drops his own long-standing opposition to a plan that would bring the railroad to town. As Chiltern was enriched by his crooked dealings years ago with the Suez Canal scheme, so Bernick would be made a millionaire by the railway line – for he has bought up all the property along the proposed route with his insider's knowledge that it could be resold to the railroad at a handsome profit. And both these inroads of progress – the canal in Wilde's play, the railroad in Ibsen's – are viewed to some extent as symbols of a corrupt, materialistic age to which the old, vital truths have been sacrificed. In stooping to dishonesty in the matter of the canal, Sir Robert Chiltern pleads that he has simply fought the nineteenth century "with its own weapons," because to succeed in modern life "at all costs one must have wealth" (p. 178). In *Pillars of Society* the coming of the railroad is associated with the importation of new ideas, with America and its mania for dollars, and with a new age of machinery and corrupt modern cities.

Against this backdrop of a society attacked by moral rot, Ibsen's Bernick and Wilde's Chiltern try to shirk responsibility for their actions by showing that others are as guilty as they. "Look into any man you please, and you will find at least one dark spot that must be kept out of sight," Bernick rationalizes (p. 338). Chiltern argues that those who would condemn him if they knew the truth are "men who every day do something of the same kind themselves. Men who, each one of them, have worse secrets in their own lives" (p. 177). Both Ibsen's and Wilde's heroes spell out their guilt to a confidant; but when the idea of a purgative *public* confession arises, both men draw back, chilled by the prospect of what a hypocritical society would do to them. It would, says Bernick, "crush me to the very dust" (p. 341). Says Chiltern: "It would ruin me" (p. 183). In any case, both men reason, they harmed no one by their crimes. "Whom did it hurt, then?" asks Bernick. Asks Chiltern: "Whom did I wrong by what I did?" And for both heroes the confidant has the same answer. "Yourself, Robert," says Chiltern's friend Lord Goring (p. 177). "Look into yourself," Lona Hessel tells Bernick, "and see if it has not hurt you" (p. 338). But even if it had not hurt them in that way, both these "pillars of society" – Chiltern and Bernick – have written incriminating letters many years ago which their adversaries now possess and threaten to use to expose them!

These parallels are so numerous and central that one wonders whether Willam Archer, when he wrote his review of *An Ideal Husband*, really failed to notice them – or just politely overlooked Wilde's foraging upon this early realist play of Ibsen. And yet the similarities are at least partly thrown in shadow when seen against the differences between Wilde's play and *Pillars of Society*. The aristocratic characters in *An Ideal Husband* and the aloof comedy of their dialogue carry few reminders of the middle-class earnestness which sets the tone of Ibsen's work. Wilde's lively creations Lord Goring and Mrs. Cheveley have no counterparts in *Pillars of Society*, either in style or substance. Sir Robert Chiltern is much more a convincing character than Ibsen's wooden Karsten Bernick, and the misguided but energetic Lady Chiltern completely overshadows Bernick's wife Betty, virtually a cipher in *Pillars of Society*. Formulaic and conventional, this minor work by Ibsen presented Wilde with an opportunity to challenge the Master on advantageous terms, to answer him with the same corrective reversals which Wilde more often applied to his English rivals. Archer himself had written in his introduction to *Pillars of Society* that Bernick "seems almost a lay-figure" and that even Lona Hessel, the next most important character, never becomes "a living and breathing woman." The play's ending, with its contrived happy solution to Bernick's difficulties, seemed totally unsatisfactory to the man who had adapted it and translated it into English. At this still early stage of his career, Archer said, Ibsen "instinctively thought of a play as a storm in a tea-cup, which must naturally blow over in the allotted two hours and a half" – a prejudice he would overcome in greater works like *A Doll's House* and *Ghosts* (pp. xix, xxii).

But the differences between Wilde's and Ibsen's plays go further and deeper. In fact *An Ideal Husband* is one of those dramas of the English 1890s which in some sense answer or revise what Ibsen had already written. In *Beata* Austin Fryers wrote a new beginning for *Rosmersholm*; in *An Ideal Husband* Oscar Wilde wrote, above all, a new ending for *Pillars of Society*. If, as Wilde would say later, he sought to "out-Kipling Henley" when he composed *The Ballad of Reading Gaol*, with *An Ideal Husband* he tried to "out-Ibsen Archer" or even surpass Ibsen himself.[38] Nowhere is this more apparent than in the different ways that Wilde's and Ibsen's plays depict a plan to expiate the "ideal" politician's secret shame and resolve the conflicts of the plot. In *Pillars of Society* Lona Hessel instructs the hero that the only atonement he can make is publicly to confess what he has done, although Bernick is certain that society will "crush" him and force him into retirement if he follows this advice. In *An Ideal Husband* Lord Goring instructs the hero to confess at least to his wife, but advises against a public confession because "it would ruin you." And when Lady Chiltern learns the truth about her husband, she urges him as a matter of "duty" to resign his position in the government and live alone with her in the country or somewhere abroad. Indeed Sir Robert Chiltern's very name has been Wilde's way of foreshadowing the possibility – a morally conventional one – that the hero must pay for his crime by retiring from office, if not by public disgrace. Applying for the "Chiltern Hundreds" is the standard practice of a member of Parliament who resigns his seat.[39]

But Wilde chose Chiltern's name with apparently ironic purpose – to predict what his hero will *not* do, rather than what he will. Actually the name Chiltern could have been worn with more accuracy by Consul Bernick than by Wilde's clever politician who never pays the moral debt he owes society. The ending of Ibsen's play, with Bernick's public confession of his wrongs, supports after all the conventional view that dishonesty in high office must be accounted for, that a cover-up cannot be justified even years after an offense by a well-meaning and essentially decent man. So Bernick confesses his guilt in the matter of the railroad and in the old scandal that ruined his friend Johan. "How else can you atone?" Lona Hessel had asked, urging him to take this step. The possibility that the consul will have to resign public office remains open at the end of the play, but his confession has so disarmed townspeople that it seems likely this pillar of society, although standing on "quicksand," will be permitted to remain.

Just as Lona Hessel pressed Bernick to confess to redeem himself from crime, so Lord Goring urges a limited confession (to his wife) upon Sir Robert Chiltern. But Chiltern never makes that confession – his wife finds out the truth from Mrs. Cheveley. And when Lady Chiltern calls it her husband's duty to withdraw from public life, she is argued out of her idea that the crime of a public official, even if he is her husband, must somehow be paid for. Not only will he decline to confess and withdraw from public life, Chiltern at the end of the play will accept a seat in the cabinet. He utters some mushy and illogical regrets about having "built up my life upon sands of shame" – the pillar of society in Ibsen's play rested on "trembling quicksand" – but is entirely unwilling to do anything about this sense of guilt. For a time Chiltern almost subsides into Karsten Bernick; he is truer to himself when he tells his friend Lord Goring that it was not really "weakness" which led him to sell a state secret years ago: "There are terrible temptations that it requires strength, strength and courage, to yield to" (pp. 181, 224). Chiltern had that courage, and with it made a fortune which brought him the power he coveted.

In both Ibsen's and Wilde's plays a woman counsels a plenipotentiary to add up the cost of his crime and pay it. Consul Bernick takes that advice, Sir Robert Chiltern refuses it. Several years earlier, when he was editing a women's magazine and writing in favor of a larger role in society for women, Wilde might have ended his play differently. In reviewing a book called *Darwinism and Politics* in 1889, Wilde approved the author's speculation that the development of a more advanced society would mean a larger sphere for women. To bring women into political life would bring, Wilde wrote hopefully, "the family ideal" to the State. "It would mean the moralisation of politics. The cultivation of separate sorts of virtues and separate ideals of duty in men and women has led to the whole social fabric being weaker and unhealthier than it need be."[40] That statement shows Wilde contemplating, long before he wrote *An Ideal Husband*, some vital connection between politics and certain "ideal" conceptions of men and women. Surprisingly, he makes the same point in the review as Ibsen in *Pillars of Society*, where the woman, Lona Hessel, touches public life in just the way Wilde imagined possible – namely, to bring about the "moralisation of politics." But when he wrote *An Ideal Husband* five years later, Wilde had decided that politics required no "moralisation" after all. The "family ideal," as Wilde termed it in his review of *Darwinism and Politics*, is the one thing most grotesquely out of place in the dilemma which embarrasses Sir Robert Chiltern. A cover-up, not the "moralisation of politics," is what is wanted. Instead of meddling in the man's world of dirty politics, Lady Chiltern learns simply to leave it alone, acknowledging that "a man's life is of more value than a woman's" because it has "larger issues, wider scope, greater ambitions" (pp. 264–5). Her function – "all the world wants of women, or should want of them," says Lord Goring – is not to make politics conform to her high moral standard, but simply to keep her husband's love and to love him in return. A more thorough reversal of the "modern" position that Wilde took in his review of *Darwinism and Politics*, or a more smashing rejection of Ibsen's advanced ideas about women, would be hard to imagine.

IV

But Wilde's conclusion to *An Ideal Husband* thwarts in more than one way Ibsen's solutions to the knotty problems raised in *Pillars of Society*. Exposing a conservative, even reactionary vein, Wilde portrays politics as beyond the ken of women – but offsets this unexpected embrace of an old-fashioned sexual ideal by shattering others which even Ibsen did not care to touch. He points, like the Norwegian, to the hidden "quicksands" upon which the pillars of society stand, only Wilde is content to leave his "ideal" politician in the moral swamp where he finds him. The courage of his crime, and its success, are excuse enough for what Chiltern did and place him beyond the irrelevant morality of women. Where once he had hoped women might raise men to a higher level of political conscience, Wilde now views this project with dread. The selfish lie and the crime are masculine strategies by which Sir Robert Chiltern can realize himself and even render valuable service to the society he defrauded.

If Wilde sought to "out-Ibsen" the Ibsenites with *An Ideal Husband*, then to a degree he succeeded. William Archer, iconoclast though he was, was disoriented by the falling of idols that Ibsen had left unmolested. He did not like Wilde's ending, and proposed a new one in his review of *An Ideal Husband*. Sir Robert Chiltern, he argued, ought not submit to Mrs. Cheveley's blackmailing demand that he either support the Argentine Canal scheme or be exposed for his old treachery in the Suez business. He should instead "send Mrs. Cheveley to the right-about and prepare to face the music." Archer adds:

Alas! this is not at all Mr. Wilde's view of the matter. Sir Robert Chiltern does not send Mrs. Cheveley to the right-about. On the contrary, he licks the dust before her, and is quite prepared to involve his country in a second Panama catastrophe in order to save his own precious skin. This is giving away the whole case. It may be a mistake to hold a man disabled by his past from doing service to the State; but this man is disabled by his present. The excellent Sir Robert proves himself one of those gentlemen who can be honest so long as it is absolutely convenient, and no longer; and on the whole, in spite of Mr. Wilde's argument, I am inclined to think it is a wise instinct which leads us (so far as possible) to select for our Cabinet Ministers men of less provisional probity.[41]

86

So Archer proposes that Wilde should have ended *An Ideal Husband* in just the way Ibsen ended *Pillars of Society* – by depicting his fallen politician as being prepared to "face the music" of public exposure, but leaving the door open for continued "service to the State" because of his great abilities and well-meaning nature. Sir Robert should have heeded Lady Chiltern, in other words, precisely the way Bernick heeded Lona Hessel in Ibsen's drama.

None of this can efface the fact that Wilde, despite his denials, still worked in the shadow of Sardou. But the tools of the French dramatist were the stock-in-trade of practically everybody writing plays – including Shaw and Ibsen, who in *Pillars of Society* finds a place for such familiar devices of the well-made play as the woman with a past, the incriminating letter, the misunderstanding, the confidant, and a quickening rhythm of suspense which ends with a too effortless resolution of difficulties posed by the plot. If anything, Wilde was probably less backward-looking in the mechanics of plot construction in *An Ideal Husband* than was Ibsen in *Pillars of Society*. And in substance, Wilde's play is undoubtedly a less conventional production – that is, a more daring assault upon society's system of ideals – than the play by Ibsen which preceded it. The patched-together happy ending, by which the guilty Sir Robert Chiltern retains both his good wife and his good name, is at the same time subversive and dramatically unconvincing (Wilde had no dramatic precedent to go by in framing such a conclusion). Shaw alone seems to have understood the revolutionary nature of Wilde's play, observing with relish that "the modern note is struck in Sir Robert Chiltern's assertion of the individuality and courage of his wrong doing as against the mechanical idealism of his stupidly good wife, and in his bitter criticism of a love that is only the reward of merit."[42] This play demeans practically every ideal but love itself, and *The Importance of Being Earnest*, Wilde's next and last, would blithely mock even that.

No wonder, then, that Wilde was appalled to find *An Ideal Husband* subjected to comparisons with *Dora*, and himself advertised as "the English Sardou." Impatient with critics who wanted to link him with the past, with the tradition of Scribe and Sardou, Wilde knew himself to be, in the phrase of fellow dramatist Sydney Grundy, a "playwright of the future."[43] If comparisons with his work were in order, he implied, they should be looked for in the productions of Ibsen, whom he rewrote at least as much as he imitated in *An Ideal Husband*. It remains perhaps Wilde's most under-rated play, although admittedly a flawed one. R. K. Miller's judgment that it is the best of Wilde's society dramas is notable because such a view has so rarely been expounded.[44]

It is a play which can still startle us today, producing the same kind of moral vertigo as, say, *Ghosts* or *Mrs. Warren's Profession*, because the ideals under assault, although ancient, are perennially green. In *Lady*

Windermere's Fan, by contrast, the naughtiness of Mrs. Erlynne does not really threaten prevailing values in the modern world, or perhaps even speak to them. But is the modern world prepared for Wilde's assault upon the ideal of the honorable public servant, or for his cool endorsement of criminal bravado in high places? In *An Ideal Husband* Wilde's shaking of the pillars of society produces shock waves capable of reaching us today, as only some of Ibsen's plays can. Here, more than in any other drama, Oscar Wilde lives up to his ambitious self-conception as the "peer of Ibsen."

6

An Ideal Husband: *resisting the feminist police*

Surely you don't share this new-fangled folly that a man's life must
be immaculate?
Sir Philip Marchant to his wife in Sydney Grundy's play *A Bunch of Violets* (1894)

I can't think what's come over women. They never used to make this
fuss.
Admiral Darby in *The Case of Rebellious Susan* (1894)

I

"By that curious rule which ordains that it shall never rain without pouring," wrote the *Era*'s dramatic critic in early 1895, "we are having just now
quite a little crop of political plays."[1] Part of this odd theatrical harvest was
An Ideal Husband, whose title must also have suggested associations that
were not strictly parliamentary. A major theme of Victorian comedy, as
Michael R. Booth points out, was that of the ideal wife, an "angel of truth
and goodness" whose devotion to husband and children was unqualified.[2]
In Tom Taylor's *Victims* (1857), for example, Mrs. Fitzherbert cheerfully
works long hours as a dressmaker to finance the extravagance of an
unfaithful and idle husband. This was the "domestic ideal" fostered by
mid-century comedy: the wife bound to a code of perfection, the husband
allowed gross lapses from virtue before being reclaimed, finally, by the
wife's goodness.

The dramatic basis of *An Ideal Husband* – Lady Chiltern's demand that
her ambitious husband be "pure" and "without stain," her "ideal" – is a
complete reversal of Victorian tradition (p. 210). From a late twentieth-
century perspective the wife's obsession with male virtue is likely to seem
preposterous instead of merely antiquated, for it assails the ubiquitous idea
that in Victorian times the woman, not the man, was enshrined upon a
moral pedestal. The modern spectator, therefore, may well be perplexed
when Sir Robert Chiltern declaims to his wife, with all sincerity:

Why can't you women love us, faults and all? Why do you place us on monstrous
pedestals? . . . Let women make no more ideals of men! let them not put them on

89

altars and bow before them, or they may ruin other lives as completely as you . . .
have ruined mine!

(pp. 210–11)

His speech undercuts the view, expressed even in Victorian marriage
manuals, that society "may shut its eyes . . . or may even smile" in the case
of a man's "lapse from virtue," but never a woman's.[3]

Yet the late Victorian stage is crowded with Sir Robert Chilterns. In one
play after another, most never published or long out of print, a man (often
a politician or diplomat) is placed upon a "monstrous pedestal" by the
woman who loves him. Phrases such as "ideal husband" and "model
husband" turn up with strange frequency. In Sydney Grundy's *A Debt of
Honour* (1890), for example, the young hero must expiate a sin which
would bar his becoming the "admirable husband" he is expected to be.[4]
Camilla, heroine of A. W. Pinero's *Lady Bountiful* (1891), declines to wed
self-indulgent Dennis Heron until he has gone to America, espoused noble
aims, and lived up to what she calls her "ideal of a husband."[5] Offstage,
too, these beatified husbands and fiancés abound. Among them is the
abominable Kurtz, who in Joseph Conrad's *Heart of Darkness* (1899) is
reverenced blindly by the Intended as a man of high purpose, "generous
mind," and "noble heart," one whose "goodness shone in every act."[6]

To some extent, as Carol Christ has observed, the idea of an ennobled
male is inherent in the Victorian belief that women could, in Coventry
Patmore's phrase in *The Angel in the House*, make "brutes men, and men
divine." A woman like Dickens's Agnes Wickfield or the mother of the
Prince in Tennyson's *The Princess*, with "Angel instincts, breathing
Paradise," might redeem the sensual male – feminizing him into a "gentleman" with enough delicacy, sympathy, and disinterestedness to satisfy
Matthew Arnold or John Ruskin.[7] But the notion of a perfected male, as
Elaine Showalter has shown, was given a different interpretation by
certain New Women writers at the end of the nineteenth century. Instead
of rejecting the stereotyped womanly values of chastity and maternal love,
they sought to foist these same values on "degenerate male society." A
new generation of women and fictional heroines intensified, if anything,
the Victorian insistence on female purity, but insisted that men live up to
the same high standard.[8]

In Rhoda Broughton's novel *A Beginner* (1894) there is the "World
Women's Federation for the Regeneration of Men." In Sarah Grand's *The
Heavenly Twins* (1893) the militant Evadne refuses to marry Major Colqu-
houn when she learns of his "past life." Her widowed aunt, by contrast,
takes the more traditional view: "I know that if I could have my husband
back with me, I would welcome him, even if he were – a leper . . . I should
think only of his future. I should forgive the past." But Evadne replies:

That is the mistake you good women all make . . . you set a detestably bad example.

So long as women like you will forgive men anything, men will do anything. You have it in your power to set up a high standard of excellence for men to reach in order to have the privilege of associating with you.[9]

Kathleen Blake has remarked that this "ascetic aspect" of Victorian feminism, although important, is "only beginning to be well understood."[10] It goes far toward explaining why Wilde made Lady Chiltern in *An Ideal Husband* a member of the Women's Liberal Association and advocate of votes for women, while at the same time emphasizing that her marriage to Sir Robert Chiltern had produced no children. It is what Thomas Hardy represents so unnervingly in the secular celibacy of Sue Bridehead, what George Gissing suggests in his choice of name for Rhoda Nunn in *The Odd Women*, and what Shaw captures in Vivie Warren, the cigar-smoking accountant from Newnham College whose disgust with the flesh sounds the troubling last note of *Mrs. Warren's Profession*. By contrast, for Herminia, the heroine of Grant Allen's notorious *The Woman Who Did* (1895), feminism meant primarily the loosening of Victorian sexual restraint upon the woman – the right to live with a man not her husband.

By the 1890s the virtue of men – whether sexual, political, or more generally moral – had become an issue of increased moment. But some Victorians, not unlike the character in *Joseph Andrews*, recoiled with dismay at the joining of maleness and purity. "Your Virtue!" exclaims a skeptical Lady Booby when Joseph cites it as his reason for resisting her overtures:

Your Virtue! Intolerable Confidence!. . . Did ever Mortal hear of a Man's Virtue! Did ever the greatest, or the gravest Men pretend to any of this Kind![11]

By the end of the nineteenth century, however, "a man's virtue" had been heard of with some emphasis. The surprised outrage of Lady Booby gave way in some cases to acceptance, but opposition to the "new," feminized man was intense.

II

The "ideal husband" plays of the 1890s are the products, therefore, of more than a theatrical fashion. They belong to a heated debate, carried on in late-Victorian literature and journalism, which makes clear that time-honored ideals of marriage and relations between the sexes were being challenged as never before. After Mona Caird published her articles "Marriage" and "Ideal Marriage" in the *Westminster Review* in 1888, London's *Daily Telegraph* opened its pages for readers to respond to her argument that marriage was a "vexatious failure" whose remedy was thorough reorganization. The newspaper received an astonishing 27,000 letters in response, and a selection of them formed a book – *Is Marriage A Failure?* – edited by Harry Quilter.[12]

In 1895, the year *An Ideal Husband* was staged, a writer who signed herself "E. M. S." saw marriage and man-woman relations at a crossroads. New ideas about marriage, the author said in a *Westminster Review* article, were beginning to challenge the traditional rule that woman must attain a pure standard of morality while the man "can and does stray from the straight and narrow way." In the press and in literature, wrote E. M. S., "modern ideas" on the subject were being widely discussed:

Periodicals of all descriptions are bursting with them; novels and plays, with and without a purpose, dealing with the many problems that centre round marriage, are springing up with mushroom growth in this and other countries.[13]

But E. M. S. found the threat to traditional values taking two radically divergent paths in journalistic and literary discussion. There were those – like Thomas Hardy in *Tess of the D'Urbervilles* and Grant Allen in *The Woman Who Did* – who argued in effect for lowering woman's stardard of behavior to match man's. Others, she pointed out, pulled in the opposite direction, struggling to elevate men to the feminine standard of purity.

Wilde himself reviewed one of the proliferating marriage manuals of the day, the ironically titled but serious-minded *How To Be Happy Though Married*. The anonymous author cautions women against unscrupulous men who lie and cheat, suggesting that the "model husband" would be one who "touched the furthest verge of human virtue" and embodied in his mild temperament the apogee of "home affections."[14] In 1895 the H. B. Marshall firm announced a new book called *Ideal Husband: Papers on the Qualities in a Man Which Conduce to Happiness in Married Life*.[15] Another marriage manual lamented the prevailing view that "impurity" was excusable in a man. "A pure, noble wife is the best gift this world holds for any man," Dr. H. S. Pomeroy reflected, "and he can pay for it only in kind; position, wealth, and all else besides that he may offer, count but as the small dust of the balance in comparison."[16] Like the sensational views of Mona Caird on "ideal marriage," these were signs that fundamental notions about man, as well as woman, were being rethought. Perhaps relatively few agreed with Caird that marriage should be abandoned in favor of a so-called free contract in which the closest bonds between men and women could be dissolved with no more inconvenience than accompanied their formation. But on one point reformers could be united: "Why should there be one law for men, and another for women!" as Jack Worthing puts it in *The Importance of Being Earnest*.

The notion of a perfect man – not merely good, but "pure" and "unstained," as Lady Chiltern says in Wilde's play – may be, in part, the reflection of a utopian vein in Victorian feminist thinking. In *Marriage; As It Was, As It Is, and As It Should Be*, Annie Besant attacked "barbarous" marriage laws which authorized a husband to inflict corporal punishment on his wife, and worse. Her remedy, far from proposing an ethical ideal of the male, was to create a "Marriage Reform League" to work for systematic change in statutes governing relations between men and women. Yet politically minded feminists often viewed the changes they advocated as the prelude to transfiguration of men no less than women. In the reformed future, concludes Annie Besant, "men and women will rise to the full royalty of their humanity, and hand in hand tread life's pathway."[17] Earlier, John Stuart Mill had foreseen the "moral regeneration of mankind" issuing from the struggle for equality of the sexes.[18]

But in the chorus which advocated one morality for both sexes, the tones of radicals and traditionalists were strangely mingled. Conservatives could join in because it was nothing new to demand that men be as good as women, although the idea had become anachronistic among many Victorians. Marriage, complained Mona Caird, had developed into a kind of "Eastern despotism" in which the woman was a "slave-girl" chained to man by economic dependency and thwarted by ideals of purity and duty from which the husband was exempt. One result, she pointed out, was raging prostitution in England, and with it "the division of women into two great classes" – one satisfying man's conception of the ideal woman, the other satisfying his animal desires.[19]

But if New Women and the authors of conventional marriage manuals agreed that there ought not to be "one law for men, and another for women," not everyone saw eye to eye on whether to make the law easier for women or more demanding of men. In Sydney Grundy's popular comedy *The New Woman* (1894) two advanced women stake out opposite positions – Enid Bethune arguing that men should be better, Victoria Vivash that women should be worse.

> *Victoria*: I want to be allowed to do as *men* do.
> *Enid*: Then you ought to be ashamed of yourself; there!
> *Victoria*: I only say, I ought to be allowed.
> *Enid*: And I say that a man, reeking with infamy, ought not to be allowed to marry a pure girl –
> *Victoria*: Certainly not! She ought to reek with infamy as well.[20]

Grundy, however, shows little sympathy with either of these reformers. His hero marries a traditional young woman in the last act, abandoning his book-in-progress about "the Ethics of Marriage" and dropping his feminist friends who would, in one way or another, overthrow the double standard of morality. The joke, of course, is on the woman's movement, which in general fared poorly in the male-dominated world of play writing. The same year *A Doll's House* was first staged in London, William Archer said of the new Pinero play, *The Weaker Sex*: "I remember how amazed I was, even in 1889, to find that the phrase, *The Weaker Sex*, was not used ironically."[21]

In *The Case of Rebellious Susan* (1894) by Henry Arthur Jones, the heroine, like Lady Chiltern in Wilde's play, imagined her husband "perfect" when she married him. When she learns her mistake, Lady Susan Harabin decides to repay her unfaithful husband in his own coin, making herself, as Grundy's character would put it, "reek with infamy" as much as he. Rather than see his wife claim this male liberty, Harabin capitulates to reform of another kind. "If I can only get Sue to settle down comfortably again with me," he vows, "I'll reform and make a model husband for the rest of my life." In the last act his good intentions consume Harabin. "I have thoroughly determined to be the best of men in the future," he announces. Again, several speeches later: "I intend to be the best of husbands."[22] Similarly, in an unpublished play called *The Future Woman* (1896) the husband, Jenkins, decides never to "go astray" again, and in return his wife determines to give up the "Society for the Advancement of Woman's Rights."[23]

The Victorian ideal of woman is thus salvaged, but at the cost of making it apply equally to men – and this was more than some traditionalists could swallow. In their play *Husband and Wife* (1891), F. C. Philips and Percy Fendall make sport of the feminist Mrs. Greenthorne, founder of the "Married Women's League" which, she explains, "we started for the amelioration of men's morals." The aim is "to elevate the standard of husbands to a degree of refinement and purity" previously associated with women only. Among the League's successes is the founder's own spouse, termed a "model husband," who spends his days hemming dusters, washing babies, and pushing perambulators.[24] *Husband and Wife* thus presents what is meant to be an unthinkable feminization of the male. To measure man by the standard of "purity" usually applied to women – to make him a "model husband" – is to devastate his sexual identity. The men in Philips and Fendall's play can realize their manhood only by throwing off the yoke of "model husband" and resuming old privileges. "Men are very weak, and their temptations are very great," says an antifeminist woman in the play. "We should therefore do our best to remember this and make excuses for them."[25]

Being "perfect" taxed the nerves of these idealized men just as it put a strain upon pure women. In a novel by James Payn, for example, the hero is revered by his wife and friends as "the Best of Husbands," but under an appearance of domestic perfection conceals the fact that years ago he killed his own brother in self-defense. One night, threatened with discovery, the "Best of Husbands" ages more rapidly than Dorian Gray, his features becoming sunken and worn, his eyelids dark, his hair white in a matter of hours. Like guilty young women from Victorian novels of an earlier date, John Millbank wastes away with remorse and leaves England at last for the anonymity of foreign shores. "It was well in him to have left her," Payn concludes with no trace of irony; "she confessed she could never have taken that hand in hers again," although "she pitied him, and she loved him."[26]

Not always, however, did the husband bow so compliantly to the refined stardards which his wife thrust upon him. "You have been exhausting yourself in vain efforts to raise me to your level," cries an exasperated husband to his spouse in a novel called *Divorce* (1889). "The thing must end!" Oscar Wilde, who reviewed the book for *Woman's World*, singled out the scene as "finely conceived," calling it a needed antidote to the increasing perversion of art by "pamphleteers" and "reformers."[27]

If sexual reform is mocked or ignored in *Divorce* and in plays like Grundy's *New Woman*, it is accorded much greater weight in other treatments. Often the author sympathizes with a heroine who turns the tables on the male by scrutinizing his past to make sure his reputation and character are spotless. In George Gissing's *The Odd Women* (1893) Rhoda Nunn plans not only to demand "flawless faith" of her husband after marriage, but even before they met (the same demand men customarily made of their wives). When she hears of Everard Barfoot's past indiscretions, therefore, Rhoda scorns the idea of marriage with him, preferring at this stage of her life to be one of the unmated "odd women" of the book's title.[28] In Shaw's play *The Philanderer*, written in 1893, Grace Tranfield, a New Woman, refuses to marry Leonard Charteris because of a libertine career which has made him unable to respect even a woman he loves. "I have refused his offer to marry me," Grace tells Julia Craven, former mistress of Charteris. "I will not give myself to any man who has learnt how to treat women from you and your like."[29] Thus emancipated women become lonely defenders of a new faith with an "ascetic ideal," as Gissing's character calls it – "Propagating a new religion, purifying the earth." Only a moral elite among men will be good enough to espouse women of these puritanical views. "The majority of men are without sense of honour," Rhoda Nunn points out in *The Odd Women*. "To be bound to them in wedlock is shame and misery."[30]

Although women like Rhoda Nunn feel thwarted because they are unable to find an ideal husband, others regret that they did. In Pierre Leclerq's unpublished *This Woman and That*, staged at the Globe in 1890, Lady Agnes Ingleside is enviably wed to a man "incorruptible, unique," the only man anyone knows who is truly "faultless." As one of the characters explains to the heroine: "You are a happy woman, Lady Ingleside, to have secured him for your husband." Near the end of Act I, however, the audience finds the fortunate wife with a lover who passionately kisses her hands while she reproaches herself with betrayal of an ideal husband. "He – he is faultless. . . but – *I do not love him*," she says. Indeed Sir George, the ideal husband, is so good that he can do what few other Victorian males in his position were capable of. He forgives his wife when he learns the truth – once she has shown contrition by shooting herself with a pistol. The bullet only grazes her skin, however, leaving her the strength to cry: "My noble husband!"[31]

With all this Oscar Wilde has no more patience than the put-upon husband of the novel *Divorce*, who chafes under his wife's demand that he be good. In *Lady Windermere's Fan* Lord Darlington laments that in the modern age men have abdicated purity and innocence, leaving them entirely to "good women" such as Margaret Windermere. "My dear fellow," rejoins the dandy Cecil Graham, "what on earth should we men do going about with purity and innocence? A carefully thought-out buttonhole is more effective" (pp. 65–6). In *An Ideal Husband* one of the minor characters complains of her husband: "My Reginald is quite hopelessly faultless. He is really unendurably so, at times! There is not the smallest element of excitement in knowing him" (p. 151). To Lady Chiltern's sister Mabel, an "ideal husband" is not an attractive possibility – "it sounds like something in the next world" (p. 270). Indeed the very idea of a faultless man seems to strike Wilde as quite unnatural. "Men become old," says the delightful Duchess of Berwick in *Lady Windermere's Fan*, "but they never become good" (p. 19).

Thus did the late Victorians – increasingly uncomfortable with the double standard – hesitate between raising man to the level of idealized woman or letting her "reek with infamy" alongside him. To one kind of feminist as well as to old-fashioned moralists it seemed better to raise the standard for men rather than lower it for women. Such reformers had little pity for "the woman who did" – for a Tess Durbeyfield or a Paula Tanqueray. Having sinned once, redemption for them became, with justice, impossible. The right course was not to make things easier for the woman who erred, but more difficult for the man who did – precisely the revolutionary change that the very modern and reformist Lady Windermere proposes to Lord Darlington:

> *Lord Darlington*: Do you think seriously that women who have committed what the world calls a fault should never be forgiven?
> *Lady Windermere*: I think they should never be forgiven.
> *Lord Darlington*: And men? Do you think that there should be the same laws for men as there are for women?
> *Lady Windermere*: Certainly!
>
> (p. 11)

With this policing of male sexuality Oscar Wilde would concern himself again, and more centrally, in *An Ideal Husband*.

III

As applied to the Victorian woman, bound almost exclusively to the function of wife and mother, the idea of perfection was ineluctably linked with the sexual impulse. The endeavors of the Victorian male enjoyed wider scope, with the result that reformist attempts to define the perfect man or "ideal husband" encompassed more than sexual purity without excluding it. Thus Henry Arthur Jones was the exception, not the rule, in dramatizing what he called the "model husband" exclusively in terms of sexual ethics in *The Case of Rebellious Susan*. Despotic power, Mona Caird said, had become the identifying mark of the Victorian male. So it is not surprising to find the ideal husband conceived in relation to his management of power, often unaccompanied by concern for sexual protocol as such. It is this, perhaps, which explains the peculiar fact that so often plays about perfect men and model husbands have as their focal characters a type (exclusively male in Victorian times) whose business was the exercise of political power. In one such play after another the hero is a member of Parliament, holds a Cabinet post, or serves as a diplomat – his claims to ideal masculinity tested by his means of seizing, and keeping, the special entitlements of his position.

Although nearly all ideal-husband dramas were written by men, most seek to dilute the drives for ambition and power with an admixture, at least, of "feminine" virtue and domesticity. A very typical and early instance is Tom Taylor's play *The House or the Home* (1859). Like Chiltern in Oscar Wilde's play thirty-six years later, Chetwynd in Taylor's comedy is an M. P. and an undersecretary of foreign affairs whose unswerving devotion to his political career is the cause of his failure to live up to a husbandly ideal. "I only wish he were as good a model of the husband as he is of the M.P.," says a friend who observes Chetwynd's neglect of his young wife. "The House encroaches sadly on the Home."[32] Even though Wilde's undersecretary of foreign affairs is guilty of taking a bribe while Taylor's has only ignored his wife "shamefully," both politicians have flouted the values by which their wives judge them. Lady Chiltern and Lady Chetwynd alike seem to retaliate by considering the idea of taking lovers. In both plays the wife is interrupted by an unexpected caller just as a scene with the would-be or apparent lover is about to unfold. In both, the politician-husband receives a misdirected, unsigned letter to or from his wife, and in both a piece of jewelry functions ironically to bring about the denouement. But unlike the politician in *An Ideal Husband*, who draws back just in time, the M.P. in Taylor's comedy is won over to his wife's side, made to understand "how a woman's heart will pine for sympathy and fellowship – how its treasure of tenderness must be bestowed somewhere."[33]

Taylor's play reaches what would become on stage a routine solution to woman's discontent with a standard which arrogated power exclusively to the male and domestic tenderness and virtue to the female. Rather than see woman desert the ideal of sexual purity, her portion in the double standard, the power-oriented male consents to be domesticated, embracing hearth and home and consenting to be governed, at least to a degree, by what Wilde regarded in his maturity as the sentimental morality of women. At the end of *The House or the Home* Chetwynd is about to become the "model of the husband" by which he was measured in Act I, but to do so must devote less of himself to the masculine world of the House and much more to the feminine one of Home.

A similar compromise is reached in the unpublished *The M.P.'s Wife*, staged at the Opera Comique in February 1895 while Wilde's *An Ideal Husband* was playing the Haymarket. The M.P. of this anonymous play, John Armitrage, concerns himself only with politics and "scarcely notices" his young wife.[34] He cannot fail to notice, however, when she becomes entangled in a scandal involving not only illicit love but murder. In the end both husband and wife see their error and give one another a second chance – he to become a suitably domesticated husband, like the M.P. in Taylor's play, and she to live up to the standard of purity which, although strained, remains intact at the curtain. Instead of encouraging women to become more like men to equalize their discrepant conditions, this play, like *The House or the Home*, finds it preferable to nudge the male into the feminine orbit.

An M.P.'s Wife and its much more successful competitor at the Haymarket, Wilde's *An Ideal Husband*, were contrasting products of one social and artistic impulse. By the late 1880s, at least, the theatrical agenda – from farce to Ibsenite realism – reflects an evidently intense concern to curb the excesses of the puissant male. In their various ways, and with unequal success, dramatists created a host of politicians whose drive for power was challenged by wife, daughter, or fiancée in the interest of higher or more homely values. Scarcely "ideal," the husband is portrayed – in one way or another – as a polluter of the domestic hearth. He stoops to corruption to further his career, assumes a sexual liberty never granted a "good" woman, or simply neglects wife and family to bestow all his energies on the pursuit of power. A usual outcome is that of *The House or the Home* and *The M.P.'s Wife*: the male becoming the "ideal man" or "model husband" of his wife or fiancée's imagining.

Frequently such plays end with the guilty husband not only repenting, but atoning for his misdeed by "taking the Chiltern Hundreds" – official jargon for resigning from Parliament. Released from the amoral, male preserve of politics, these sanitized men look forward to retirement in the country under the corrective surveillance of a woman's eye. But the hero of Wilde's play, although actually called "Chiltern," behaves in a way that belies his name. After wavering, he rejects in the last act his wife's idea that he resign his post – take the Chiltern Hundreds. And there he parts company with most others of his type, men who consent finally to the feminizing changes which will make them, as Tom Taylor put it, "a model of the husband." What Wilde resists in *An Ideal Husband* is thus not only a set of generic conventions, but the domestic authority of women – what Nancy Armstrong has described as an emerging feminine "power" that transformed nineteenth-century fiction and culture by both complementing and softening harsher forms of authority in the male-dominated political sphere.[35] It is precisely this collaboration between the political and domestic – between male and female – that Wilde wants to foreclose.

Ibsen's *Pillars of Society* can thus be seen as a typical incarnation of the "ideal husband" myth – presenting the soiled politician redeemed by the police authority of a truly good woman. Other playwrights, in productions a far cry from Ibsen's, worked their own variations on the theme. In the unpublished farce *The Candidate* (1888), for example, Justin H. McCarthy depicts an M.P. who in the third act declares "I will apply for the Chiltern Hundreds tomorrow," abjectly returning to his wife and home after using politics as an excuse to escape them.[36] In Arthur Wing Pinero's *The Times* (1891) an M.P. decides to resign his seat and live abroad when his political double-dealing is exposed. It is not his wife's preaching but his own growing recognition that leads him to pronounce, at the end of the piece, "It is 'getting on in the world' that has ruined me."[37] In *The Dean's Daughter* (1888), by F. C. Philips and Sydney Grundy, the diplomat Sir Henry Craven is regarded as "a model husband" although in fact a "heartless and wicked man."[38] But he resists his wife's call to virtue, and she proceeds to do what Lady Chiltern in Wilde's play stops short of – she engages herself to another man and (surprisingly for a play of this kind) marries him after her divorce.

The secretary of foreign affairs in actor-dramatist Neville Doone's unpublished *A Modern Marriage* (1890), softened by his daughter's pathetic appeal, learns to regret his "misspent" life as a "hardened, selfish man of the world" and devotes himself entirely to "good deeds and kind actions."[39] In Pinero's *The Notorious Mrs. Ebbsmith* (1895) and Henry Arthur Jones's *The Liars* (1897), young men almost wreck their careers in public life by becoming involved in illicit love affairs, but recognize before it is too late what Jones calls the "tow-path of duty."[40] Ibsenite "problem plays," farces, and melodramatic potboilers had little else in common, but they could agree in placing the politician under the surveillance of an authority that was both domestic and feminine, even at times monastic. For them the man of public life must be, as for Lady Chiltern in Wilde's *An Ideal Husband*, "something apart from common life, a thing pure, noble, honest, without stain" (p. 210).

Victorian literature had not always treated the related ideals of "model husband" and unblemished politician with such respect. Dickens laughed in *Martin Chuzzlewit* at the demand for perfect rectitude in public life, finding in it something alien, distastefully American. It was the New York newsboy who cried:

Here's the Sewer's exposure of the Wall Street Gang, and the Sewer's Exposure of the Washington Gang, and the Sewer's exclusive account of a flagrant act of dishonesty committed by the Secretary of State when he was eight years old; now communicated, at a great expense, by his own nurse. Here's the Sewer![41]

Nurses, wives, fiancées, and daughters might be shaped (and were by Dickens) to the mold of "angels in the house," but men, while not encouraged to be bad, were not expected to be perfect or homelike. The very idea of the "ideal husband," in fact, evoked for many authors the ridiculous figure of a male in petticoats, unsexed by passionless perfection or by involvement in household routine. Thus in the farce *A Model Husband* (1853) the laughter comes at the expense of the title character, called a "perfect" male, who cooks, cleans, builds fires, and otherwise assumes the woman's conventional role as his own.[42]

Later Victorian authors – although persuaded for the most part that it was wrong to have "one law for men, and another for women" – also saw the "ideal husband" and perfect politician at times as comically feminine men. An impressive novel by Wilde's friend Elizabeth Robins, *George Mandeville's Husband* (1894), calls its hero a "model husband" and shows him thoroughly dominated by his feminist wife with her demand that men live up to the "virtue" and "purity" traditionally required of women. This ideal husband, Ralph Wilbraham, begins and ends the novel with the applause of women for his "particular virtue," but (says the narrator) "he has grown too numb and rigid to be warmed or tempted by beauty, happiness, or love."[43] The man referred to as a "model husband" by the advanced women of Fendall and Philips's *Husband and Wife*, staged in 1891, spends his days playing with and caring for his children – and is therefore the object of laughter. A one-act piece by Arthur Conan Doyle, *Foreign Policy* (1893), makes fun of its hero – a cabinet minister – for being confined to his house with gout and being easily led by his wife. Doyle's farce relies upon the audience to see as incongruously funny the spectacle of a man of power unable to budge from the domestic hearth and incapable of resisting the views of a woman. But whether his audience of 1893 appreciated the joke is unclear. *Foreign Policy* closed after only six performances at Terry's.[44]

IV

"Scandals used to lend charm, or at least interest, to a man," says Mrs. Cheveley in *An Ideal Husband*, "now they crush him" (p. 161). Everyone, she says, but especially a man in public life, must "pose as a paragon of purity" or be laid open by a high-minded and vigilant press. It is against this keen awareness of a new demand for perfection in men that the mushrooming political plays of the early to middle 1890s should be seen. These mostly forgotten or dimly remembered dramas often present a politician who has been less than perfect, and so must pay the price for deviating from the highest standards. To a startling degree the best-known of these plays, *An Ideal Husband*, simply takes its characters and dramatic situations ready-made from the curious type it belongs to. At the same time, however, it denies the new morality on which most dramas of the kind

100

were founded. Thus Wilde's play, like one of his epigrams, begins conventionally enough before turning the tables on an undoubtedly surprised mid-1890s audience. This rhetorical whiplash, as in a paradox, is indispensable to the desired effect of *An Ideal Husband*, but few can have felt it in our own time.

One of the plays which anticipates *An Ideal Husband* even in details is Pinero's *The Cabinet Minister* (1890), which like Wilde's comedy depicts an M.P. compromised in a canal-building project. In Pinero's little-known play the adventuress Mrs. Gaylustre seeks secret information on the Government's decision on the Rajputana Canal Question so she can profit in financial speculation. In *An Ideal Husband* Mrs. Cheveley, a character of the same type, seeks to influence the report of Chiltern on the soundness of the Argentine Canal Company in order to ensure her own investment in it. The wife of Pinero's Cabinet minister has become implicated in the schemes of Mrs. Gaylustre, leaving her husband no alternative (or so he imagines) but to depart public life. "We must hope for a cottage, and a small garden," he counsels, asking his spouse to "resign yourself to a peaceful, rural life" and saying he will "ask for the Chiltern Hundreds."[45] It is the politician's finely tuned conscience (not his wife's, this time) which influences him, even in a farcical comedy, to write *finis* to a brilliant career. But Wilde's politician, similarly situated, can better resist the lure of perfection. Tempted briefly to resign and take the Chiltern Hundreds himself, to live "abroad perhaps, or in the country" (p. 259), as his wife urges, Sir Robert Chiltern soon perceives that such an abdication would be unworthy. Thus Chiltern accepts a seat in the Cabinet at the end of the play – unlike Pinero's hero, who resigns one – on grounds that the emotional idealism of women should not be allowed to restrain his passion for power. "Women are not meant to judge us," explains Chiltern's friend Lord Goring. "A woman who can keep a man's love, and love him in return, has done all the world wants of women, or should want of them" (pp. 263–4). An ideal husband is even worse, therefore, than what Shaw called the "womanly woman." With his sentimental conscience, the ideal husband is a womanly man.

To defend his politician against radical demands for male purity, Wilde recultivated an eroding sexual stereotype of the Victorian era – that women are intellectually the inferiors of men, unequipped for ambition and action, but well-suited for the homelike virtues of mercy and love. Thus one way to protect against "modern" demands for purity in men was to remind feminist reformers like Lady Chiltern that woman has her own place, man his. But a much more egregious instance of getting the guilty politician off the hook by diverting attention to his wife is provided in *The Idler* (1891) by C. Haddon Chambers. The main character again is an M.P. with visions of a Cabinet seat; again he is thought of as a "perfect" husband but has a blot on his past – he has killed a man.[46] But this central issue of the play is suddenly displaced in Act II when Sir John Harding discovers his wife alone with the "idler" who knows the secret of his past and is prepared to use it against him. Although Lady Harding went there to ask the blackmailer to spare her husband, her protestations that "I am innocent" have little effect on her spouse, outraged by the impropriety of her being in another man's rooms. "Don't touch me," cries the indignant murderer. "It is all over." And later, to a friend: "I have no wife. . . For me she has ceased to exist."[47] Thus *The Idler*, which begins with tension between the "perfect" politician and his sordid past, becomes virtually a different play in the third act. In the end, incredibly, it becomes a question of whether an innocent wife will be forgiven by her criminal husband, the concept of ideal man having surrendered with little resistance to the more familiar one of perfect woman.

If *The Idler* solves the problem of the ideal husband by forgetting about it, most of the plays which followed did not. Usually the offending politician-husband pays for his crime, either by taking the Chiltern Hundreds or by penalties even more severe. In Sydney Grundy's *A Bunch of Violets* (1894) the parliamentary candidate Sir Philip Marchant is guilty not only of fraud and bribery, but of sexual misdeeds also. He is blackmailed by a witty adventuress, like so many men in ideal-husband plays, and like Wilde's politician is found out by his highly principled and prosecutorial wife. "Surely," complains Grundy's hero to his unbending spouse, "you don't share this new-fangled folly that a man's life must be immaculate?"[48] But she does, and the only dissenting note is struck by the adventuress, Mrs. Murgatroyd: "I'm sure it's very bad to be too good," she says. "If I were as good as Lady Marchant I should commit some horrid crime, I know I should. Simply for contrast's sake."[49] But her Wildean attitudes are swamped by the sentimental ending in which, facing public exposure and deserted by his family, the guilty Sir Philip quaffs poison and falls dead upon the stage.

Just as Wilde was writing *An Ideal Husband* – perhaps already had finished it – a play by his old friend Maurice Barrès opened in Paris in February 1894 under the title *Une Journée parlementaire*.[50] Wilde was in Paris at about the time the play was produced at the Théâtre Libre, and if he was in the audience must have been stunned by the likeness of this piece to his own – if he had finished it by then.[51] Barrès provides a parliamentary hero, André Thuringe, deputy for Anjou, who has risen to wealth and power by having accepted a bribe for 100,000 francs, just as Wilde's Chiltern builds a splendid career on a bribe of £110,000. Both men dread the public humiliation with which blackmailers threaten them, but both fear more that the truth will become known to their wives, who idolize them. When the deputy hints to his wife that his past might not be spotless, Madame Thuringe responds with a French version of Lady Chiltern's speech in a nearly identical situation:

Je t'aime parce que tu es incorruptible, loyal, généreux et franc . . . et je me refuse à envisager l'hypothèse que tu me proposes d'un Thuringe sans honneur; je ne connais pas cet homme-là! . . . Toi . . . es ma parure et mon orgueil . . .[52]

Lady Chiltern, too, loves her politician-husband because his perfection demands it; he has earned it with a strenuous virtue. "To the world as to myself," she intones, "you have been an ideal always. Oh! be that ideal still . . . don't kill my love for you, don't kill that!" (p. 172). And like Chiltern, the politician in the play by Barrès looks forward to being a cabinet minister – but without fulfillment in his case. Unable to slough off his past as Chiltern can, Thuringe withdraws into the library in Act IV and fires a bullet into his head – choosing to kill himself rather than his wife's love for him.

While *An Ideal Husband* played the Haymarket in the winter and spring of 1895, at least five other plays on the "ideal husband" theme were being, or were about to be, staged in London. Among them was one by R. C. Carton called *The Home Secretary*, in which Julia Neilson acted a part remarkably similar to her role as Gertrude Chiltern in *An Ideal Husband*. Lewis Waller, who played Sir Robert Chiltern in Wilde's play, having taken over the Haymarket while Beerbohm Tree toured in America, was likewise a performer in *The Home Secretary*. Carton's hero is – like Chiltern, Thuringe, and many others – set upon a moral "pedestal" by his idealistic wife, elevated, complains Home Secretary Duncan Trendel, "far above my reach."[53] Gradually, like the demanding wife of Wilde's play, Rhoda Trendel learns to doubt her husband's virtue, suspecting by the end of Act I that he would "forsake any principle . . . to still hold the reins of . . . power."[54] Like Lady Chiltern, Trendel's wife cannot live with such a man, and to retaliate she drifts toward an extramarital intrigue. But in *The Home Secretary* the politician-husband is entirely innocent. He finds her alone with another man, who turns out to be the anarchist Dangerfield, and to save his wife's good name must set free the very man sought in a manhunt that he himself organized. "In giving freedom to that reckless madman, I was untrue to my duty," says the Home Secretary, ready to take the Chiltern Hundreds at the final curtain. "My career is at an end."[55] At a time when the stage was becoming crowded with poisoned and pistoled "ideal" husbands, the Home Secretary let himself off rather lightly.

But the easy tolerance of Sir Robert Chiltern toward his guilty past in *An Ideal Husband* is without parallel in these dramas of immaculate men. Not only does he fail to drink poison or shoot himself, he even refuses the hint supplied by his own name – that of taking, like Carton's Home Secretary, the Chiltern Hundreds. He thinks of his decision years ago to accept Baron Arnheim's bribe as the mark of distinctive "strength and courage," not weakness (p. 181); and at the end is prepared to accept the Prime Minister's offer of a Cabinet post, suppressing the impulse to retire to the country like Pinero's compromised Cabinet minister. It was this innovation that disturbed the critics, even William Archer, who complained that Chiltern did not deserve his happy outcome because he could be honest only "so long as it is absolutely convenient."[56] And the review in the *Era*, never reprinted, is ablaze with indignation:

It is arranged – and this without any indication of sly underlying irony – that Chiltern shall, as a Cabinet minister, enjoy his ill-gotten gains, and the respect and admiration of the world . . . He wanted money, and so he betrayed his trust; and when he thought he was in danger of being found out and exposed he was very uncomfortable. This kind of thing happens every day, and the results are duly reported in the newspapers. But we are not asked to cultivate a fellow feeling with the sordid rogue, to listen to his cowardly and contemptible excuses, and to finally witness the drugging of what he calls his conscience and his maintenance by a process of sophistry in the world's esteem and in that of his wife.[57]

But by breaking the mold of the then-familiar "ideal" stage husband, Chiltern at least created dramatic excitement. No one complained, as *The Times* had of Pinero's Cabinet minister, that he was "a feeble creature," having "little more to do than lounge through the piece in a condition of advanced senility."[58]

If the audacious Chiltern makes a more vigorous hero than usual in ideal-husband plays, the major weakness of Wilde's drama is nevertheless one of characterization, deeply rooted in the now-obscure traditions of this genre. Peter Raby, for instance, has suggested that Lord Goring, the witty dandy, "needs to be in another play to find someone suitable to talk to."[59] From the beginning, moreover, critics complained that Goring "unexpectedly turns philosopher and moralist" later in the play.[60] A figure like Goring appears in many such plays; for if the hero cannot confess an evil past to his uncompromising wife, he needs a confidant – someone like Harker in *A Bunch of Violets* or the co-conspirators in *La Journée parlementaire*, if only to let the audience know what he has done. Tension is required between Chiltern and Goring to make their conversations dramatic, and this the author supplies by thrusting upon the dandy Goring, all too suddenly, the role of moral tutor to his friend. As Ian Gregor has pointed out, Goring's adoption of an active role in the intrigue of politics is not well-suited to his "post of vantage" as dandy – all the less so, in fact, when he speaks with moral indignation.[61] Thus in the scene which finds Chiltern congratulating himself upon having the "strength and courage" to embrace crime, Goring, whose lively but irresponsible wit animated the first act, asks his friend "how could you have sold yourself for money?" (p. 178).

There is a sense in which Goring, by becoming a rather conventional hero who punishes the wicked and promotes the good, deals a blow to the stereotyped characterization of dandies by such authors as Grundy and Jones. But this overturning of audience expectation comes at great cost to the integrity of Goring's own nature. From dandy in Act I to moral monitor in the middle of the play, Goring becomes again the foe of Victorian earnestness in Act IV. When Chiltern declares his short-lived intent to resign from Parliament out of "duty," Goring, a dandy now, sneers that the politician's contriteness is "what is called nowadays a high moral tone" (p. 262). Indeed he is instrumental in arguing Lady Chiltern out of her views on the masculine ideal. The dandy and the New Woman were rightly linked in the consciousness of the 1890s, as Linda Dowling has shown, so it is not surprising to find Goring in deep collaboration with Lady Chiltern, childless feminist, agitator for votes for women, and member of the Women's Liberal Association.[62] What seems improbable in the context of the times is that he so quickly persuades her to discard a key element of her radical feminism – the ascetic insistence upon male purity. Moreover, as John Stokes has observed, "Goring's altruism is enough to make one wonder if he should be counted among the Dandies at all."[63] Brilliant though he is, what can we make of a dandy who links love and politics so sentimentally, who preaches such a retrograde sexual ethic as the one he expounds to Lady Chiltern, and who ends the play by choosing a domestic life in preference to any other?

At other times, too, the almost threatening presence of the dramas which preceded it seems to obstruct Wilde's purpose and damage the integrity of *An Ideal Husband*. An integral feature of many of these political plays is the hero's dawning recognition of the importance of being perfect – the prelude to his reformation in some dramas, to his abject withdrawal from public life or even suicide in others. In Act II Chiltern seems bound for another destination, boasting of his crime as being a token of "strength and courage" and hurling defiance at his wife for having made him "the ideal of your life":

Women think that they are making ideals of men. What they are making of us are false idols merely. You made your false idol of me, and I had not the courage to come down, show you my wounds, tell you my weaknesses. I was afraid that I might lose your love, as I have lost it now . . . Let women make no more ideals of men! let them not put them on altars and bow before them, or they may ruin other lives as completely as you . . . have ruined mine!

(p. 211)

But when he appears next on stage, in Act III, Chiltern speaks more like the creation of Pinero or Grundy than the proud sinner of Act II. "The woman I love knows that I began my career with an act of low dishonesty," he whines. "I would to God I had died before I had been so horribly tempted" (pp. 224–5). Although E. H. Mikhail has pointed out that the conflicts within Chiltern may reflect the author's own "inner torment," in Wilde's play there is no dramatic basis for such a change; it is without motivation and entirely at odds with the beginning and ending of

105

the piece.[64] For one act – nearly a disastrous one – the magnetic force of Wilde's predecessors seems to have wrested control of the drama from its author.

So instead of converting the lapsed husband to an ideal of the man – a usual outcome in plays of this type – Wilde turns the tables and unconverts the wife just before the curtain drops on the last act. So much time had been wasted, however, on the uncontrolled vacillation of Chiltern that none remained to make credible this unexpected and sudden change in his mate. She is merely taken aside by Goring, who whispers in her ear that "Robert has been punished enough" and should not be pressed to resign from office. This improbable dandy adds the conventional Victorian wisdom that men are made for intellect and ambition while women, made of emotions, "are not meant to judge us, but to forgive us when we need forgiveness." That is why, he says complacently, "a man's life is of more value than a woman's" (p. 264). Once exposed to these remarks, Lady Chiltern, the ardent feminist, suddenly tears up with her own hands the letter of resignation she persuaded her husband to write. It is an awkward and unconvincing scene, disturbingly similar to the better-prepared conclusion of a novel by "Rita" – *A Husband of No Importance* – published a year earlier, in 1894. In that reactionary story the feminist Mrs. Rashleigh is disappointed in her quest for "an ideal of manhood . . . a combined essence of Hercules and Apollo, with a dash of King Arthur thrown in."[65] But in the last chapter this "Emancipated Woman" is forced, in a cleverly drawn scene, to recognize the genius and worth of her scorned husband. "The woman's sphere begins with love, and by love alone she reigns," says the chastened modern wife, giving up, like Lady Chiltern, her misguided surveillance of the male.

One of the strange features of *An Ideal Husband*, reflective of its historical moment, is that simultaneously it seeks to dismantle and to preserve the double standard as it applies to women. Like Lady Windermere in an earlier play, Lady Chiltern must develop tolerance for the moral lapses of other people – indeed the righteous feminist becomes her husband's accessory, joining the cover-up to shield him from the lawful consequences of his crime. She, like her husband, must find the strength of character to be bad. The demand for perfection in women needs to be relaxed, Wilde seems to say, rather than applied equally to men as some were urging by 1895. Wilde by now had scrapped the position he took as editor of *Woman's World* – an idea he shared with Beatrice Webb and other progressives of the day – that society should empower women politically because to do so would infuse "the family ideal" into the state and bring about "the moralisation of politics."[66] This yielding to domestic authority no longer attracts Wilde in *An Ideal Husband*; it is what he fears rather than hopes. To stop the feminization of man, he is prepared to embrace the Victorian idea of women as creatures of vast feeling, but scant intellect, properly confined to the domestic sphere and the expression of that womanly love which bonds marriages and families. While proposing to free women from the expectation of angelic purity, he joins the Victorian chorus which charged them, as John Stuart Mill complained, "to have no life but in their affections."[67]

This unlikely mixture of ideas, swallowed without a murmur by Lady Chiltern, is sure to puzzle audiences today almost as much as the play's anxiety over the concept of "an ideal husband." We have lost the context which would light up these dark places of Wilde's drama, but even that context cannot save *An Ideal Husband* from its contradictions – it can only make them comprehensible. The play was part of an energetic discussion – in journalism, in fiction, in the popular theatre – of a doomed scheme to make the sexes equal by enforcing upon men as well as women the most austere standard of virtue. Wilde, however, wished to pursue an opposite course, to encourage a new masculinism by shattering ethical constraints upon the male rather than multiplying and strengthening them. Such a man is Sir Robert Chiltern, who trespasses without remorse upon forbidden ground, and flourishes because of it. He has the full blessing of the author and ultimately of the modern wife Lady Chiltern.

On stage there were many "ideal husbands," many of them in the sexually exclusive world of politics, but few, if any, like Chiltern. In part *An Ideal Husband* is a clever mockery of its prolific species, and it owes at least some of its appeal to Wilde's reversal of the expectations attached to this aristocratic type of play. Regenia Gagnier has argued persuasively that "the dramatic action consists in the unmasking of the upper classes, showing their sham if not obliterating their power."[68] Yet Chiltern is dramatically effective largely because he does not, like most of his kind, wither with self-reproach into an uninteresting lump of moralizing. Nor does he shoot himself or take the Chiltern Hundreds. But its sources are the spinal column of *An Ideal Husband*, and at times they seem to exert almost as much control over the play as Wilde himself. The unfortunate Act III stands at the crossroads of mere imitation and original work, Chiltern almost slipping through Wilde's fingers to become the abject penitent so familiar in these plays. Although it never fully recovers from that loss of control, *An Ideal Husband* remains for us one of the handful of notable Victorian plays. It illuminates and survives its historical niche. Meanwhile the thronging ideal husbands of the late Victorian stage, so wittily mocked in Wilde's comedy, have dwindled to oblivion along with the idea which gave them life – "this new-fangled folly that a man's life must be immaculate."

7

The importance of being at Terry's

> The Foundling is an ingeniously constructed farce, full of ludicrous
> complications and boisterous fun, so cleverly sustained as to keep the
> audience in continuous merriment.
>
> From a review in the *Stage*, 6 September 1894

I

Although no biographer records it, one day near the end of August or
beginning of September 1894 Wilde may have ventured into Terry's
Theatre in the Strand to see a rollicking three-act farce that would alter the
course of his career. The play was *The Foundling*, written by actor and
author W. Lestocq in collaboration with actor E. M. Robson, and it was
welcomed with gales of laughter at Terry's, where one successful farce after
another was produced in the mid-1890s.[1] The critic for the *Era* wrote: "If
uproarious applause and calls before the curtain for actors, authors, and
manager be any indications of success, *The Foundling* at Terry's Theatre is
destined to achieve the same."[2]

Lestocq and Robson's play never would reach the heights of *Charley's
Aunt* – Brandon Thomas's farce was easily the most popular play of the
1890s – but it held the stage at Terry's for nearly two months, from 30
August to 26 October 1894. Soon after closing it enjoyed a week's revival
at the Grand Theatre, Islington. In London, with five or six plays opening
in a typical week, this was no small achievement.[3] A New York production, at Hoyt's Theatre, was mounted the following April. But after that *The
Foundling* disappeared, leaving few reminders of its brief existence in the
footlights. It survives now in typewritten versions – the Lord Chamberlain's licensing copy (dated 11 August 1894) and the script for the New
York production.[4]

Wilde does not mention *The Foundling* in his published letters or other
work, but Lestocq and Robson's farce opened at Terry's just as *The Importance of Being Earnest* was being written – or about to be written. Wilde
rented rooms at Worthing in late summer 1894 (the exact date is not
known) and hoped, he said in a letter, "to do work there."[5] At about this

time Wilde wrote an undated letter to George Alexander, the actor-manager of the St. James's Theatre, asking for an advance of £150 on a "slight" comedy "with lots of fun and wit" in it.[6] Once started, he wrote *The Importance of Being Earnest* very fast – "in three weeks," he reportedly told Frank Harris.[7] And it was exactly three weeks from the opening night of *The Foundling* to 19 September 1894 – the date stamped on the first typed copy of *Earnest* by Mrs. Marshall's Typing Service, which worked from Wilde's handwritten draft.[8]

Scholars who have identified the date of composition for *The Importance of Being Earnest* have done so in general terms such as "August 1894" or "during August–September."[9] Although the date of the first typescript of the play is identified by the stamp of the typing agency, no one knows exactly when Wilde went to Worthing to do the actual writing. Rupert Hart-Davis, editor of *The Letters of Oscar Wilde*, suggests that the move to Worthing took place in August 1894 and that Wilde remained there with his family through September.[10] In any case Wilde wrote "5 Esplanade, Worthing" above a letter which reported he was "just finishing a new play which, as it is quite nonsensical and has no serious interest, will I hope bring me in a lot of red gold."[11] But the letter carries no date, and the hypothetical one assigned by Hart-Davis, "August 1894," is unsupported by evidence. In fact none of Wilde's surviving communications from Worthing can be dated precisely except a telegram of 22 September and letters of 1 and 4 October, and these do not bear on the writing of *The Importance of Being Earnest*.

Wilde, if already in residence at Worthing by the end of August, could have traveled to London by train (as he did more than once) and then gone to the theatre while in town.[12] Before he saw *The Foundling*, therefore, Wilde could have been working on his own play at Worthing for several days without having imposed any final form upon it. According to his friend, the artist Charles Ricketts, Wilde originally intended to write a comedy with a plot "much more complicated" than *Earnest* turned out to be, and set "in the period of Sheridan."[13] Perhaps it was seeing *The Foundling* that turned him from the idea of a "complicated" costume comedy to one with a contemporary setting and a plot based on a young man whose comic difficulties in romance are caused by having "lost" his parents. In any case Wilde could have seen one of the first performances of *The Foundling* and spent the next two or three weeks in Worthing writing the first draft of a farce that would long outlive its forerunner.

Although nearly all memory of *The Foundling* expired with the end of its run on stage, Lestocq and Robson's farce is a play of some merit. Simply as a piece of writing it ranks above the average dramatic work of the 1890s. "Incident follows incident at such headlong speed," wrote the critic for the *Theatre*, "complication succeeds complication with so little pause, that the spectator has barely time to draw breath before from one imbroglio he is hurried into another. All this tends to make *The Foundling* a popular success."[14] A popular success was what Wilde wanted his own, as yet unwritten farce to be, and Terry's Theatre had built its reputation – such as it was – on farces which "brought in a lot of red gold."[15]

II

By no means, however, was *The Foundling* the sole ingredient which Wilde added to his concoction. *The Importance of Being Earnest*, wrote one acute reviewer, "is as full of echoes as Prospero's isle."[16] Long before the nineteenth century, farces had made capital of lovers' misunderstandings, confusions of identity, and such stock characters as the henpecked husband and domineering woman. In the tradition of "practical joking turned theatre," as Eric Bentley has described farce, *The Importance of Being Earnest* finds a generic context, resonating with the tricks and devices of a variety of plays rather than a single precursor.[17] Its aggressive pranks, quick-paced action, and evasion of moral responsibility produce the distinctive laughter of farce – a laughter so at odds with rationality and seriousness that to Shaw, for one, it seemed "galvanism" and "brute."[18] Viewed another way, however, *Earnest* and its farcical predecessors provided the opportunity Charles Lamb found in the amoral comedy of a century ago "to take an airing beyond the diocese of strict conscience – not to live always in the precincts of the law-courts – but now and then, for a dream-while or so, to imagine a world with no meddling restrictions . . ."[19]

Algernon Moncrieff's gluttonizing of muffins and cucumber sandwiches in Wilde's play is reminiscent generally of the ritual food gags of Victorian farce – from pouring tea in a hat in *Charley's Aunt* to throwing bacon and chops out the window in *Box and Cox*.[20] Among the French farces which Wilde might have read or seen in Paris, Labiche and Delacour's *Célimare le bien-aimé* anticipates the "Bunburying" motif in *Earnest* by presenting an imaginary invalid whose feigned illness is used to escape certain social responsibilities.[21] In Musset's *Il ne faut jurer de rien*, a favorite at the Théâtre-Français, an ingenue named Cécile – rather than Cécily, as in Wilde's play – is the reluctant pupil of her clerical tutor and falls in love with a young man pretending to be someone else.[22] In W. S. Gilbert's *Engaged* two young women turn from gushing friendship to hostility when they discover one may have inadvertently married the other's fiancé, anticipating a similar development between Cecily Cardew and Gwendolen Moncrieff in *Earnest*. And like Jack Worthing in Wilde's play, one of the characters in *Engaged* comes to stage dressed in deep mourning for what turns out to be only an imaginary death. But this device had already been used by John Maddison Morton, whose *A Husband to Order* (1859) has a character enter "*in a black costume,*" disguised as his own brother, mourning his own make-believe death.[23]

The Importance of Being Earnest, therefore, can be traced to no single source.[24] Instead Wilde formed his play by resisting many "sources" even while drawing generously, even unscrupulously, from these same plays, French as well as English. But the play on which Wilde leant most in writing his own farce may well have been Lestocq and Robson's *Foundling*. In story, in tone, even in dialogue the two plays exhibit far more in common than can be explained by coincidence or by casual relationship through the genre of farce. At the same time, however, the differences between *Earnest* and *The Foundling* are so pointed that Wilde appears at pains to distance himself from the less ambitious work of his predecessors. More generally, yet pointedly, *Earnest* is an aggression against the genre of farce as a whole.

The first act of *The Foundling* establishes a situation which would be duplicated in several respects by Wilde's farce. Lestocq and Robson introduce a domineering aunt – Miss Ussher – who seeks to thwart her niece Alice Meynall's love for a young man named Jack (not Jack Worthing, as in Wilde's play, but Jack Stanton). *The Foundling* is complicated, moreover, by the same kind of misunderstanding between a pair of lovers that causes so much mirth in *Earnest*. In Wilde's play Cecily and Gwendolen seem to be engaged to the same man, "Ernest" Worthing; in Lestocq and Robson's farce Alice Meynall becomes – to all appearances, at least – the bride of Dick Pennell, the man supposed to be engaged to her friend Sophie Cotton. And in both plays a strong-minded matriarch adds to the lovers' troubles by objecting to the doubtful lineage of the man her daughter wants to marry. To Lady Bracknell the obscure birth of wealthy Ernest (Jack) Worthing seems "to display a contempt for the ordinary decencies of family life that reminds one of the worst excesses of the French Revolution," and she forbids her daughter Gwendolen Fairfax to marry him.[25] To Mrs. Cotton in *The Foundling* the unknown origin of Dick Pennell, despite his being heir to a fortune, disqualifies him from marrying her daughter Sophie. A behemoth of respectability, Mrs. Cotton speaks at times in accents quite Bracknellian. "I will never allow a daughter of mine to marry a man who has no genealogy," she announces; "I want blood."[26]

Confusion about identity was a routine feature of Victorian farce, but the similarity of *Earnest* with *The Foundling* in this respect may be too close to be explained generically. In Act I the foundling-heroes of both plays confess their condition to the mothers of the girls they love. Says Jack Worthing in Wilde's play:

I have lost both my parents.

(p. 30)

And Dick Pennell in *The Foundling*, asked about his parents, blurts out:

I've lost them.

(p. 13)

Under pressure from the impatient mother of his fiancée, the foundling-hero in both plays attempts further explanation. When Mrs. Cotton demands of Dick Pennell that he "come to the point," he replies:

I will . . . I don't know who I am.

(p. 13)

And Jack Worthing says to Lady Brancaster, as Lady Bracknell is called in the manuscript draft of September 1894:

I don't actually know who I am.[27]

Eventually we learn in *The Foundling* that Dick Pennell was discovered and adopted by Sir Nicholas Pennell "five-and-twenty years ago" in the seaside resort of Margate (p. 18). In the first draft of *Earnest*, by comparison, Jack Worthing was "found" by Thomas Cardew "twenty-five years ago" on his way to the seaside resort of Worthing (p. 168). Once more Wilde altered his work in a way that diminishes somewhat its similarity with *The Foundling*, for in later versions of *Earnest* the infant Jack Worthing was adopted not twenty-five, but "twenty-eight years ago" (p. 175) or "twenty-nine" (in a late 1894 manuscript).

In Act I of both plays a character performs wedding music on the piano – Algy Moncrieff striking up "The Wedding March" in *Earnest*, Alice Meynall in *The Foundling* singing and playing "To-morrow I'll be married, I don't care for to-day" (p. 5). Alice's song is inspired by her secret plan to marry Jack Stanton, but her aunt Miss Ussher soon astonishes her with the news that she is actually engaged to someone else – the ridiculous Timothy Hucklebridge. Pressed to explain, Miss Ussher reveals that Alice's father and Timothy himself are her sources of information. "How do *they* know?" demands Alice, incredulous, and Miss Ussher replies:

How do *they* know indeed – who should know if not your father and the man you are engaged to?

(p. 6)

In *Earnest* this comic idea of making the young woman the last to know of her own engagement is given delightful amplification. Gwendolen Fairfax, like Alice, thinks she is engaged to a man whose name is Jack, but learns from Lady Bracknell that

. . . you are not engaged to anyone. When you do become engaged to some one, I, or your father, should his health permit him, will inform you of the fact. An engagement should come on a young girl as a surprise, pleasant or unpleasant, as the case may be. It is hardly a matter that she could be allowed to arrange for herself.

(p. 26)

Another example of Wilde's enlarging upon material in *The Foundling* is his comic use of names, a device to which *The Importance of Being Earnest* owes its title. In Lestocq and Robson's play her fiancé's name, as such, is not important to Alice, but Timothy Hucklebridge's is:

Ha! Ha! Hucklebridge! (*Leaning over back of the settee*) Fancy any self-respecting girl leaving the altar with a name like that!

(p. 7)

Gwendolen in Wilde's play also shows an aversion to certain names in connection with marriage:

I pity any woman who is married to a man called John. She would probably never be allowed to know the entrancing pleasure of a single moment's solitude.

(p. 24)

For Cecily Cardew, too, some names are strangely repellent. "But seriously, Cecily," asks Algernon, posing as Ernest Worthing, "– if my name was Algy, couldn't you love me?" Cecily is unyielding: "I might respect you, Ernest. I might admire your character, but I fear that I should not be able to give you my undivided attention" (p. 65). In *The Foundling* Dick Pennell is unable to remember Hucklebridge's actual name, mispronouncing it "Mr. Muddle-ditch" and "Mr. Tucker Breeches." Exasperated, he finally tells Hucklebridge that "a man with a confounded name like yours ought to hang it round his neck" (p. 30).

Although names are the object of scorn in both comedies, nothing in *The Foundling* matches the strange "ideal" of Wilde's young women "to love some one of the name of Ernest" (p. 23). Yet the pivot of both plays is the foundling-hero's lack of an authentic name and his determination to find one in order to wed the girl he loves. Furthermore in both *The Foundling* and *Earnest* this quest for a name raises the amusing image of a full-grown man of twenty-five being *christened* – as Jack Worthing puts it, "along with other babies" (p. 54). Thus twenty-five-year-old Dick Pennell in *The Foundling* tells Sophie Cotton:

so, darling, until I'm christened no engagement, it will be better.

(pp. 28–9)

In Wilde's play, when Jack Worthing learns that Gwendolen will marry no one but a man named Ernest, he cries:

Gwendolen I must get christened at once.

(p. 24)

113

And when Algernon discovers a similar prejudice about names in his own Cecily, he is eager to confer with the local clergyman: "I must see him at once on a most important christening – I mean on most important business" (p. 65). But the humorous incongruity of the hero's being christened appears only once, and metaphorically at that, in Lestocq and Robson's play. Wilde, by comparison, has Algy and Jack actually make appointments to be christened by Canon Chasuble and introduces baptism as a comic motif into every act of *The Importance of Being Earnest*. Thus what is used up in one humorous speech of *The Foundling* becomes practically a structural principle in Wilde's play, turning up repeatedly as a way of objectifying the heroes' aspirations to be somebody else.

In fact much of *Earnest*'s fantastic humor – its quality of having gotten free of trammeling reality – is the result of Wilde's making what are fanciful metaphors in *The Foundling* into actual events in his own farce. Thus Dick Pennell in *The Foundling* never seriously intends to get christened, but Wilde's grown-up babies, Algy and Jack, lay elaborate plans for the ceremony and have every intention of going through with it. Likewise, the foundling in Lestocq and Robson's play observes a similarity between his own story and that of a sensational novel when he explains his plight to his prospective father-in-law Major Cotton:

Listen to a novel in a nutshell and learn how truth is stranger than fiction . . .

(p. 18)

Dick proceeds to narrate his story in novelistic style, interrupted by an occasional "go on" and "most interesting" from the major. "Five-and-twenty years ago, in the ancient town of Margate," Dick begins, "Sir Nicholas and Lady Pennell, then but a few weeks married, were preparing to retire to rest, when a sound, foreign to any they had ever heard in their room, riveted their attention . . ." Dick describes how Lady Pennell "clutched at her husband," Sir Nicholas "clutched at a razor," and both advanced to the bed, "for from there this muffled cry which chilled them to the marrow, had proceeded." They threw back the bedding and discovered – but here Dick pauses:

Major: Yes, yes, discovered – go on–
Dick: To be continued in our next. How's that?

(p. 19)

Dick's sportive treatment of his foundling past as if it were sensational fiction has a counterpart – much more than echo – in *The Importance of Being Earnest*. In Wilde's play it is Miss Prism who treats the foundling-hero as a person in a novel – indeed as if he *were* the three-volume sentimental novel she wrote "in earlier days." When an irate Lady Bracknell demands

114

to know how she lost the "baby of the male sex" with whom she had been entrusted, Miss Prism recalls:

> Lady Bracknell, I admit with shame that I do not know. I only wish I did. The plain facts of the case are these. On the morning of the day you mention, a day that is for ever branded on my memory, I prepared as usual to take the baby out in its perambulator. I had also with me a somewhat old, but capacious hand-bag in which I had intended to place the manuscript of a work of fiction that I had written during my few unoccupied hours. In a moment of mental abstraction, for which I never can forgive myself, I deposited the manuscript in the bassinette, and placed the baby in the hand-bag.
>
> (p. 98)

A blurred distinction between a baby and a novel thus accounts for the comic effect of long passages in both *The Foundling* and *Earnest*. But the equation of infant and book is left on an analogic plane in Lestocq and Robson's comedy. In Wilde's the mix-up has been real – "the plain facts of the case," as Miss Prism says – and the absurdity of it produces laughter more extravagant than anything Lestocq and Robson achieved with a less imaginative use of the same device. It is an idea which, in both plays, makes fun of the standard melodramatic orphan who discovers his identity and thus surmounts obstacles in love – but Wilde's mockery is at once more daring and more original than what appeared on stage at Terry's.

Indeed Wilde reclaims and reshapes so many of *The Foundling*'s materials that a complete accounting of them would be cumbersome. They include, however:

The bill collection episode Algernon in the manuscript draft of *Earnest*, like Major Cotton in *The Foundling*, is pursued by a London collector to the countryside and presented a bill for food or drink. Both Algy and Major Cotton deny they owe money, but both collectors successfully insist upon payment before they leave. Both debtors have been, as Algy would say, "Bunburying" – leading a secret life in defiance of the proprieties represented by Lady Bracknell and Mrs. Cotton. While Algernon has run up an extravagant bill in pampering one kind of sensual appetite, Major Cotton is in debt for another – his extramarital affection for a singer known as "the Maybud," who shared his revels at the Alhambra. When, however, Wilde cut *Earnest* from four acts to three (the usual structure of a farcical comedy), he deleted the entire bill-collection scene, and with it some seventy speeches and much delightful humor. George Alexander needed extra time for a curtain-raiser, and Wilde, with perhaps too little anxiety about influence from stage managers, readily complied shortly before the play opened.

Giving Mama "the slip" Those dragons of respectability, Mrs. Cotton and Lady Bracknell, do everything they can to thwart their daughters' engagements to twenty-five-year-old foundlings.

A vexed Mrs. Cotton in *The Foundling* commands Dick:

For the present, you and Sophie are strangers.

(p. 16)

Lady Bracknell in *Earnest* lays a similar injunction on Jack:

. . . all communication between yourself and my daughter must cease immediately from this moment.

(p. 87)

Both Sophie and Gwendolen, however, elude their mothers for clandestine interviews with their suitors and reaffirm their love. Says Sophie: "Dick dear – I've given Mama the slip – I did so want to tell you again I'll *never* give you up" (p. 28). And Gwendolen tells Jack – although not in later versions – that she has fled her mother "to assure you of my unalterable devotion" (p. 124, manuscript draft). In both plays, the rendezvous are interrupted by the mothers in hot pursuit.

The mock murderers Ensnared in the complications of a double life, the role-playing young men of the two plays seem to suggest murder as a solution to their problems. Dick Pennell, masquerading as Alice's husband (so she cannot be made to marry Hucklebridge), eagerly awaits the arrival of Jack Stanton and Alice's planned elopement with him. That would free Dick to marry Sophie – but early in Act II the situation is already too tangled for the Major to sort out Dick's explanation:

Dick: . . . Major – mark my words – in a few hours I shall be rid of my wife and free to marry Sophie.
Major: (*Aside*) Heavens! He means murder – phew!

(p. 41)

Wooing Gwendolen under the mask of an imaginary brother Ernest, Jack in Wilde's play imagines he will clear up matters and drop the pose soon:

If Gwendolen accepts me, I am going to kill my brother, indeed I think I'll kill him in any case.

(p. 16)

And when Algy decides to discard his imaginary invalid Bunbury, he replies to Lady Bracknell's ironic inquiry about him: "Oh! I killed Bunbury this afternoon" (p. 87). Furthermore Algy's reference to Bunbury's "doctors" gives a literal texture and heightened absurdity to an idea which, in *The Foundling*, is but a comic misinterpretation of Dick's real meaning in predicting he would soon "be rid of my wife."

The "Baby Boy" finds his mother "Some of the loudest laughter" which

Plate 5   "Congratulate me, I've found my mother!" exclaims the young man who "lost" his parents in a scene from *The Foundling*

greeted *The Foundling*, wrote the critic for the *Era*, arose from scenes in which Dick embraces the wrong woman as his long-lost mother.[28] The point apparently was not lost on Wilde, who made one of the funniest moments in *The Importance of Being Earnest* out of Jack's embracing maidenly Miss Prism as his "mother." Each of the foundlings – Wilde's and Lestocq and Robson's – identifies the wrong woman as his parent after hearing a story of a nurse who, twenty-five years before, took a baby for a walk and lost it. In *The Foundling* the nurse was "dreadfully intoxicated" (p. 56) and could not remember, try as she might, where the baby had been mislaid ("in the wrong house," as it turns out [p. 64]). In *Earnest*, the nurse – Miss Prism – misplaced the infant in a handbag stained by an exploding "temperance beverage" (p. 100) and left behind in Victoria Station.

Although Dick in *The Foundling* views several women as prospective mothers, one of his leading candidates is Miss Ussher, a prim-and-proper spinster not unlike Wilde's Miss Prism. "Mother – kiss your baby boy," he cries, rushing to embrace her (p. 69). And Jack in Wilde's play, embracing Miss Prism, cries "Mother!" (p. 101). Miss Ussher "dodges" Dick and screams, Miss Prism recoils with *"indignant astonishment,"* and in both plays the foundling-hero ponders the consequences of having had an unmarried woman bring him into the world: "I would rather I wasn't the son of a single lady – I crave to be respectable," muses Dick in Lestocq and Robson's farce (p. 75). "Unmarried!" says Jack in Wilde's play. "I do not deny that is a serious blow" (p. 101). But neither Miss Ussher – "I who have been so careful all my life" (p. 74) – nor Miss Prism, whose idea of scandal is a chapter on the Fall of the Rupee, turns out to be the foundling's mother after all. Indeed both plays end with the foundling's discovery that his mother was a woman of rank, lawfully married, and that his father pursued a career in India![29]

III

But why would Wilde, a man of genius, incorporate so much of an ephemeral farce into a play that ranks by common consent among the greatest English comedies? Why give his own foundling-hero the same age as Lestocq and Robson's, why echo so much casual phrasing from the play at Terry's, and why make Jack Worthing's quest for a name and parents so strikingly like Dick Pennell's – down to the Indian backgrounds of the father?[30]

Such questions, I believe, go to the heart of Wilde's method as a writer and the temper of his mind. At his best he was not, as critics like Clement Scott believed, feebly dependent on the work of predecessors. Sources he had, however, and they were indispensable to his creative process. Although Wilde was planning to write a light comedy anyway, the result probably would not have been *The Importance of Being Earnest*, as we know it, had he not visited Terry's when, or soon after, *The Foundling* opened there on 30 August 1894. Probably it would have been a play with some tangible relation to the original title – *Lady Lancing*. But despite its possibly immense debt to Lestocq and Robson for characters, plot, and dialogue, *The Importance of Being Earnest* can by no means be called an imitation. Wilde's play and *The Foundling*, interleaved in dozens of specific ways, are yet separated by an abyss. Indeed *Earnest*, from one point of view, strategically reverses the elements that matter most in the earlier farce.

To turn the ordinary idea or expression inside-out was the habit of Wilde's paradoxical mind. While Ibsenites swept aside old dramatic modes to write "advanced" plays, Wilde spent his five-year theatrical career in the 1890s writing the traditional "well-made play" and farce. When the farce came, Shaw, who had liked *An Ideal Husband*, was repelled by what he considered Wilde's retreat into the unmeaning laughter of worn-out "farcical comedy dating from the seventies."[31] In fact, Shaw added tongue-in-cheek, Wilde must have written the play long ago and recently retouched it for production. "On the whole," he concluded, "I must decline to accept *The Importance of Being Earnest* as a day less than ten years old." Usually the most astute of critics, Shaw did not perceive that Wilde actually had written a kind of "anti-farce," which Shaw himself would soon do in *You Never Can Tell*. In *Earnest* Wilde takes up the devices of farce in general, of *The Foundling* in particular, and stands them upside-down.

Platitudes and popular literature were the food of Wilde's imagination. They energized his paradoxical wit by providing it a substance to work upon – a hollow sentiment, a barren idea, a depleted mode of expression. Just as his epigrams made coruscating effects by inverting commonplace ideas and clichés, so *The Importance of Being Earnest* achieves some of its brilliance by rewriting *The Foundling*, as it were, backwards. Thus what is amusingly metaphorical and even tangential in Lestocq and Robson – the christening of a 25-year-old man, the confusion between baby and book – is revived in *Earnest* as improbable but central fact. In some of its most memorable scenes, therefore, Wilde's play is almost the mirror image of *The Foundling*, owing its wonderful absurdity to the unlikely reworking of language from its predecessor.

Just as Wilde everts the language of a particular farce, turning mildly funny metaphor into zany fact, he transforms at the same time the linguistic milieu of the entire genre. With its spirited deceptions and cross purposes, *The Foundling* was recognized by critics as "an old-fashioned farce" whose emphasis fell more upon quick-paced action than expression. W. S. Gilbert had long since employed a relatively sophisticated dialogue in farce, but his example had by no means been universally followed. Indeed, wrote the critic for the *Times*, "it would be impossible to carry away from the theatre a single *mot* of Mssrs. Lestocq and Robson's dialogue worth repeating."[32] *Earnest*, aglitter with epigram and elegant phrase, leaves quite a different impression. When the *Times* reviewed Wilde's play, it correctly noted a quality in the language of *Earnest* which foiled every expectation:

Mr. Oscar Wilde's peculiar vein of epigram does not accord too well with flippant action. Its proper vein is among serious people, or so we have been taught to think. In a farce it gives one the sensation of drinking wine out of the wrong sort of glass: it conveys to the palate a new sensation, which in the end, however, is discovered to be not unpleasing.[33]

The cultured expression of Wilde's personae – the literary rhythms of their speech – is comical in itself when measured against the "flippant action" of the play. Subverting the banal style of ordinary farce, Wilde created an incongruity between expression and substance which conveyed a "new sensation" and heightened the comic effect of the piece.

Characters in *Charley's Aunt*, *The New Boy*, and *The Foundling* practice deception and undermine authority, but when it counts most they embrace the axioms of popular art and custom – for example, the ideal of a steadfast and self-sacrificial love overcoming all difficulties. Thus when the hero of *The Foundling* discloses to Sophie Cotton that his name is not really Dick Pennell, she assures him it makes no difference. "I love you for yourself alone," she says predictably, "and you will always be the same to me!" (p. 14). Her mother may bar the marriage for the time being, but Sophie will not be daunted: "Look here, Ma, I'm turned nineteen," she says, "and if Dick will wait till I'm twenty-one, I'll marry him in spite of everything" (p. 16). But constant, disinterested love does not fare so well in similar scenes of *The Importance of Being Earnest*. Cecily and Gwendolen cannot – like Sophie – overlook their lovers' names. They *must* be Ernest. Gwendolen pledges "eternal devotion," yet "may marry someone else, and marry often" (p. 38). And Cecily, forbidden to marry Algernon, cannot imagine waiting for him until she comes of age. "I hate waiting even five minutes for anybody," she confesses. "It always makes me rather cross" (p. 95).

So just where a typical farce dissolves into bland conventionality, Wilde's strikes at the root of accepted standards. Nowhere is this subversion better illustrated than in his handling of the role-playing, mistaken-identity motif so predictable in plays of this kind. Farcical characters passing themselves off as someone else – Lord Fancourt Babberley masquerading as Charley's Aunt, Dick Pennell pretending to be Sophie's husband – undoubtedly appealed to Wilde as being, as he puts it in *The Picture of Dorian Gray*, a way to "multiply our personalities" and so make drab life exhilarating and artistic.[34] The usual Victorian farce, however, after getting its laughs from mixups of identity, ends by restoring all characters to their right names and true positions. Indeed the masqueraders are made to repent their false representations as a violation of the good order and just standards of society. "I apologize all round," says Dick Pennell when he drops his disguise in *The Foundling* (p. 38). And in *Charley's Aunt*, just when the deceptions of the young Oxonians are about to bear fruit, Charley cries that he is "too sincerely" in love to go further in his falsehoods.[35] He embraces the truth, conscience-stricken, while Donna Lucia points out to him the wickedness of deceit.

In *The Importance of Being Earnest*, however, there is no such decay of lying – no decline into the ordered serenity of customary life and conventional views. Instead, the heroes are permanently liberated from their former identities – Jack really is Ernest by the end of the play, and Algernon really his brother. Far from repenting their rebellion against things as they are, Jack and Algernon exult in their gossamer lies and see them curiously transformed into truth. Instead of apologizing, Jack simply asserts in the last lines of the play the supreme virtue of "being Ernest" – of flouting sincerity, honesty, fact, steadfastness, and all the other virtues that farces in general found some way to extol.

So just as he stands on end the language of farce, Wilde turns upside down the conventional views which farce at least superficially underwrote. Prevailing ideals are emptied of their traditional content and whimsically reconstituted. The keystone Victorian ideal of earnestness – with its aura of zealous effort, sincerity, and high seriousness – becomes in the end a word signifying the opposite of what it means. To be "Ernest" is to be the "true liar" who overcomes dreary actuality with charming delusions, pursuing a life of pleasure and beauty without reference to clumsy fact.[36] Such playing with language – as an antidote to ordinary reality – was for Wilde one of the secrets of life. It was also one of the secrets of his art, for in absurdly reversing the tendencies of language in *The Foundling* specifically, in Victorian farce generally, Wilde creates the distinctive tone and really original humor that have made *The Importance of Being Earnest* a stage classic while almost all the other farces of the day – including *The Foundling* – have vanished.

IV

It may seem strange that such blatant similarities between *Earnest* and *The Foundling* escaped the notice of London's dramatic critics, who often paused in their labors to observe that some allegedly new play was the recognizable offspring of an old one. But the number of critics, distinguished though they were (G. B. Shaw, William Archer, A. B. Walkley, Clement Scott), was small, while the number of new productions in London approached 300 a year. The long interval between the last London production of *The Foundling* – a one-week revival in November 1894 at the Grand – and the first production of *The Importance of Being Earnest* on Valentine's Day 1895 would have blurred any detailed recollection of Lestocq and Robson's farce for most reviewers. They would have attended dozens of first nights between *The Foundling's* and *Earnest's*, and there was no printed text of the earlier play which a suspicious critic might check for comparison. Clement Scott, dean of critics at this time, confessed in the *Illustrated London News*: "Plays I forget twenty-four hours after I have seen them – otherwise I should go plot mad."[37] Playwrights could experience a similar amnesia, even where their own works were concerned. Asked for recollections of *Topseyturveydom*, an extravaganza he wrote in the 1870s, W. S. Gilbert bluntly confessed years later that "I don't even know what the piece was about."[38] And reviewers believed – with at least some basis – that all farces were alike anyway. Indeed the usual review of a new farce, whoever the critic might be, began by pointing out the play's debt to other farces. A notice in the *Stage* on Lestocq and Robson's play is entirely typical: "Some of the characters and incidents are reminiscent of similar works – a matter hardly to be avoided in farce!"[39] As usual in such cases, the reviewer was not specific. Probably he had in mind the familiar generic attributes of farce – lovers' disguises, absurd misunderstandings, boisterous fun, and the like. The assumption was, then, that farces were not – perhaps could not be – original, and in any case were an inferior form of drama on which the analytical powers of the critic were wasted.[40]

And yet the relationship between *The Foundling* and *The Importance of Being Earnest* did not go completely undetected. Wilde had nothing to say about it – nothing which survived, at least – but Lestocq and Robson seem to have noticed what Wilde had done and responded in kind. Other playwrights of the period who thought their work had been poached wrote the press to complain or filed suit against the supposed plagiarist.[41] Instead, Lestocq and Robson, or someone acting for them before the script was professionally typed in New York, plagiarized Wilde's play when *The Foundling* was staged in April 1895 in America – less than two months after *Earnest* had become a hit in London. Recognizing perhaps that Wilde's characters were practically their own in many respects, only with different names, the authors of *The Foundling* (or someone else who figured in the production at Hoyt's Theatre in New York) laid their hands on one of the brightest speeches of Lady Bracknell and gave it, word for word, to Mrs. Cotton. Dick Pennell, having just confessed himself a foundling, excites the disapprobation of his future mother-in-law in a scene strikingly similar to one in the first act of *Earnest*:

> *Mrs. Cotton*: . . . suppose you should ever find your parents – goodness knows who they might be – utterly vulgar and plebeian for all we know – possibly unmarried – oh! think of it!
>
> *Dick*: May I ask you what would you advise me to do? I need hardly say I would do anything in the world to secure Sophie happiness.
>
> *Mrs. Cotton*: I would strongly advise you, Mr. Pennell, to try and acquire some relatives as soon as possible and to make a definite effort to produce at any rate one parent of either sex, before the season is quite over.
>
> *Major*: Dick, my boy, I'm sorry for you, but Mrs. Cotton is right – that is a frightful prospect – find your parents.[42]

Mrs. Cotton's advice to Dick "to try and acquire some relatives" is identical to Lady Bracknell's counsel to Jack Worthing – except Wilde writes "relations" instead of "relatives" and punctuates the sentence better. In the earlier 1894 manuscript of *The Foundling* – the licensing copy typed at least six months before *Earnest* had its premiere – Dick's question "what would you advise me to do?" (also lifted from Wilde) and Mrs. Cotton's advice to "acquire some relatives" are not to be found. It is clear those speeches were added later, and without much thought, because they illogically divide Mrs. Cotton's expressed fear that Jack's parents might be "unmarried" from the Major's direct response to it: "Dick, my boy, I'm sorry for you, but Mrs. Cotton is right – that is a frightful prospect" (pp. 14–15). With Wilde's clever lines spliced into the dialogue, the Major's reaction is so far separated from Mrs. Cotton's apprehensive comment (which it immediately followed in the earlier, 1894 typescript) that the connection between the two speeches is practically lost.

Except for these lines filched from *Earnest*, the 1894 licensing copy of *The Foundling* and the 1895 New York version are nearly the same. They complete, in effect, what may be one of the oddest cross-fertilizations in literary history – one in which an earlier text influenced a later one, which in turn influenced a *second* version of the original work. But the difference between Wilde's borrowing and that of Lestocq and Robson is crucial. What *The Foundling* takes from Wilde is simply copied and inserted into the text without any regard for coherence, much less with any "anxiety of influence." *Earnest*, however, apotheosizes both the language and the thought of *The Foundling*. Admittedly it is difficult to see how Wilde's play, as we know it, could have been written without the author's having gone to Terry's Theatre one important summer night in 1894 to see the new farce by Lestocq and Robson. At the same time, however, one of the highest compliments to be paid Oscar Wilde as a dramatist is that *The Importance of Being Earnest* is not, by any true estimate, an imitation of *The Foundling*. It is, instead, an assault upon Lestocq and Robson's play, and on the genre it typifies.

8

Algernon's other brothers

Our farcical comedies are all modelled on much the same lines, we
are beginning to perceive, and novelty in their plot is becoming a rare
quality.
From the *Era*'s review of the Parisian farce *Les Ricochets de l'amour*,
5 January 1895

It has often been suggested that this play forms a genre in itself.
Epifanio San Juan Jr., in *The Art of Oscar Wilde*,
commenting on *The Importance of Being Earnest*

I

On the one hand unique, "a genre in itself," on the other *The Importance of Being Earnest* is a shameless ingathering of devices which characterized Victorian farce, especially as it came to be written and staged in the 1890s. A month after the *Era*'s theatre critic announced he was "beginning to perceive" a disturbing sameness in current farces, along came *Earnest* as if to prove his point. But it is a point difficult to substantiate today, for the farces of this period – although frequently zesty, readable, and spontaneously funny – are with few exceptions hopelessly obscure. Few were ever printed, despite great success on stage in some cases, and as a result even the names of most go unrecorded in literary history.

Like its hero, therefore, *The Importance of Being Earnest* can be said to have lost its "parents" – those forgotten farces which in a real sense gave birth to Wilde's play. In these unpretentious works, one can trace the genetic heritage with which *The Importance of Being Earnest* is endowed. Thus W. Lestocq and E. M. Robson's *The Foundling* contains the dramatic basis of *Earnest*, but not everything. What about the imaginary invalid named Bunbury, and the imaginary brother named Earnest? These cannot be discovered in *The Foundling* – but they appear in the manuscript of an unpublished farce called *Godpapa*, which amused audiences at the Court Theatre for four months in 1891–2.

Wilde could not have written *The Importance of Being Earnest* without a thorough, practical knowledge of what was being done in the lowly theat-

124

rical genre of farce in the 1890s. He would have had, without the example of his obscure forerunners, little or nothing to say. Yet *Earnest* has survived, while nearly all the others perished utterly after their moment in the footlights. What distinguished Wilde's play – besides its publication as a book – was an undercurrent of seriousness which was mostly absent among other farces of the day.

Nothing could be more mistaken than the popular and traditional view of Wilde's play as a wisp of fantasy, void of significance and unconnected even to reality.[1] As Richard Ellmann has pointed out, *Earnest* resembles Wilde's earlier work in leading toward a ceremonial unmasking, its characters, like their creator, craving to show what they are.[2] In addition to serving as a staging ground for identity, the play's concern with appearances (Algy "has nothing but he looks everything" [p. 92]) may be, in part, Wilde's comment on a society of spectacle in which "all that mattered was the authority of the participants' poses and the glitter of their props."[3] Wilde's subjects, as Eric Bentley observes, are death, money, marriage, sociology, economics, and the class system, and his "flippancies repeated, developed, and, so to say, elaborated almost into a system amount to something in the end – and thereby cease to be flippant."[4] Katharine Worth finds in *Earnest* Wilde's "supreme demolition of late nineteenth-century social and moral attitudes, the triumphal conclusion to his career as revolutionary moralist."[5] It is highly ironic that Wilde achieved such effects in *Earnest* by using the mechanisms he had employed in the society dramas, with their almost fatal hesitations between sentimental morality and the dandy's world of pure form. Here again are women with a past, "ideal" yet guilty males, motifs of hidden parentage and mistaken identity, and the pivotal plot-object (handbag rather than fan). These similarities illustrate the close relation of farce and melodrama, as Worth has shown, but also the difference between the two forms.[6] Once out of melodrama, Wilde could dissolve in the dandy's laughter the notions of sin and guilt that were so potent, and disruptive, in his previous works.

II

Affording a holiday from earnest reality, Victorian farces appropriately find their setting in a vacation resort by the sea or some other hideaway where the routine and even the values of ordinary life can be suspended.[7] Thus W. E. Suter's popular farce *The Lost Child* (1863) is set in a "garden of a Seaside Hotel at . . .," and the scene of *Tom, Dick, and Harry* (1893) is laid at the "Sea View Hotel."[8] *The Foundling* takes place at the resort town of Brighton, after its orphaned hero "lost" his parents at another coastal watering place – Margate.[9] Its predecessor, *An Innocent Abroad* – performed in January 1895 – depicts a sober broker forsaking his wife and City respectability for a card-playing lark in Brighton.[10] In *The Importance of Being Earnest*, which opened the next month, Jack Worthing's name derives from a seacoast resort in Sussex, and his problematic identity is linked curiously with luggage mislaid in Victoria Station – "the Brighton line" (p. 31).

In fact 1890s farce is obsessed with travel, whether to the sea in *An Innocent Abroad*, to foreign parts in Fred Horner's *The Late Lamented*, or to a country house in *The Importance of Being Earnest*. Occasionally a Jack Worthing visits London to escape tedium elsewhere, but more common is an Algernon Moncrieff who departs town to seek adventure at the seashore or in the country. Remarkable prominence is given to railway stations and luggage. A character in *Godpapa*, preparing to leave from Euston Station, stuffs his suitcase so full of mustard leaves and hot-water bottles that he cannot force it shut. In *Mr. Boodle's Predicament* (1890) comic mixups ensue when a lady novelist finds a handbag with her initials on it in Queensborough Station. In *The Importance of Being Earnest* confusion arises when another lady novelist *loses* a handbag with her initials on it in Victoria Station. And in *Mr. Boodle's Predicament* Theresa Babbacombe carries her manuscripts in the luggage, just as Laetitia Prism meant to do in *Earnest* – before she absent-mindedly put the draft of her novel in a bassinette and laid the baby Ernest in her handbag.[11]

En route to or from a railway terminal, carrying luggage or looking for lost bags, these travelers are in flight not only from their place, but also from their identity in time. Repeatedly they shed adulthood and revert, in one way or other, to the condition of children. Thus Wilde's young men find a way out of their romantic difficulties when they determine to get christened, as Jack says, like "other babies" (p. 54). In *Crime & Christening* (1891), a farce by two dramatists calling themselves Richard Henry, some of the incongruous humor arises from the notion that aging Uncle Gribble is about to undergo baptism.[12] In *Adoption* (1890), by the same authors, an engaged couple without income advertises in the *Times* for "any wealthy bachelor or spinster who would adopt them."[13] *The Magistrate* (1885), by Arthur Wing Pinero, presents a youth whom everyone believes to be fourteen, but is actually nineteen years old, displaying an unseasonable interest in liquor and sex.[14] In Arthur Law's *The New Boy* (1894), one of the biggest hits of the mid-1890s, a grown man mistaken for a schoolboy goes about smoking, ordering whiskey, and muttering "I'm damned!!!"[15] Adults masquerade as children, and the chasm which opens between appearance and truth forms the basis for laughter. But the prominence of christening and other infantile imagery makes sense, too, in its kinship with the impulse by which these characters become ardent travelers and vacationers. Beginning the world again in a comic fantasy of childhood is one way they gratify the need to be somewhere else, somebody else. Without being self-consciously thematic, these farces make life a seaside holiday in which adult cares and duties can be postponed or set aside as characters become, in effect, perpetual children.

Escapes into childhood, to the seacoast, and to the country are insepar- able in late Victorian farce from what Algernon Moncrieff calls "Bunbury- ing." His creation of an imaginary "dreadful invalid" enables Algy to plead the excuse of visiting a sick friend in order to evade responsibility and do as he likes. "If it wasn't for Bunbury's extraordinary bad health," he explains to Jack, "I wouldn't be able to dine with you at Willis's to-night, for I have been really engaged to Aunt Augusta for more than a week" (p. 15). The concept of Bunburying – and its name – could have been suggested to Wilde by the recent success of *Godpapa*, a farce at the Comedy Theatre in which young Reggie describes the imaginary ailment of an acquaintance named Bunbury in order to indulge his own whims without interference:

The fact is he's under the slavery of drink just now. It's something he's read about in the papers and he's trying it as an experiment.[16]

Not only does Bunbury's affliction enable the hero to conceal a disrepu- table double life, as in *Earnest*, but there is an absurdly premeditated quality about the illness in both plays. In *Godpapa* Bunbury – played by Charles H. E. Brookfield – becomes a drunk because "it's something he's read about in the papers," while in *Earnest*, as Algy says,

The doctors found out that Bunbury could not live . . . so Bunbury died.

(p. 87)

One Bunbury shows unusual reliance on journalism in health matters, while the other, as Lady Bracknell sardonically observes, "seems to have had great confidence in the opinion of his physicians" (p. 87).

But Bunburying, if not the name itself, is highly characteristic of late- century farce. Characters form imaginary identities or engage in fictitious activities which enable them to invigorate their respectable but humdrum lives. In the country, in his position as guardian to Cecily, Jack Worthing must "adopt a very high moral tone on all subjects" – so he invents a disreputable brother Ernest whose "dreadful scrapes" give him an excuse to escape to London as often as he wishes (p. 14). The successful farce *Jane* (1890), by W. Lestocq and Harry Nicholls, features a hero who creates a mythical spouse and uses her supposed extravagance as the pretext for extracting money from a wealthy relative.[17] Pinero's *The Schoolmistress* (1886) has a prim heroine who leads a double life as a music-hall singer, leaving her husband every night on the excuse "that I am visiting a clergy- man's wife at Hereford."[18]

But in one of the rare farces by a woman, the popular *Our Flat* (1893) by Mrs. Musgrave, a wife decides she has "no genius for the domestic arts" and decides to enter the masculine world of play writing. "I'll not act in a play but I'll *write* one," Margery Sylvester determines, thus entering secretly into competition with her husband, a struggling writer of melodramas.[19] Her play, a farcical comedy written from her own life, becomes a huge success, with the result that thereafter she and her husband will collaborate on joint productions. "Bunburying" in *Our Flat* is more, therefore, than an essentially harmless lark. In this play written by a woman it becomes, as it would in *Earnest*, a means of developing alternatives to the stifling roles that society imposes on individuals. Margery writes her way to a new and unconventional identity as feminine playwright, the equal of her husband, and thus at the curtain, not unlike *Earnest*, the creatively fashioned *alter ego* dissolves into the actual self of the Bunburyist.

The sheer illicit fun of the secret life is what most farces emphasize, and in these mostly male-written plays the "Bunbury" amounts to little more than a husband's philandering. Often the action centers round a shady hotel – the Hôtel Macotte in *A Night Out* (1896) or the Hôtel des Princes in *The Magistrate* – where the complications of a secret assignation were played out. In Fred Horner's farce *The Late Lamented* (1891), which ran for 230 performances, the late Godfrey Nicholson leaves *two* widows – one in London, one in Cyprus, where he visited regularly under the assumed name of "Mr. Webb," supposedly on business.[20] The hero of Sydney Grundy's *The Arabian Nights* (1887), desperate to evade his tyrannical mother-in-law, disguises himself as Caliph Haroun al Raschid and goes about London doing good deeds and ingratiating himself with pretty girls. The idea came to him when – "in order to escape that eye" of his wife's mother – he shut himself in his bedroom with a volume of *The Arabian Nights*. "My imagination was fired," explains Arthur Hummingtop. "I felt myself every inch a Caliph. In my excitement, I disguised myself."[21]

In addition to Bunbury himself, *Godpapa* introduces – nearly four years before Wilde's play – an evidently imaginary brother named "Ernest." In the farce of 1891 an ingenue makes observations of a very forward kind, but protects her feminine dignity by referring them to a "brother" who never appears or supplies any other token of existence. Thus, when she learns she is being wooed under false pretenses, Maria Browne comments:

Gentlemen & men of honour – don't assume – bogus names – when they go mashing – as my brother Ernest would say.

Again, when Reggie Foster throws her over for another woman:

I am not by nature vindictive, but this young man has fairly given me the needle – as my feather-brained brother Ernest would say.[22]

Like the brother Ernest imagined by Jack Worthing in Wilde's farce, Maria Browne's in *Godpapa* makes feasible an impropriety of expression or behavior at odds with the "high moral tone" expected of his creator. Thus Maria – and Jack, as Algy mischievously remarks – is a "serious Bunburyist," one who lies artfully to evade prevailing notions of responsibility and self-restraint. The young Oxonians in *Charley's Aunt* (1892) are serious

Plate 6   George Alexander and Allan Aynesworth in a scene from the original production
of *The Importance of Being Earnest*

Bunburyists, too, as is John Mags in Fred Horner's *Two Johnnies* (1893), who pretends to be his prosperous cousin in order to win the heart of Clara Bulman.

Characters in these plays not only sprout dual identities and fictitious relatives, they sometimes advance conflicting claims to a single name or personality. There are two persons calling themselves Ernest in Wilde's play, two Donna Lucias in *Charley's Aunt*, two John Magses in *Two Johnnies*, two William Joneses in *The Lost Child*. Frequently an absurd situation arises when a character's identity is misperceived by others rather than misrepresented by himself. In *Mistaken Identity* (1886), an unpublished farce by Alfred Murray, the hero calls upon the designated lover he has never met – only to be received as a valet looking for a place.[23] Carried to extremes, these mixups can be more bewildering than comic. The audience of *Cousin Jack* (1891) – written by Wilde's old elocution coach, the actor Hermann Vezin – would have had to take notes to be sure who is making love to whom. One vital distinction between Vezin's forgotten and unpublished play, which expired after one London performance, and *Charley's Aunt*, which ran four years, is that the successful farce confuses its characters without entirely baffling the audience.

Even when the audience escapes confusion, therefore, the *dramatis personae* assuredly do not. In many cases they virtually lose their grasp of self-identity, as if intoxicated by their own deceptions. This fundamental disorientation makes for one of the brightest moments in *Earnest* – when Jack Worthing asks:

Lady Bracknell, I hate to seem inquisitive, but would you kindly inform me who I am?

(p. 101)

As Katharine Worth says, such a question looks forward to Pirandello and Beckett. At the same time, however, it looks backward to Wilde's immediate predecessors in farce. In *Charley's Aunt*, still playing to packed houses when *Earnest* made its debut, Lord Fancourt Babberley must pose questions of the same basic kind:

What did you say my name was? . . . What am I? Irish? . . . have I any children?[24]

In *Uncles and Aunts* (1888) a character complains:

You see I don't quite know who I am.[25]

In W. S. Gilbert's *Tom Cobb* (1875):

I declare I don't know who I am.[26]

In *The Foundling*:

I don't know who I am.[27]

And in *Two Johnnies*:

Clara: John, who are you? – Tell me.
John: I don't know.[28]

The real answer to Jack's inquiry of Lady Bracknell – "would you kindly inform me who I am?" – is thus more complicated than audiences today can appreciate. His identity cannot be disentangled, any more than his language, from that of the stock hero of late Victorian farce whose holiday frolic leaves the customary verities in turmoil, not least his own sense of self.

Tokens of identity clutter the stage – the engraved cigarette case in *Earnest*, initialed bags in *Mr. Boodle's Predicament* and *Earnest*, handkerchiefs with names embroidered on them in *The Arabian Nights*, a portrait presiding enigmatically over the set of *The Late Lamented*. In Seymour Hicks's unpublished but spectacularly popular *A Night Out* (1896) an ebony brush initialed "H. P." encourages a character to believe, with comic results, that it belongs to the "Hotel Proprietor."[29] In Jerome K. Jerome's *New Lamps for Old* (1890) an umbrella – "green alpaca, no ferrule, knobbly handle" – only seems to hold the key to one of the characters' secret life.[30] F. C. Burnand in *Mrs. Ponderbury's Past* (1895) provides a handkerchief "marked with an 'L' in blue" to unlock the embarrassing history of his title character.[31] This was the age of Dorian Gray and Dr. Jekyll, and the plastic natures depicted in 1890s farce resemble them in more than a superficial way. An Algernon Moncrieff or Arthur Hummingtop becomes a comic Dorian, fashioning an alternative identity – a "double" within whose robes he can transgress accepted standards and satisfy desires which authority would restrain. Like the young people of *The Importance of Being Earnest*, the heroes of such plays seem always in conflict with their elders, who espouse conventional values and demand obedience. "I positively forbid you to aspire to the hand of my ward," the inflexible guardian tells the young man in *Tom, Dick, and Harry*.[32] This tone of absolute authority is adopted by Lady Bracknell in *Earnest*, by Hummingtop's mother-in-law in *The Arabian Nights*, and by many an eagle-eyed aunt, mother, father, and guardian in farces of the period. To evade these tyrants, the heroes conceive the importance of being someone else – they dress in costume, change their names – and so the masquerade and the mixups begin.

Thus the epidemic of mistaken identity in Victorian farces arises from a context of repression and revolt. The despotic parent is defied, and with him or her the constellation of authorized values in whose name obedience is exacted. In rebelling against Lady Bracknell in *Earnest*, for instance, the young people oppose custom itself as well as the stout woman who so brilliantly exacts conformity to it. Among the casualties of this conflict in Wilde's play is the Victorian ideal of the young girl – modest, unassertive, naive. Cecily Cardew and Gwendolen Fairfax become aggressors, capable of prodding an indecisive man through a marriage proposal or even writing his love letters for him. Cecily, indeed, goes so far as to fall in love and engage herself to a man she never met.

The two girls are sexual revolutionaries in the comic mode, but by 1895 their type had become a cliché in Victorian farce, influenced as it was by the topsy-turvydom of W. S. Gilbert. "How long you have been about it!" complains Gwendolen as Jack Worthing works his way nervously to an offer of marriage. "I am afraid you have had very little experience in how to propose" (p. 37). Her forwardness in matters romantic recalls an ingenue in Israel Zangwill's farce *Six Persons* (1893) who remarks after a similar occasion:

Even the way he proposed wasn't original. I've been proposed to far better.[33]

In Pinero's *Dandy Dick* (1887) this exchange occurs when Darbey asks Sheba to marry him:

Sheba: All I ask is time – time to ponder such a question, time to know myself better.
Darbey: Certainly, how long?
Sheba: Give me two or three minutes.[34]

Cecily Cardew in Wilde's play is no less bold, and in a sense no more original, than other young ladies of her type. She writes Ernest's love letters, just as in Sydney Grundy's *Man Proposes* (1878) the heroine dictates a marriage proposal from her young suitor to herself.[35] Enamored of a total stranger, Cecily becomes his fiancée before she meets him – a situation already presented in W. S. Gilbert's *Tom Cobb* (1875), and in *Two Johnnies*, in which Clara exclaims:

Do you know, darling, Father and I admired you oh, so much before we ever heard of you . . . [36]

Propriety ordained a certain detachment of a young girl from her fiancé, as Lady Bracknell explains to Gwendolen – but not to know him at all was an absurd parody which turned Victorian reticence inside-out.

The obsession with engagements forms part of the domestic milieu of these farces. Even their titles announce with remarkable frequency an interest in family relations, from *Charley's Aunt* to *Cousin Jack* to *Uncles and Aunts*. Victorian farce, however, derives much of its humor from overturning current ideas of a wholesome domesticity. In marriage-proposal scenes, therefore, the women are predatory and the men yielding, almost feminine in the Victorian sense; indeed, Lord Fancourt Babberley in *Charley's Aunt* is dressed in drag. A man marries two women (in *The Late Lamented*) or a woman becomes engaged to two men (*Box and Cox*). Children not only defy their parents, they "lose" them like Jack Worthing in *Earnest* or Dick Pennell in *The Foundling*. As a character in *Godpapa* puts it:

I always think it's the first duty of a marriageable girl to lose her mother, to take her out and lose her altogether.[37]

In *Jane*, Nicholls and Lestocq have fun with the related idea (as Wilde would in *Earnest*) of parents losing their children, even forgetting their existence. Shackleford can recall nothing about his supposed young son:

Shackleford: . . . I've forgotten all about it.
　Jane: How old is it?
Shackleford: I don't know.
　Jane: A boy or a girl?
Shackleford: That I can't tell you.[38]

Love, instead of being the lasting foundation upon which families are raised, is unstable and transient. Thus in *Adoption* a long engagement ends abruptly:

Theodosius: I did love you fondly, nay, more so – until this morning.
Constantia: And I loved you with a devotion which mere words would but faintly express – until 10.15.[39]

This is the tone Wilde catches in Act III of *Earnest*:

Cecily: Algy, could you wait for me till I was thirty-five?
Algernon: Of course I could, Cecily. You know I could.
Cecily: Yes, I felt it instinctively, but I couldn't wait all that time. I hate waiting even five minutes for anybody.

(pp. 94–5)

Similarly Gwendolen tells Jack that although "I may marry someone else, and marry often, nothing . . . can possibly . . . alter my eternal devotion to you" (p. 38).

The family ideal is conspicuous throughout Victorian literature, which indeed makes a special point of the homeless child – an Oliver Twist or Jane Eyre – whose difficulties are resolved by assimilation into a harmonious domestic circle. The unhappy waif typically finds a mother or father or in due time becomes a parent herself, establishing – like Esther Summerson in her tiny "Bleak House" – a shelter from the rough winds of the world outside. John Strange Winter's story *Bootle's Baby* (1885) was one such work which achieved spectacular success with the late Victorians. Oscar Wilde, like everyone else, had read it, and once remarked mockingly in a letter:

What a great passionate splendid writer John Strange Winter is! How little people understand her work! *Bootle's Baby* is *une oeuvre symboliste*: it is really only the style and the subject that are wrong. Pray never speak lightly of *Bootle's Baby* . . . [40]

The victim of Wilde's irony was a story whose heroine, a little girl with "short golden curls" named Mignon, is left by her mother in the quarters of a captain of the Scarlet Lancers. He rears her as his own daughter and years later falls in love with the woman who turns out to be – who else? – Mignon's mother. They marry, and the foundling is reunited with the lost parent in a rapture of familial emotion. The novel was turned into what the *Times* called "a strong, pathetic play" in 1888, its success "attested by the applause of a crowded house."[41]

The great Victorian myth of the foundling assigns urgent significance to finding a home for the homeless child, for here, in the warmth of the fireside, humane values could prosper in a Darwinian world. Farce, however, mocks this ideal of domesticity and the foundling who is so integral a part of it. The "babies" become worldly Oxonians, as in *Charley's Aunt*, or twenty-five-year-old men about town, as in *The Importance of Being Earnest* and *The Foundling*. They desperately seek "one parent of either sex, before the season is quite over," but only to satisfy the punctilios of a Lady Bracknell or Mrs. Cotton about "blood."[42] Otherwise they seem comfortably reconciled to the loss of father and mother, and recovery of the lost parent does not bring the sacramental results that attend it elsewhere in Victorian literature. So the apocalyptic moment of the foundling myth is deflated – all the more so when the young hero cries "Mamma!" or "Mother!" when embracing, as in *Charley's Aunt* or *The Foundling* or *Earnest*, a dignified woman of no relation to him. This is the distinctive tone of late Victorian farce, which – not unlike Ibsen's plays in this respect – treats all ideals, including that of domesticity, from the point of view of absurdity. But an even earlier work such as *The Lost Child* handles such materials irreverently. An anxious father in that mid-Victorian farce, having sought his missing child in vain, "starts up and stands paralyzed" when a waiter at a seaside hotel uncovers the cold-meat tray and rolls the lost infant onto the dinner table before him.[43]

To someone like Henry Arthur Jones, who hoped the theatre would take over the religious and moral functions of a dying English Church, it was disheartening that so many plays were content to be "foolishly dallying with the great issues of human life as with a child's box of wooden toy men."[44] Farcical playwrights, from Jones's viewpoint, neglected their sacerdotal duty when they brought up high ideals and great themes merely to insult them with giddy laughter. Their characters were invariably in flight from serious effort – vacationing, or Bunburying, or – like Jack in *The Importance of Being Earnest* – smoking cigarettes as their life's work. They respond to sublime crises – baptism, love, death – with commonplace physical hunger. "When I am in trouble," explains Algernon Moncrieff, feasting on muffins, "eating is the only thing that consoles me" (p. 79). Even love cannot quell an appetite for cucumber sandwiches in Wilde's play, but this was a trick Pinero had already played to perfection in *The Magistrate*, in a scene in which Captain Vale complains to Colonel Lukyn of a recent disappointment in romance:

Lukyn: Great loss – have a cigarette.
Vale: Parascho's?
Lukyn: Yes. Was she – full grown?
Vale: Just perfection. She rides eight stone fifteen, and I have lost her, Lukyn. Beautiful tobacco . . . By Jove, it's broken my heart, old fellow. I'll go right on to the champagne, please.[45]

This flippant attitude in late-century farce suggests a disillusionment as profound, in its way, as that exhibited in the scabrous dramas of Ibsen. Playwrights were the heirs of priests, Henry Arthur Jones argued in the 1890s; but before English drama could fulfill its Arnoldian destiny as spiritual advisor to the nation, the twin evils of farce and Ibsenism would have to be outrooted.

Even when characters in these plays manifest some organizing focus in their lives, or some ideal, it is certain to be craven or absurd or both. This parody of purpose can be seen, for example, in *Two Johnnies* when the ingenue's father welcomes a new suitor, a grocer masquerading as a famous lawyer:

The dream of my life has been for my daughter to marry a celebrated man! Take her! She's yours.[46]

And in Pinero's *The Schoolmistress* the heroine's dream is fulfilled when she marries a broken-down aristocrat known as the Honourable Vere Queckett:

It had been a long-cherished ambition with me, if ever I married, to wed no one but a gentleman. I do not mean a gentleman in a mere parliamentary sense; I mean a man of birth, blood, and breeding.[47]

The ideals so important to these characters are silly, but at least have a certain plausibility. In other plays, however, ideals are mere words emptied of content. Thus in Justin H. McCarthy's *Your Wife* (1890) a man is fanatically devoted to the idea that his infant nephew be christened "Livingston Burton Speke," after Africa's "most illustrious explorers."[48] In Wilde's play great urgency is attached to "being earnest" – but in name rather than fact. As Gwendolen explains it to her new fiancé:

My ideal has always been to love some one of the name of Ernest. There is something in that name that inspires absolute confidence. The moment Algernon first mentioned to me that he had a friend called Ernest, I knew I was destined to love you.

(p. 23)

As in *Your Wife*, furthermore, the dramatic crisis arises when it is learned that the person with the "ideal" name is really called Jack.

This mockery of official values – from male earnestness to modest femininity – is accompanied in many plays by a suggestion of outlawry and even revolution. Indeed the policeman is one of the stock characters of

Victorian farce. In *The Magistrate* the first scene of Act III takes place in a police court, and in *Dandy Dick* the dean of a cathedral is jailed. Two leading characters are arrested by a bungling policeman in *Crime & Christening*, a curtain-raiser whose synoptic title captures the essence of 1890s farce. The title character of *Mr. Boodle's Predicament* is taken into custody when, by mistake, he claims a piece of luggage with an anarchist's bomb in it. And in *The Importance of Being Earnest* – in a scene eventually cut from the play – Algernon is threatened with imprisonment in connection with an unpaid bill for luxurious dinners in the West End. Most suggestively of all, Lady Bracknell, that fortress of conventionality, discovers in the unorthodox young lovers "a contempt for the ordinary decencies of family life that reminds one of the worst excesses of the French Revolution" (pp. 31–2). She understood, and so did Oscar Wilde, that the upside-down attitudes of farcical characters were as much a threat to custom and authority as the dynamite of socialists.

III

If Wilde supplied himself with characters, situations, and speeches from the ample warehouse of *fin-de-siècle* farce, he also instilled his play with qualities which distinguish it from other comedies of the kind. *The Importance of Being Earnest* is characterized, above all, by an intellectual coherence and thematic solidity which are notably absent in its precursors. It is, as the playwright subtitled it, "A Trivial Comedy for Serious People."

By the 1890s the rough-and-tumble slapstick which typified older farces like *Box and Cox* (1847) and *The Lost Child* had abated considerably. Hurling chops across the stage and rolling infants off meat platters were devices too crude to suit the kind of play which drew large crowds to Terry's, the Court, the Criterion, and (in the case of *Earnest*) even the dignified St. James's. Pinero, however, was capable of having characters gorge themselves on jujubes and slip on a floor littered with nuts in *The Magistrate*, and even Wilde included the ritual food gags and suitcase business in *Earnest*. Boisterous farce in the tradition of *Box and Cox* continued to be written by playwrights like Mark Melford, who had a man run across the stage in his underwear in *A Screw Loose* (1893). In Melford's *Kleptomania* (1888) an agitated General Blair *"throws a book"* and *"smashes a vase"* before a general melee breaks out in the next act.[49] But by the late Victorian period, farce in general had become more verbal and less physical, finding its basis in the expression of an absurd idea more than in simple horseplay.[50] Humor sprang from the incongruity of a 25-year-old "baby" looking for his mother, a girl engaging herself to a stranger, a schoolmistress singing in the music halls, a young man mistakenly thinking himself a child. The knockabout style of *Box and Cox* was absent even from the most physical scenes of plays such as *Charley's Aunt* or *The Importance of Being Earnest*. Jack Worthing, it is true, dresses up in mourning garments, and Lord Fancourt Babberley dresses up in woman's clothing – but in both plays the Oxonian backgrounds and aristocratic eloquence of the characters prevent mere physical exuberance from taking command. The idea of the absurd is the keynote of 1890s farce, and often it finds expression in the ironic counter-pointing of physical comedy (Jack in "mourning," Lord Fancourt in a dress) with the effete dignity of patrician drawing rooms.

The familiar judgment that *The Importance of Being Earnest* differs from other farces in being less "physical" is thus only partly true, for in de-emphasizing slapstick Wilde was unquestionably following recent trends in farcical drama. But he went further than his predecessors. Not only is Wilde's comedy more verbal than physical, it brings to the surface what was only incipient in the farces which preceded it. A cigar-smoking young man is made up as a woman, or girls comport themselves in the most outspoken fashion, but the typical farce only invites laughter at such dis-turbances of good order. Characters typically do not reflect upon the impli-cations of their absurd behavior, and so the subversive possibilities of these plays – which derive their comedy from the discomposure of prevailing standards – remain for the most part latent. In *Earnest*, however, Wilde makes his characters think as well as act, with the result that absurdity becomes more than a theatrical style. An exchange between the two heroes at the end of Act I crystallizes the nihilism which lay just beneath the surface of late Victorian farce:

> *Jack*: If you don't take care, your friend Bunbury will get you into a serious scrape some day.
> *Algernon*: I love scrapes. They are the only things that are never serious.
> *Jack*: Oh, that's nonsense, Algy. You never talk anything but nonsense.
> *Algernon*: Nobody ever does.
>
> (p. 40)

Wilde's characters have serious views, if not actual philosophies, and from these their foolishness of word and deed develops. They generalize, and in doing so awaken to self-consciousness and the world outside the play. For Algy, therefore, Bunburying entails a critique of existence, but for the unreflecting Reggie in *Godpapa* it is simply an expedient to get what he wants.

In 1895, the year *Earnest* was staged, Henry Arthur Jones brought out *The Renascence of the English Drama*, admonishing playwrights to provide their audiences with an "interpretation of life" rather than merely "funny or sensational theatrical things."[51] Wilde's play satisfies this standard, although not in the way intended by Jones, who wished theatres to become the cathedrals of a secular age. Neither Jones himself, imbued with ideas of Arnoldian culture, nor the farcical dramatists who preceded Wilde would have permitted their heroes to assert, as Jack Worthing does, that "a high moral tone can hardly be said to conduce very much to either one's health or one's happiness" (p. 14). But it is language of this sort which makes *The Importance of Being Earnest* more than merely "funny." All through its dialogue runs a current of generalization which bestows upon the characters and their behavior a significance beyond themselves.

Cynical it may be, but what Jones would call an "interpretation of life" emerges from scene after scene in which the moral imperatives of Victorian society are reversed. "You musn't think that I am wicked," Algy assures Cecily in Act I – to which she replies:

> If you are not, then you have certainly been deceiving us all in a very inexcusable manner. I hope you have not been leading a double life, pretending to be wicked and being really good all the time. That would be hypocrisy.
>
> (p. 46)

Lady Bracknell, on the other hand, defends custom with a majesty of speech which makes her utterance almost theological. When Jack admits to smoking, for example, she is "glad to hear it," for "a man should always have an occupation of some kind" (p. 27). The tyrannical matriarch in *Earnest* becomes the embodiment of a system, and the contest between her and the young people is really a conflict between Victorian earnestness and conscious revolt against it. Mary Lydon's remark that in Wilde's work mothers are "monstrous" is true of *Earnest*, but in a sense equally true of *The Foundling* and other farces of the time.[52] Young people struggle to establish themselves against repression by the old, to clear a space for enactment of the self, even in the typical farce of the 1890s. The difference in Lady Bracknell resides in her speech – like much of Wilde's writing, "it is the language of the Apollonian law giver," withdrawn, as it were, into "aristocratic sequestration." The generalized formulations of Lady Bracknell, indeed of all the characters, provide not only magisterial personae for themselves (and indirectly for their author), but also make it necessary for them to think beyond themselves to the large issues of life beyond the play.[53] The power of generalization in *Earnest* is one of the qualities which most emphatically divides it from its farcical predecessors.

If the characters of Wilde's forerunners ever reflect on the significance of their tricks and disguises, it is done belatedly and with remorse. "Forgive me," pleads the forward young lady in *Man Proposes*, while in *Your Wife* the young people suddenly, near the end, become "very much ashamed of our deception."[54] Says a character in *A Night Out*: "This is a lesson for me. I'll never get myself into such a scrape again."[55] The hero in *Charley's Aunt* realizes just before the final curtain that his stratagems have been incompatible with the responsibilities of a sincere lover. But these characters have little to apologize for – at least in comparison with Jack Worthing and Algernon Moncrieff – for their revolt against authority has been unpremeditated, the product of high spirits rather than calculated defiance.

Not only do Jack and Algernon understand their own positions from the beginning, they do not succumb to any sudden or improbable conversion at the end. Reproached by Lady Bracknell for displaying "signs of triviality," Jack replies in the last speech of the play: "On the contrary, Aunt Augusta, I've now realized for the first time in my life the vital Importance of Being Earnest" (pp. 104–5). It was common to end a farce with this kind of tag line, often a self-quotation of the play's title. But in a more conventional work such as the unpublished, anonymously written *Never Again* (1897), the tag speech confirms the characters' return to normative behavior. "But remember," says Vignon, just before the curtain falls. "I swear it," responds Ribot, "– Never again!"[56] Wilde's play concludes on the note of revolt with which it began, leaving its heroes in a state of clear-headedness which was unprecedented in such comedies.

The revolutionary use which Wilde made of farce does not answer the objection that too much of *Earnest* is not his own – a good deal less, in fact, than has been imagined by his harshest critics. Almost everything of importance came into the play ready-made, from Bunburying to the imaginary brother named Ernest to the comic idea of a grown man frantically seeking his mother and planning to be christened. *The Importance of Being Earnest*, from one point of view, provides the strongest evidence for the *Era*'s complaint in early 1895 that originality in farces was "becoming a rare quality." Other English farceurs often modelled their plays on a single source – as Justin McCarthy adapted *Prête-moi ta femme* under the English title *Your Wife*, or Fred Horner made *The Late Lamented* out of Bisson's *Feu Topinel*. In *Earnest*, as in his other dramas, Wilde adapted not a particular play, but an entire genre – practically cataloguing its varied devices, yet somehow creating a fresh impression rather than only collocating what others had done before him. Absurdity is a wonderful joke for Wilde, but also a weapon of the critical intelligence. *The Importance of Being Earnest* resonates with significance, and it is this distinction more than anything else which divides it from the irreclaimable bog of its numerous but only "funny" precursors.

Epilogue

If I can write a play . . .

Oscar Wilde, 1897

Long after the death of Oscar Wilde, one of his rivals in the theatre of the 1890s derided *The Importance of Being Earnest* in these terms: "Could any but a diseased brain have conceived so contemptible a pun?" asked Sydney Grundy. "Is this the definite re-union of the English Theatre with English Letters? Muffins!"[1] Even admirers of Wilde must be disheartened to find in one of the reputedly great comedies of the language such dialogue as occurs early in Act I:

Algernon: Come, old boy, you had much better have the thing out at once.
   Jack: My dear Algy, you talk exactly as if you were a dentist. It is very vulgar to
       talk like a dentist when one isn't a dentist. It produces a false impression.
Algernon: Well, that is exactly what dentists always do.

(pp. 12–13)

Humor of this kind belongs less in spirit to *The Importance of Being Earnest* than to Victorian farces of another kind. It would be more comfortably at home in a play called *Love and Dentistry*, a more typical entry in the London theatrical season of 1895, than in Wilde's subtle comedy for "serious people." In such passages – and there are several – Wilde merely sinks to the level of the genre in which he is writing. "From the top of one of the hills quite close one can see five counties," says Cecily in Act II. "Five counties!" Gwendolen exclaims – "I don't think I should like that. I hate crowds" (p. 71).

These generic jokes represent a temptation which, for the most part, *The Importance of Being Earnest* withstands. They are what happens when for a moment the play slips back into the orbit of tradition. The real distinction of *Earnest*, by contrast, arises from an evasion of influence through its paradoxical relation to other farces of the time. Gwendolen, for instance, refuses to call a spade a spade because, as she complacently notes, "I have never seen a spade" (p. 70). Although Wilde was not above the sort of

140

"contemptible pun" that Grundy accused him of, Gwendolen's dry remark is of another kind, reorganizing a cliché into deflation of an ideal hallowed by Captains of Industry and Marxists alike. Punning in farces – including puns on the word "spade" – was not usually so ambitious or disruptive. In Mark Melford's *Kleptomania*, for example, Professor Smalley proposes to refer frankly to the strange compulsion of General Blair's wife:

Smalley: Let us call a spade a spade.
General: My wife's not a spade, sir.[2]

The mere jokes of farce are transformed in *Earnest* to challenge the unreflective laughter, conventional morality, and prosaic expression that were the identifying marks of its predecessors. In his last play Wilde brazenly copies from numerous, if mostly forgotten playwrights, yet surrenders less to his sources than ever before. One does not find in *Earnest* whole acts of indecision, the nearly disastrous hesitations between his own voice and that of another, which disfigure *Lady Windermere's Fan* and *An Ideal Husband*. In the end, at least, the two earlier comedies overcome what was to Wilde, if not to us, the thoroughly familiar example of plays about wanton mothers and stainless men. Two other notable dramas – *Salomé* and *A Woman of No Importance* – never declare themselves as individuated works, although at times they seem about to. What distinguishes *Earnest* among Wilde's plays is not that it was conceived independently of sources, but that it so effortlessly masters so many of them. In this way *Earnest* brilliantly undermines the foundation upon which plays of its kind were built.

Why did Wilde write no more plays after *Earnest*, the triumph of his career? The question may seem too obvious to require an answer, and indeed the usual explanation – that Wilde's artistic powers were extinguished by the hard life of prison – is probably true, or contains truth.[3] But it should not be forgotten that the author of *Earnest* was in exile after his release from Reading Gaol, banished from the London stage which had been so influential, for both good and bad, upon his own plays. He was able to produce a quantity of poetry and autobiography after the catastrophe of April 1895, but plays, although he attempted several, were now beyond his reach. "Tomorrow I begin the *Florentine Tragedy*," he writes in a bright moment in 1897 in Naples. "After that I must tackle *Pharaoh*."[4] In Naples he could feel himself a dramatist again; in its theatre he could see Sarah Bernhardt play Tosca, as he had in London, and meet her after the performance – "she embraced me and wept, and I wept, and the whole evening was wonderful."[5] This far surpassed Bernéval-sur-Mer, where Wilde lived earlier in 1897 and where there was no theatre at all, but even in Naples, as anywhere else on the Continent, he was hopelessly distant from the vital forces which contributed most to his success in drama. In London, in the shadow of the Haymarket and the St. James's, breathing the atmosphere of an ephemeral but stimulating English theatre, Wilde had written plays with comparatively little effort. His masterpiece had been begun and completed within three or four summer weeks of 1894. Three years later, away from England, he could only hope to write for the stage – not actually do it. "C'est là qu'il veut écrire ses drames; son *Pharaon* d'abord, puis un *Achab* et *Jésabel*," wrote André Gide after being shown Wilde's "charmante petite maison" in secluded Bernéval.[6] But these plays were apparently never written, or even begun, while only fragments of others survive.

"If I can write a play," Wilde began half-confidently in a letter to Robert Ross in 1897 – but by that time, unfortunately, he could not.[7] In *A Florentine Tragedy*, or rather the few lines which survive under that title, he returns for some bizarre reason to the exhausted mode of blank-verse drama which he first tried with uninspiring results in *The Duchess of Padua*. "Ah!" cries Guido to Bianca in lines not of the nineteenth century, much less of Wilde, "loose the falling midnight of your hair, / And in those stars, your eyes, let me behold / Mine image, as in mirrors."[8] These used-up devices cannot give life to an interesting plot idea in which a husband and wife are awakened to passion for one another only when the husband murders his rival. In a scenario that Wilde sold to, among others, Frank Harris, who turned it into a play called *Mr. and Mrs. Daventry*, the pivotal scene comes straight from Scribe's *Une Chaîne* – a wife, asleep in a darkened room, awakes to overhear her husband making love to another woman. The plot takes a radical and promising turn when Mrs. Daventry avails herself of the same sexual liberty her husband claims, falls in love and becomes pregnant by another man, and at the end embraces her lover passionately when she learns her husband has killed himself. But Wilde could only talk about such a play, not write it, after his release from prison and self-exile from England. In *La Sainte Courtesane*, of which only a scene survives, a bejewelled and deadly female tries to seduce the ascetic Honorius. It is, in the condition Wilde left it, another Sarah Bernhardt play – the title itself in French, although not the text this time, and the dialogue reminiscent of *Salomé* with its chanted measures:

Come with me, Honorius, and I will clothe you in a tunic of silk. I will smear your body with myrrh and pour spikenard on your hair.[9]

Explicitly for Bernhardt, Wilde imagined writing a play in which the French actress would play the role of Queen Elizabeth. As he explained to Charles Ricketts, "She would look wonderful in monstrous dresses covered with peacocks and pearls."[10]

These fragmentary relics and stillborn projects were conceived and in part written before Wilde was jailed. Like all his dramas, they have their beginning in earlier plays; but unlike his completed plays of the 1890s, they never develop to the point where the contest with the source is decisively joined. Out of conflict with tradition, with the lively theatrical scene surrounding him, had come Wilde's notable plays earlier in the decade. Even a work as unsuccessful as *A Woman of No Importance* had been enlivened by a struggle with precedent, although one in which Wilde was ultimately defeated. This strife, although there are tantalizing hints and sketches of it, never develops in Wilde's projected and fragmentary dramas, and the dramas themselves do not.

Wilde had inhaled the spirit of the 1890s stage, marked as it was by notable collaborations – Sims and Buchanan, Pettitt and Harris, Nicholls and Lestocq – and by spirited parodies of dramatists from Ibsen to Jones to Wilde himself. Wilde's "collaborators" were unwitting, but would *The Importance of Being Earnest* have been the same play without the contribution of W. Lestocq? *Earnest* and all his best plays, on the other hand, are mockeries of his fellow playwrights, failing only when Wilde's antagonism, as in *Salomé*, remains so unformed that he does not speak distinctively. Removed from London and the West End stage, Wilde was deprived of an arena of cooperation and conflict which had been essential to his work as playwright.

The author of *Salomé*, stung by the Lord Chamberlain's condemnation of his play, threatened in 1892 to leave England and its theatre so he could survive as an artist. Had he gone, the result might have been other than Wilde expected, for his dramatic genius was not the self-sufficient thing he imagined, or assured the press it was. Five years later, when circumstances forced his departure, Wilde's exile only compounded the difficulties he faced in returning to drama. Lord Alfred Douglas believed Wilde still had the ability to write plays, and, if he had lived, would have written them in numbers to rival Shaw.[11] But his relation to the London theatre of the 1890s had been decisive; absent from the turmoil of that scene, separated by barriers of time and distance, Oscar Wilde was left with nothing to answer, nothing to contend with, and, alas, nothing to say.

Appendix: Dramatists of the 1890s

These brief entries for approximately 100 playwrights whose works were produced in London in the 1890s do not include the most familiar from that era – Shaw and Wilde – or other major figures such as Tennyson or Hardy who had some of their dramas produced then. The listing is an attempt to bring together for the first time, in a compact space, the most basic facts pertaining to the work of popular playwrights in a decade which saw the rise of Ibsenism and a play writing elite whose status derived more from aesthetic or political considerations than success with audiences.

Authors who worked mainly in pantomime and musical productions are omitted, as well as foreign playwrights (other than a few Americans with English ties). Even so, the listing omits many dramatists – particularly those whose plays were limited to staging in the provinces, and others who had only one or two plays produced during the decade. The entries include all the English playwrights of the 1890s mentioned in preceding chapters, but many others, especially women, have been added to give some indication of the throng of writers who supplied London theatres with the several hundred new plays staged each year.

Birth and death dates are noted whenever available, along with names of representative plays and notable biographical facts. Birth names of women writers, when known, are supplied in brackets when the playwright is identified by a better-known pseudonym or married name. Pseudonyms are placed within quotation marks and bracketed if the writer was best known by another name. If best known by a pseudonym, the author is so listed with the birth name bracketed behind it.

No single source, new or old, contains information about all the authors listed here. I have relied in particular, however, on theatrical reference works dating from the 1890s and the early twentieth century – W. Davenport Adams's *A Dictionary of the Drama* (1904), Erskine Reid and Herbert Compton's *The Dramatic Peerage* (1892), Brompton Hunt's *The Green Room Book* (1906 and after), as well as early volumes of *Who's Who in the Theatre* and *Who Was Who*. Biographical notices in the *Era*, the theatrical trade newspaper, were often used, as were obituary notices in the *Times* of London. In addition, later references have provided some material, especially Allardyce Nicoll's *Late Nineteenth Century Drama 1850–1900* (1959) and J. P. Wearing's *The London Stage 1890–1899: A Calendar of Plays and Players* (1976) and *American and British Theatrical Biography* (1979).

JANET ACHURCH (1864–1916) After acting in melodramas like *The New Magdalen*

144

and *Lady Audley's Secret*, Achurch played the parts of Hester Prynne and, more famously, Nora in the first English production of *A Doll's House* – the latter at the Novelty Theatre where she was manager. Her acting in plays by Ibsen and Shaw thereafter overshadowed her own attempt at play writing in *Mrs. Daintree's Daughter*, a work which anticipates in many respects *Mrs. Warren's Profession* although it was not produced until 1903. She collaborated with her husband, actor Charles Charrington, on an adaptation of *Frou-Frou* (1886).

CHARLES HAMILTON AIDÉ (1830–1906) A novelist who wrote an occasional play, Aidé was the author of a successful adaptation from the French – *Dr. Bill* (1890), a farce which ran for 210 performances at the Avenue and was revived in 1894. His one-act French play – *Un Rayon dans les ténèbres* – was performed in London by Sarah Bernhardt at the St. James's in 1899.

F. ANSTEY (Thomas Anstey Guthrie, 1856–1934) Although his best-known novel, *Vice Versa*, was adapted for the stage by Edward Rose, Anstey did some dramatic work himself – including an adaptation of his own *The Man from Blankley's* (1900) and some travesties of Ibsen under the title *Mr. Punch's Pocket Ibsen* (1893).

WILLIAM ARCHER (1856–1924) The most prominent of English Ibsenites, Archer was not only theatrical critic for the *World* but editor and translator of the texts used in productions of Ibsen in London. His translation of *A Doll's House* was used in the landmark production at the Novelty in 1889, and it was his version of *Ghosts* that scandalized London in 1891. In *The Old Drama and the New* (1923) Archer sought to establish a canon that reflected his own theatrical agenda without ignoring the contribution of traditional playwrights.

DR. EDWARD B. AVELING ("Alec Nelson") A supporter of the Ibsen movement who lived in "free union" with Karl Marx's daughter (Eleanor Marx Aveling) – herself one of Ibsen's translators – Aveling was the author of one of several dramatic adaptations of *The Scarlet Letter*, a play that drew praise from Shaw. His comedy *The Jackal* was staged at the Strand in 1889, and *Judith Shakespeare* played at the Royalty in 1894. At the Playgoers' Club Aveling gave enthusiastic defenses of Ibsen, and as theatre critic for *Time* argued for a new drama focusing on the class-struggle.

WILSON BARRETT (d. 1904) As an actor-manager, Barrett specialized in melodrama, realizing huge successes with the long run and world tour of G. R. Sims's *The Lights o' London* (1881) and with H. A. Jones and Henry Herman's *The Silver King* (1882). His own hit play, *The Sign of the Cross* (1896), brought him a fortune and played for 438 performances at the Lyric in 1896–7 with Barrett in the starring role of Marcus Superbus. Although one of the most spectacular successes of the 1890s, *The Sign of the Cross* was never published.

JAMES M. BARRIE (1860–1937) The farce *Walker, London* (1892) launched the success of Barrie's theatrical career with 497 performances at Toole's, making it one of the most popular plays of the 1890s. *Ibsen's Ghost* (1891) held the stage briefly at Toole's. His best-known work – *The Admirable Crichton* (1902) and *Peter Pan* (1904) – belongs to the next decade.

FLORENCE E. E. BELL (Mrs. Hugh Bell [Olliffe]) (1852–1930) For the Independent Theatre Society Mrs. Bell and Elizabeth Robins wrote *Alan's Wife*, produced on two occasions at Terry's in 1893 and published as the second in the Independent Theatre Series of Plays. She translated *Karin* by Swedish dramatist Alfhild Agrell, a *Doll's House*-like play staged at the Vaudeville in 1892, and wrote theatricals for the drawing room under the title *Chamber Comedies* (1890). In a comic vein Bell authored *Nicholson's Niece* (1892) and *Between the Posts*, a one-act piece that lasted 119 performances at the Comedy in 1893.

ARTHUR BENHAM (1872–95) In an obituary notice the *Era* lamented the death of Benham "at an age so early that the general public knew practically nothing of his rare promise as a dramatist" (14 September 1895, p. 10). The young playwrights's nurse in his final illness was his sister, Estelle Burney, an actress and dramatist who collaborated with him on *The Awakening* (1892) and *The County* (1892). His *Theory and Practice* (1893) was produced by the Independent Theatre Society at Terry's and is evidently the only one of his plays to have been published. The *Era* noted in its obituary that "Mr. Charles Wyndham and Mr. Hawtrey are said to have a drama and a farcical comedy of his writing which sooner or later they will produce" – but apparently never did (*Era*, 14 September 1895, p. 10).

MRS. OSCAR BERINGER (Aimée Beringer [Daniell], 1856–1936) Born in America of English parents, Beringer collaborated with Henry Hamilton on the comedy *That Girl* (1890). Perhaps the most notable of her several plays was *A Bit of Old Chelsea*, which ran for seventy-five performances at the Court in 1897 as the curtain-raiser for a play by Robert Buchanan.

DION BOUCICAULT (1822–90) The author of numerous mid-century melodramas, Boucicault was frequently revived in the 1890s. Among the plays staged in *fin-de-siècle* London were *The Corsican Brothers*, *The Colleen Bawn*, *The Streets of London*, *After Dark*, and *Formosa the Most Beautiful; or the Railroad to Ruin*. *Jimmy Watt*, apparently his last play, was staged for the first time in 1890, the year of Boucicault's death.

ARTHUR BOURCHIER (1863–1927) Best-known as an actor and theatre manager, Bourchier also adapted a number of plays from the French in the 1890s. The most successful of these, and evidently the only one to be published, was *The Chili Widow* (written with Alfred Sutro), which ran for 223 performances at the Royalty in 1895–6 with himself in the leading role of Sir Reginald Delamare.

MARY ELIZABETH BRADDON (Mrs. John Maxwell, 1837–1915) In addition to scores of novels, Braddon wrote a number of plays – several of them still unpublished, including *The Loves of Arcadia*, *A Model Husband*, *Griselda*, and *Genevieve*. Her novels *Lady Audley's Secret* and *Aurora Floyd* were adapted for the stage by male playwrights such as C. H. Hazlewood and Benjamin Webster Jr., as well as anonymous authors. Her last play, *For Better, For Worse*, was produced in 1891 in Brighton.

GEORGE H. BROADHURST (1866–1952) The founder and manager of the Broadhurst Theatre in New York was born in England, but emigrated to the United States where he managed theatres in Milwaukee, Baltimore, and San Francisco and edited a newspaper in North Dakota. In the 1890s he achieved success as a playwright with the farcical comedy *What Happened to Jones?* (1898), which ran for 325 performances at the Strand – one of the most popular plays of the decade.

CHARLES H. E. BROOKFIELD (1857–1913) Beginning his career as an actor and ending it as the official censor, Brookfield wrote plays himself in the 1890s – including a travesty on Wilde, *The Poet and the Puppets* (1892), with James Glover. *Godpapa* (1891), which he wrote with F. C. Philips, shows curious similarities with *The Importance of Being Earnest*. Brookfield later helped collect evidence used to convict Wilde, and with friends entertained the Marquess of Queensberry to celebrate the verdict.

ROBERT BUCHANAN (1841–1901) Known for his attack on Rossetti and the Pre-Raphaelites in "The Fleshly School of Poetry," Buchanan was a prolific dramatist as well as novelist and poet. His melodramas and farces were among the works most successful with 1890s audiences. *An English Rose*, written with G. R. Sims, enjoyed a long run at the Adelphi in 1890–1, and *The Trumpet Call* (1891), also written with Sims, had similar prosperity there. *The Strange Adventures of Miss Brown* (1895), a farce written with Harriett Jay, ran for 256 performances at the Vaudeville. Only a few of his approximately fifty plays were published.

F. C. BURNAND (1836–1917) The man who edited *Punch* from 1880 to 1906 was also the author of some 200 pieces for the stage, including a number dating from the 1890s. These include *Mrs. Ponderbury's Past* (1895), an amusing adaptation that enjoyed modest success at the Avenue and later when it was revived at the Court. Burnand also adapted John Maddison Morton's farce *Box and Cox*, with music by Arthur Sullivan, and wrote *The Colonel* (1881), in which Beerbohm Tree appeared as Lambert Streyke, a Wilde-like aesthete.

FRANCES HODGSON BURNETT (Mrs. Stephen Townsend, 1849–1924) In addition to her sentimental play *The Real Little Lord Fauntleroy* (1888), revived in the 1890s, Burnett also wrote *The First Gentleman in Europe* (1897) and, with her husband Stephen Townsend, *Editha's Burglar* (1890) and *A Lady of Quality* (1897). She had scored a great success in children's fiction with *Little Lord Fauntleroy* (1886), on which the play of 1888 was based. In successfully prosecuting a pirated dramatic version of the novel, Burnett established the right of authors to make dramatic adaptations of their own work.

ESTELLE BURNEY An actress, Burney performed in plays she wrote with her

Appendix

brother Arthur Benham – *The County* (1892) and *The Awakening* (1892). The latter has been ascribed to Benham alone, but on the title page of the licensing manuscript Burney is listed as co-author. She also wrote *An Idyll of the Closing Century* (1896), *Settled out of Court* (1897), and *The Ordeal of the Honeymoon* (1899).

J. W. COMYNS CARR (1849–1916) Theatre manager and art critic for the *Pall Mall Gazette*, Carr in the 1880s collaborated with Thomas Hardy on an adaptation of *Far From the Madding Crowd*. The farcical comedy *Nerves* (1890), perhaps Carr's most popular work, is an adaptation from the French. With C. Haddon Chambers he wrote *Boys Together* (1896), and with A. W. Pinero *The Beauty Stone* (1898).

S. MURRAY CARSON ("Thornton Clark") (1865–1917) In collaboration with Louis N. Parker, Carson wrote a number of melodramas and comedies, including *David* (1892), *Rosemary* (1896), *The Jest* (1898), and *Change Alley* (1899). He was also an actor.

R. C. CARTON (Richard Claude Critchett) (1853–1928) An actor until 1885, Carton, as he called himself, collaborated with Cecil Raleigh in that year on a drama called *The Great Pink Pearl*. By the 1890s he was writing plays alone, the most popular being *Lord and Lady Algy* (1899), a society comedy that ran for 304 performances. *The Home Secretary* (1895) is one of many plays of the time, including Wilde's *An Ideal Husband*, which concerns itself with the fashionable concept of the "perfect" male. Carton also wrote *Liberty Hall* (1892), an adaptation called *The Squire of Dames* (1895), and *A White Elephant* (1896), among other plays.

C. HADDON CHAMBERS (1859–1921) A stockrider in the bush of New South Wales as a young man, Chambers came to England in 1880, then returned to live in London permanently two years later. He worked as a journalist for a time before turning to the theatre, writing apprentice dramas in the late 1880s before his breakthrough in 1891 with *The Idler*, which ran for 173 performances at the St. James's. Also popular were *John a Dreams* (1894); *The Fatal Card* (1894), written with B. C. Stephenson; and an accomplished society drama, *The Tyranny of Tears* (1899).

ALICE CHAPIN The author of *A Woman's Sacrifice* (1899), Chapin collaborated with E. H. C. Oliphant in writing *Shame* (1892) and *Dresden China* (1892), both presented as matinees at the Vaudeville.

MRS. W. K. CLIFFORD (Lucy Clifford [Lane]) (1854–1929) The daughter of publisher John Lane was both a novelist and playwright. Perhaps her most popular play was *The Likeness of the Night*, staged at the St. James's in 1900. *A Supreme Moment* (1899) enjoyed the unusual distinction of being published in the *Nineteenth Century* after its stage production, and another play, *The Long Duel*, appeared in the *Fortnightly* in 1901. She also wrote *A Honeymoon Tragedy* (1896) and, with Walter Herries Pollock, *An Interlude* (1893).

GEORGE CONQUEST (1837–1901) The manager of the Surrey Theatre, and earlier of the Grecian, Conquest was an actor and acrobatic performer as well as

148

playwright. Many of his melodramas were written in collaboration with Henry Pettitt and Arthur Shirley, and a number were performed in theatres outside the West End. His long career as a dramatist began in 1853 and continued into the 1890s with such plays as *The Work Girl*, which played at the Surrey in 1895.

Mrs. Montague Crackanthorpe (Blanche Alethea Crackanthorpe [Holt], 1846–1928) The mother of *fin-de-siècle* short story writer Hubert Crackanthorpe was an early devotee of Ibsen who wrote some fiction and on at least one occasion authored a play. The drama that bears her name, *The Turn of the Wheel*, was banned by the Lord Chamberlain, probably because of its sympathetic portrait of a mother who abandons her child.

Walter Stokes Craven An actor and stage manager, Craven was also a writer of farce. His most notable plays were *An Innocent Abroad* (1895), which enjoyed a moderate run at Terry's, and *Four Little Girls* (1897).

Augustin Daly (1838–99) Born in North Carolina, Daly was a New York journalist and drama critic who opened a theatre on Broadway – Daly's Theatre – which he managed until his death. In 1893 he opened a Daly's Theatre in Leicester Square, but the plays he wrote – comedies and farces, especially – appeared at a number of theatres in London: *The Great Unknown* (1891) at the Lyceum, *Love in Tandem* (1893) at Daly's, *The Countess Gucki* (1896) at the Comedy, and *Love on Crutches* (1896) at the Comedy.

J. Herbert Darnley (d. 1938) A writer of farces, Darnley was the author of *Wanted, a Wife* (1890), *Mrs. Dexter* (1891), and *The Solicitor* (1891), his most popular play of the 1890s. It ran for 146 performances at Toole's.

Neville Doone Actor and playwright, Doone was the author of a society drama called *A Modern Marriage* (1890). Perhaps his most successful work was *Summer Clouds*, a one-act comedy that had a modest run at Toole's.

Arthur Conan Doyle (1859–1930) After launching his Sherlock Holmes stories in the late 1880s, Doyle tried his hand at play writing in the next decade. *Halves* (1899) ran for sixty performances at the Garrick, and a comic opera on which he collaborated with J. M. Barrie and Ernest Ford (who wrote the music), *Jane Annie; or, the Good Conduct Prize* (1893), was staged at the Savoy fifty times. Doyle's one-act play *A Story of Waterloo* (1894) was performed frequently in the 1890s with Henry Irving in the cast. With William Gillette he wrote a stage version of *Sherlock Holmes*, whose 213 performances at the Garrick made it one of the major hits of 1903. Less successful was *Foreign Policy*, a one-act political-domestic comedy that lasted but six performances at Terry's in 1893.

Henry V. Esmond (Henry Vernon Jack) (1869–1922) An actor who performed in *The Second Mrs. Tanqueray*, Esmond was the author of a number of plays of his own in the 1890s, including *The Divided Way* (1895), a comedy staged at the St.

149

James's; *Cupboard Love* (1898), a farce produced at the Court; and *Grierson's Way* (1898), a Haymarket comedy.

CHARLES S. FAWCETT (1855–1922) As both actor and playwright Fawcett specialized in comedy and farce. His plays include *For Charity's Sake* (1891) and *Beauty's Toils* (1893).

PERCY FENDALL (d. 1917) With F. C. Philips he wrote several comedies and farces – *Husband and Wife* (1891), *Margaret Byng* (1891), and *Fireworks* (1893). His duologue *Fashionable Intelligence* (1894) was presented at the Court.

GEORGE MANVILLE FENN (1831–1909) In addition to numerous novels, Fenn was the author of plays including *The Foreman of the Works* (1886), *Her Ladyship* (1889), and *The Tin Box* (1892). He collaborated with J. H. Darnley on two farces, *The Barrister* (1887) and *A Balloon* (1888), and left a little-known volume of reminiscences, *Friends I have Made* (c. 1900).

MICHAEL FIELD (Katharine Bradley, 1846–1914, and Edith Cooper, 1862–1913) In addition to published but unstaged verse dramas such as *The Father's Tragedy* (1885) and *Stephania* (1892), Michael Field was the author of *A Question of Memory*, produced by the Independent Theatre Society at the Opera Comique in 1893.

AUSTIN FRYERS (William Edward Clery) *Beata* (1892) was Fryers's revision of Ibsen's *Rosmersholm*, a domestication of the New Drama that was produced at the Globe in 1892 with unhappy results. He was also the author of *Gentle Ivy* (1894), *A Human Sport* (1895), and *The Dead Past* (1895).

SARAH GRAND (Frances Elizabeth Macfall [Clarke], 1862–1943) The feminist novelist and essayist was co-author of a play, *The Fear of Robert Clive*, staged at the Lyceum in 1896, but apparently never published.

CLOTILDE GRAVES (1863–1932) After collaborating with Edward Rose and W. Sidney on a dramatization of *She* (1888), Graves wrote *Katherine Kavanagh* (1891) with Mrs. Oscar Beringer and, on her own, *The Physician* (1893; later staged as *Dr. and Mrs. Neill*) and the popular farce *A Mother of Three* (1896). With Gertrude Kingston she wrote *A Matchmaker* (1896).

JOHN GRAY (1866–1934) The friend of Oscar Wilde and reputed original for Dorian Gray wrote *The Kiss*, an adaptation staged by the Independent Theatre Society at the Royalty in 1892. He wrote the libretto for *Sour Grapes* (1894) and a complicated society drama, *The Blackmailers* (1894), with his friend André Raffalovich.

JACOB THOMAS GREIN (1862–1935) The founder of the Independent Theatre Society was also a drama critic and the author of several plays of his own, including *A Man's Love* (1889; with C. W. Jarvis), *Spring Leaves* (1891; with Jarvis), *Reparation* (1892), *Make-Beliefs* (1892), and *The Compromising Coat* (1892).

LADY VIOLET GREVILLE (Beatrice Violet Greville [Graham], 1842–1932) A novelist and playwright, Lady Violet Greville was the author of *The Baby; or, a Warning to Mesmerists* (1891), which ran for ninety-two performances at Terry's. *An Aristocratic Alliance* (1894), an adaptation from the French, enjoyed a modest success at the Criterion, and with Arthur Bourchier she co-authored *Justice* (1892). She also wrote conduct books and novels.

SYDNEY GRUNDY (1848–1914) A barrister and son of the mayor of Manchester, Grundy's first play was a comedietta, *A Little Change* (1872), staged at the Haymarket. Afterward, he wrote a number of successful comedies and society dramas, including *In Honour Bound* (1880), *The Glass of Fashion* (1883; with G. R. Sims), *The Arabian Nights* (1887), *The Dean's Daughter* (1888; with F. C. Philips), *A Pair of Spectacles* – a major hit of 1890, *Sowing the Wind* (1893), *A Bunch of Violets* (1894), *The New Woman* (1894), *The Late Mr. Castello* (1895), and *The Degenerates* (1899). Grundy's career crested in the 1890s, when the number and magnitude of his hit plays gave him some claim to be regarded as the most popular playwright of the day. In *The Play of the Future, by a Playwright of the Past* (1914) he berates both Wilde and Shaw.

HENRY HAMILTON (d. 1918) After retiring as an actor in 1886, Hamilton devoted himself to the writing of plays – especially melodramas for the Drury Lane in collaboration with other authors. His most popular work of the 1890s was *The Derby Winner*, written with Cecil Raleigh and Augustus Harris, which opened at the Drury Lane in 1894 and ran for 140 performances. He collaborated with Raleigh again on *The White Heather* (1897) and *The Great Ruby* (1898), both of which were successful at the Drury Lane. With Mark Quinton he wrote *Lord Anerley* (1891), and with Mrs. Oscar Beringer *That Girl* (1890). He adapted Sardou's *La Tosca* in 1889.

AUGUSTUS HARRIS (1852–96) Manager of the Drury Lane from 1879 until his death, Harris specialized in the production of melodramas (including his own), pantomimes, and elaborate Christmas shows. Among his own most popular plays were *A Million of Money* (1890), written with Henry Pettitt; *The Prodigal Daughter* (1892), with Pettitt; *A Life of Pleasure* (1893), with Pettitt; and *The Derby Winner* (1894), with Cecil Raleigh and Henry Hamilton.

FRANK HARVEY (1841–1903) Many of Harvey's plays were staged in the provinces and at theatres outside the West End like the Surrey and Pavilion. His plays often dealt melodramatically with women and the working class, and included *False Glitter; or, The Manchester Girl* (1875), *A Woman's Vengeance* (1888), *A Daughter of the People* (1891), and *Shall We Forgive Her?* (1894). Most of Harvey's plays were never published, and virtually nothing has been written of him.

WILLIAM HEINEMANN (1863–1920) A publisher influential in renewing the practice of printing plays in book form (his editions of Pinero were one of the landmarks of the period), Heinemann on two occasions wrote plays of his own, although neither was performed. As books, however, he brought out *The First Step* (1895) and *Summer Moths* (1898).

Appendix

RICHARD HENRY (Henry Chance Newton, 1854–1931, and Richard Butler) The collaborators who wrote as Richard Henry were most successful with *Crime & Christening* (1891), which played for 112 performances at the Opera Comique. In addition they wrote, in a farcical vein, *Adoption* (1890), *Letters Addressed Here* (1893), and *The Newest Women* (1895) as well as a number of burlesques. Newton was a drama critic, writing under the name Carados for the *Referee*. Also an actor, he published his reminiscences as *Cues and Curtain Calls* (1927).

HENRY HERMAN (1832–94) With Henry Arthur Jones, Herman bowdlerized *A Doll's House* under the title *Breaking a Butterfly* (1884) at about the time their joint effort on a different kind of play, *The Silver King* (1882), was paying off handsomely for Wilson Barrett's company. He collaborated with Jones again on *Chatterton* (1884), a play revived several times in the 1890s with Barrett himself acting the title role. By that time Herman's new plays were being staged mostly in the provinces, but *Eagle Joe* (1892) had a brief engagement at the Princess's. Herman, also a novelist, lived for a time in the United States where he fought as a Confederate soldier in the Civil War.

SEYMOUR HICKS (1871–1949) An actor-manager who built and opened the Aldwych and Globe (originally Hicks) theatres, Hicks was also a successful playwright near the turn of the century and after. *A Night Out* (1896), a farce adapted from the French, was one of the longest-running plays of the 1890s with 525 performances at the Vaudeville. *The New Sub* (1892) and *One of the Best* (1895), the latter written with George Edwardes, enjoyed less spectacular but solid prosperity. In his *Me and My Missus; Fifty Years on the Stage* (1939) Hicks recalls pleasant evenings spent with Wilde, and recollects attending the last day of his trial in 1895 so that Wilde would see at least one sympathetic friend among the crowd of spectators.

JOHN OLIVER HOBBES (Pearl Mary Teresa Craigie [Richards], 1867–1906) The most successful play by John Oliver Hobbes, as she was known, was *The Ambassadors*, a Wildean society comedy that ran for 104 performances at the St. James's in 1899. She collaborated with George Moore on *Journeys End in Lovers' Meeting* (1894) and adapted *The School for Saints* (1896) from her own novel. Other plays included *A Repentance* (1899) and *Osbern and Ursyne*, never licensed or staged but published in 1900. For *The Yellow Book* she co-authored with George Moore *The Fool's Hour: The First Act of a Comedy* (1894).

FRED HORNER Although he wrote prolifically for the London stage, little is known of Horner, who specialized in farcical comedy. Among his plays are *The Two Johnnies* (1889), an adaptation; *Happy Returns* (1892); *The Other Fellow* (1893), another adaptation; *The Sunbury Scandal* (1896), and *On Leave* (1897). Horner's most popular play seems to have been *The Late Lamented* (1891), an anglicized French farce that ran for 230 performances at the Court.

FERGUS HUME (1859–1932) *Teddy's Wives*, a farcical comedy that played at the Strand in 1896, was Hume's most popular play of the 1890s. He also wrote *The Mystery of a Hansom Cab* (1888) and *The Fool of the Family* (1896).

152

JEROME KLAPKA JEROME (1859–1927) Reared in East London, the son of a failed ironmonger, Jerome spent his apprentice years in the theatre envying the status of West End insiders – then became one himself. Although Jerome's modest fame rests mainly on his fiction, especially *Three Men in a Boat* (1889), he worked briefly as an actor and in 1886 had his first play produced – a one-act piece called *Barbara*. Success came with a full-length farce, *New Lamps for Old* (1890), which ran for 160 performances but was never published. *Miss Hobbs* (1898) is a notable play on the New Woman, but it, and all Jerome's theatrical work of the 1890s, is overshadowed by *The Passing of the Third Floor Back* (1907), his best-remembered drama. *Stage-Land* (1889) and *On the Stage – and Off* (1885) contain Jerome's reflections on the late Victorian theatre.

HENRY ARTHUR JONES (1851–1929) Jones worked in a draper's shop, in a warehouse, and as a commercial traveler for ten years before one of his plays was finally staged in 1878 – *It's Only Round the Corner*. His reputation was made by *The Silver King* (1882), written with Henry Herman for Wilson Barrett, which ran for 189 performances at the Princess's. Jones's later work was less obviously melodramatic than *The Silver King* but never eradicated its influence. *The Dancing Girl* (1891) was a major success for Herbert Beerbohm Tree at the Haymarket (266 performances), and *The Case of Rebellious Susan* (1894), *The Liars* (1897), and *Mrs. Dane's Defence* (1900) were fashionable society dramas that dealt with controversial subjects in a tentative manner. In *The Renascence of the English Drama* (1895) Jones called for a serious English theatre to fill the void left by a dying English Church.

BENJAMIN LANDECK (1864–1928) A frequent collaborator with Arthur Shirley, Landeck chiefly turned out melodramas for theatres outside the West End – especially the Pavilion, Surrey, and Parkhurst. His plays include *A Guilty Mother* (1894), *Women and Wine* (1897), and *A Daughter's Honour* (1894), the latter two written with Shirley. Almost nothing has been written of Landeck, and few of his plays were printed.

ARTHUR LAW (1844–1913) After writing a thrilling melodrama for the East End to begin his play writing career (*Hope*, performed at the Standard in 1882), Law turned with great success in the 1890s to farcical comedy. One of the most popular plays of the decade was *The New Boy*, which ran for 428 performances at Terry's and the Vaudeville in 1894–5. *The Judge* (1890) prospered earlier at Terry's, and *The Lady's Idol* (1895) had a respectable engagement at the Vaudeville. But Law told the *Era* in an interview that he preferred "serious plays," and disclosed that he had written almost twice as many plays (sixty, he claimed) as had actually been produced (*Era*, 10 March 1894, p. 11).

PIERRE LECLERQ (d. 1932) The older brother of Rose Leclerq, the original Lady Bracknell, Leclerq tried his hand as a dramatist from 1888 to 1891. *Illusion* (1890) and *This Woman and That* (1890) contain interesting similarities with *Lady Windermere's Fan*. Leclerq also wrote *The Rule of Three* (1891). None of his plays was ever published.

W[ILLIAM]. LESTOCQ (William Lestocq Boileau Woolridge, d. 1920) An actor early in life and the London representative of Charles Frohman later on, Lestocq wrote several farcical comedies in the late 1880s and 1890s. The most popular was *Jane* (1890), written with Harry Nicholls and frequently revived. *The Foundling* (1894), on which Lestocq collaborated with actor E. M. Robson, has pointed similarities with *The Importance of Being Earnest.* He wrote *Uncles and Aunts* (1888) with Walter Everard and was the author of *The Sportsman* (1893).

RALPH R. LUMLEY (d. 1900) The little-known Lumley, who died at thirty-five, was once termed "the youngest of our prominent dramatists" (*Era,* 7 April 1894, p. 11). A barrister, he wrote *Aunt Jack* (1889), *The Volcano* (1891), *The Best Man* (1894), and *Thorough-Bred* (1895). All were farces or comedies, and the two latter enjoyed engagements of more than 100 performances.

R. FENTON MACKAY (d. 1929) A writer of melodrama and farce, Mackay was the author of *Black Diamonds* (1892), *The Life We Lead* (1892), *Qwong-Hi* (1895), and *The J. P.* (1898).

CHARLES MARLOWE (Harriett Jay, 1863–1932) An actress and novelist (e.g. *Through the Stage Door,* 1884), Marlowe, as Jay called herself, acted in the plays of Robert Buchanan, her brother-in-law, and collaborated with him in writing the melodrama *Alone in London* (1885) and the farce *The Strange Adventures of Miss Brown* (1895). The latter, which ran for 256 performances in 1895, was among the most popular plays of the 1890s. Her biography, *Robert Buchanan: Some Account of His Life,* was published in 1903.

A. TEXEIRA DE MATTOS (1865–1921) Primarily a translator, Texeira de Mattos's renderings of continental drama were staged on several occasions by the Independent Theatre Society: *Thérèse Raquin* in 1891, *The Goldfish* in 1892, *The Cradle* in 1893, and *The Heirs of Rabourdin* in 1894.

MARK MELFORD (d. 1914) An actor as well as writer of old-fashioned, physical farce, Melford was the author of *Kleptomania* (1888), *Turned Up* (1891), and *A Screw Loose* (1893).

DAVID CHRISTIE MURRAY (1847–1907) Collaborating with J. L. Shine, Murray wrote *The Puritan* (1894) and *Ned's Chums* (1891). *An Irish Gentleman* (1897), like the others a comic drama, was written by Murray alone.

MRS. H. MUSGRAVE The author of farces and comedies, Mrs. Musgrave, whose full name is not known, was most successful with *Our Flat,* performed in 1889 as a matinee and revived in the 1890s with some success – 118 performances at the Strand in 1894. Her other plays were *Cerise and Co.* (1890) and *Dick Wilder* (1891).

G. STUART OGILVIE (1858–1932) The little-known Ogilvie wrote *Hypatia* (1893), an adaptation of Kingsley's novel; *The Sin of St. Hulda* (1896); *The White Knight* (1898); and *The Master* (1898).

MRS. R. PACHECO *Tom, Dick, and Harry,* a farce that ran for 105 performances at the Trafalgar after its premiere in Manchester, is the only play credited to Mrs. Pacheco, whose full name is not known.

LOUIS N. PARKER ("Thornton Clark," 1852–1944) Musician, playwright, and designer of historical and patriotic pageants, Parker was among the most popular playwrights of the late Victorian and Edwardian periods. He left his job as music master at a school in Dorset in 1892 to devote himself entirely to the theatre. With his frequent collaborator, Murray Carson, he wrote *Rosemary* (1896), which ran nearly 200 performances, and *Gudgeons* (1893), which enjoyed a modest success at Terry's and helped launch his career. His autobiography, *Several of My Lives,* was published in 1928.

W. J. PATMORE A writer whose work was staged outside the West End at theatres such as the Surrey, Britannia, and Pavilion, Patmore was the author of *Lured to London* (1894; with L. B. Moss), *Capital and Labour* (1891; with Moss), *Sons of Erin* (1893), and *A Daughter of Ishmael* (1897; also known as *Miriam Gray; or, the Living Dead).* None of Patmore's plays seems to have been published and little is known of his life.

HARRY MAJOR PAULL (1854–1934) A writer of farce and comedy, H. M. Paull was the author of *At a Health Resort* (1892), *The Gentleman Whip* (1894), *Hal, the Highwayman* (1894), *Poor Mr. Potton* (1895; with Clarence Hamlyn), and *Merrifield's Ghost* (1895), among others.

HARRY PAULTON (1842–1917) A comic actor and dramatist, Paulton was best known for the extravaganza he wrote with his brother, Edward Paulton – *Niobe (All Smiles)* (1892), whose 535 performances at the Strand made it the second longest-running play of the 1890s. *A World of Trouble in a Locket* (1895) gained a less spectacular success at the Strand in 1895.

HENRY PETTITT (1848–93) After humble beginnings as an East End dramatist with the play *Golden Fruit* (1873), Pettitt achieved great success in collaboration with some of the leading writers of melodrama in the 1880s and early 1890s. He wrote *A Million of Money* (1890) with Augustus Harris, *Master and Man* (1889) with G. R. Sims, and *The Prodigal Daughter* (1892) with Harris. Most of his melodramas were staged at the Drury Lane, but *Carmen up to Date,* a burlesque he co-authored with Sims, ran for 240 performances in 1890–1 at the Gaiety.

F. C. PHILIPS (1849–1921) Journalist, novelist, and playwright, "Eff Cee Pee" collaborated with Sydney Grundy on *The Dean's Daughter* (1888; an adaptation of his own novel), with Percy Fendall on *Husband and Wife* (1891), with Charles H. E. Brookfield on *Godpapa* (1891), with Seymour Hicks on *Papa's Wife* (1895), and with Brookfield on *A Woman's Reason* (1895). Philips wrote his memoirs under the title *My Varied Life.*

EDEN PHILLPOTTS (1862–1960) After starting life as a clerk in an insurance office, Phillpotts began writing in the 1880s and became a popular novelist as well as dramatist for decades to come. His first play was a farce, *The Policeman* (1887), written with Walter Helmore. In his 1890s work for the stage Phillpotts was the collaborator of Jerome K. Jerome – on *The Prude's Progress* (1895) and *The MacHaggis* (1897) – in addition to writing plays of his own such as *The Love of Prim* (1899) and *A Pair of Knickerbockers* (1899). His comedy of rural life, *The Farmer's Wife* (1916), ran for more than 1,300 performances at the Court in the 1920s. Phillpotts also wrote a book of reminiscences – *One Thing and Another* (1954).

ARTHUR WING PINERO (1855–1934) Of Portuguese-Jewish descent, Pinero was apprenticed to the law at age ten but by 1874 had joined the company of the Theatre Royal, Edinburgh, as an actor. He performed for ten years and had his first play – *Two Hundred a Year* (1877) – staged at the Globe. But his real popularity came later, with the production of *The Magistrate* (1885) at the Court. Pinero followed that success with a series of farces, all produced at the Court, including *The Schoolmistress* (1886), *Dandy Dick* (1887), and *The Cabinet Minister* (1890). In the meantime *Sweet Lavender* (1888), a sentimental drama, had become one of the most popular plays of the late 1880s, and *The Profligate* (1889) had given Pinero an occasion to try his hand at "unpleasant" drama. But it was *The Second Mrs. Tanqueray* (1893), with Mrs. Patrick Campbell in the starring role, that startled London with its sympathetic portrayal of a woman with a past, making clear that a new age was dawning in the theatre. Unlike the productions of Ibsen's plays, moreover, it was a popular success – perhaps because Pinero was able to keep his discussion of controversial matters within the range of what was publicly acceptable.

WALTER HERRIES POLLOCK (1850–1926) A novelist and critic, Pollock collaborated on several plays during the 1890s – *The Ballad-Monger* (1890) with Walter Besant (adapted from the French), *An Interlude* (1893) with Mrs. W. K. Clifford, *St. Roman's Well* (1893) with Richard Davey (an adaptation of Scott's novel), and *The Were Wolf* (1898) with Lillian Mowbray. His novel *The Picture's Secret* (1883) is laced with premonitions of *The Picture of Dorian Gray*.

PAUL M. POTTER (1853–1921) Potter was known for his adaptation of George Du Maurier's novel *Trilby*, which opened at the Haymarket in 1895 and ran for 254 performances. Less successful was *The Conquerors* (1898). Born in Brighton, Potter worked for the New York *Herald* – as foreign editor, London correspondent, and drama critic – and for the Chicago *Tribune*.

CECIL R. RALEIGH (1856–1914) An actor and drama critic for various magazines (including *Vanity Fair* and *The Lady*), Raleigh typically wrote melodramas in collaboration with other playwrights. With R. C. Carton he authored *The Great Pink Pearl* (1885) and *The Treasure* (1888), with G. R. Sims *The Grey Mare* (1892) and the farce *Fanny* (1895), and with Augustus Harris and Henry Hamilton *The Derby Winner* (1894). *The Great Millionaire* (1901), a Drury Lane melodrama, was written independently.

ALICIA RAMSAY (1864–1933) Virtually unknown, Ramsay was the author of *Gaffer Jarge*, staged at the Comedy in 1896, and *Monsieur de Paris* (1896; staged in the provinces earlier as *The Executioner's Daughter*) and *As a Man Sows* (1888). The two latter were collaborations with Rudolph de Cordova. Ramsay's novel about New Women, *Miss Edizabeth Gibbs*, was published in 1915.

ELIZABETH ROBINS ("C. E. Raimond," Mrs. G. R. Parkes, 1862–1952) Born in Louisville and educated in Zanesville, Ohio, Robins was befriended by Oscar Wilde when she came to London as an actress in the 1880s. She was Martha Bernick in the first London production of *Pillars of Society* (1889), Mrs. Linden in *A Doll's House* in 1891, and Hedda Gabler in 1891. She played many Ibsen roles, but also acted in farces and melodramas, from *Dr. Bill* to *Diplomacy*. She retired from the stage in 1897 to write fiction, a labor she had already begun with *George Mandeville's Husband* (1894) and *The New Moon* (1895). Her feminist play, *Votes for Women*, was produced at the Court in 1907. She also wrote *Theatre and Friendship* (1932), *Both Sides of the Curtain* (1940), and *Raymond and I* (1956), among others.

E. M. ROBSON (d. 1932) An actor who did everything from Ibsen to Shakespeare to French farce, Robson collaborated with other writers on two plays: *Faithful unto Death* (1881), with Edward Compton, and *The Foundling* (1894), with W. Lestocq.

CHARLES ROGERS (d. 1900) Author of the antifeminist *The Future Woman, or Josiah's Dream* (1896), a farcical comedy that ran briefly at the Strand, Rogers wrote other plays staged mostly in provincial theatres. They included *Reality* (1889), *The Democrat* (1893), and *Sherlock Holmes* (1894), which preceded Conan Doyle's own dramatization of the fictional detective.

EDWARD ROSE (1849–1904) Rose's career as a playwright began in the 1870s (*Our Farm*, 1872), continued in the 1880s (e.g. *Two Women* [1885] and *A Girl Graduate* [1886]), and flourished in the 1890s with two hit romantic dramas: *The Prisoner of Zenda* (1896; an adaptation of Anthony Hope's novel) and *Under the Red Robe* (1896; adapted from Stanley Weyman's novel), both performed more than 250 times.

MADELEINE LUCETTE RYLEY (Mrs. J. H. Ryley, 1865–1934) Born in London, Ryley resided and acted in America and wrote a number of plays produced in the West End of London in the 1890s – *Jedbury Junior* (1896), *A Coat of Many Colours* (1897), *An American Citizen* (1899), and *The Vanishing Husband* (as it was called in the provinces; staged at the Strand in 1900 as *The Mysterious Mr. Bugle*). Ryley wrote mostly comedy and farce.

WALTER SAPTE A writer of farce, Sapte was the author of *A Lucky Dog* (1892), *Uncle's Ghost* (1894), and *There She Goes* (1896). Some of his plays were staged in the provinces and never reached London.

CLEMENT SCOTT ("Saville Rowe," 1841–1904) One of the most influential drama critics during his nearly thirty years on the London *Daily Telegraph*, Scott was an implacable foe of Ibsenism and particularly hostile toward *Ghosts*. He was editor of the *Theatre* and critic for the *Illustrated London News* in addition to writing plays himself. His *Diplomacy*, an adaptation of Sardou's *Dora*, was first performed in 1878 and revived in 1893 with great success. He also adapted Sardou's *Odette* (1894) and collaborated with Brandon Thomas on *The Swordsman's Daughter* (1895), an Adelphi melodrama. His farce *Off the Line* (1871) was revived in 1890.

ARTHUR SHIRLEY (1853–1925) The prolific Shirley, who began as an actor, wrote more than 120 plays, mostly in collaboration with G. R. Sims, Fred Leslie, Sutton Vane, Benjamin Landeck, and others. His first play evidently was *Reparation* (1882), soon followed by *Saved; or, a Wife's Peril* (1885) – a work with interesting similarities to *Lady Windermere's Fan*. Shirley's farce *As Large as Life* (1890) played at Terry's in 1890, but mostly he was known for melodrama such as *False Witness* (1890; also called *The Cross of Honour*), *The Star of India* (1896; written with Sims), and *Straight from the Heart* (1896) written with Benjamin Landeck and performed at the Pavilion.

GEORGE ROBERT SIMS (1847–1922) Famous as a columnist for the *Referee* (writing as Dagonet) as well as for his plays, G. R. Sims was among the most productive of later Victorian dramatists. He was known especially for his melodramas, often written in collaboration with other authors. *The Lights o' London* (1881), one of the major hits of the period, was successfully revived in 1891. Sims collaborated with Sydney Grundy on *The Glass of Fashion* (1883), with Henry Pettitt on *The Harbour Lights* (1885) and *Master and Man* (1889), with Robert Buchanan on *The Trumpet Call* (which ran for 220 performances at the Adelphi in 1891), and with Arthur Shirley on *The Star of India* (1896) and *The Gipsy Earl* (1898). He also wrote fiction (e.g. *A Missing Husband and Other Tales*) and sketches of East End life such as *How the Poor Live* (1887) and *Horrible London* (1883). In 1900 appeared *Without the Limelight: Theatrical Life As It Is* and, in 1917, *My Life: Sixty Years' Recollection of Bohemian London*.

B. C. STEPHENSON ("Bolton Rowe," d. 1906) After collaborating with Clement Scott on *Diplomacy* (1878) and *Peril* (1876), Stephenson joined with Haddon Chambers in writing the successful melodrama *The Fatal Card*, which ran for 167 performances at the Adelphi in 1894–5. Some of his other plays were acted in provincial theatres and never reached London.

ROBERT LOUIS STEVENSON (1850–94) Although written and published in the 1880s, two plays by Stevenson had their first production in the 1890s. *Admiral Guinea* was staged at the Avenue in 1897, *Beau Austin* at the Haymarket in 1890, as a matinee.

ALFRED SUTRO (1863–1933) Of Sutro it was said that he looked to the drama as a popular art and tried to keep it so. He succeeded with *The Chili Widow*, a comedy written with Arthur Bourchier, adapted from Bisson and Carré. The play, which opened at the Royalty in 1895, ran for 223 performances. Sutro quit his family's wholesale business and moved to Paris where he made the acquaintance of Maeterlinck and became his translator, eventually introducing many of the Belgian's plays to English readers. Maeterlinck himself wrote an introduction to Sutro's play *The Cave of Illusion* (1900). Sutro collaborated with George Meredith on a dramatization of *The Egoist* which apparently was never produced, and scored a major success in 1904 with *The Walls of Jericho*.

ARTHUR SYMONS (1865–1945) The Welsh critic, poet, and writer of fiction was also the author of a play staged on 4 March 1892 by the Independent Theatre Society – *The Minister's Call*. It was acted at the Royalty, where it shared the bill with John Gray's *The Kiss* and William Archer's *A Visit*.

BRANDON THOMAS (1856–1914) Far and away the most popular play of the 1890s was Thomas's *Charley's Aunt*, which ran for 1,469 performances in an engagement that spanned approximately four years, beginning in 1892. An actor as well, Thomas played the title role in revivals of the play, although W. S. Penley took the part in the original production. His other plays, not nearly as successful, include *Comrades* (1882; written with B. C. Stephenson), *A Gold Craze* (1889), *Marriage* (1894; the immediate successor of *Charley's Aunt*), and *The Swordsman's Daughter* (1895; with Clement Scott).

DR. JOHN TODHUNTER (1839–1916) The Independent Theatre Society produced Todhunter's *The Black Cat* at the Opera Comique in 1893. The Irish physician's *Comedy of Sighs* was staged in 1894, and *The Poison Flower* in 1891 as a matinee.

SUTTON VANE (d. 1913) Most of Vane's plays were staged outside the West End, but his melodramas occasionally had mild success in established theatres. *The Cotton King* played at the Adelphi in 1894; *The Sight of St. Paul's*, written with Arthur Shirley, was staged at the Princess's in 1896; and *The Span of Life* was produced at the Princess's, also in 1896. Little of his work for the stage was ever published.

HERMANN VEZIN (1829–1910) An actor and one-time elocution coach to Oscar Wilde, Vezin's attempts at play writing include two farces: *Cousin Jack* (1891) and *Mrs. M. P.* (1891), the latter an adaptation. Born in Philadelphia, Vezin moved to England in 1850 to stay. He was manager of the Surrey Theatre, known especially for his Shakespearean roles.

ISRAEL ZANGWILL (1864–1926) The Jewish writer's *Six Persons* had a run of ninety-two performances at the Haymarket in 1893. Two farces – *The Great Demonstration* (1892; written with L. Cowen) and *Threepenny Bits* (1895) – were less fortunate. Zangwill's adaptation of his own *Children of the Ghetto* had an abbreviated engagement at the Adelphi in 1899. Later, however, *The Melting Pot* (1914) prospered in both New York and London.

Notes

1 Rewriting the past

1   I have identified the relative popularity of plays on the basis of playbills in J. P. Wearing, *The London Stage 1890–1899: A Calendar of Plays and Players* (Metuchen, N.J.: Scarecrow, 1976), which note dates of the engagements of plays of the period, thus providing a statistical basis for estimating their public appeal. About thirty major London theatres are represented in Wearing's compilation, which omits provincial theatres and some in London, especially those outside the West End. In general, the dates I give for English plays refer to their first London production.

2   Many plays were published in privately printed acting editions which have not survived. At the Lyceum, for instance, Henry Irving regularly had texts of the plays he produced set in type for the use of actors.

3   Quoted in the *Era*, 6 August 1892, p. 8.

4   W. MacQueen-Pope, *Haymarket: Theatre of Perfection* (London: Allen, 1948), p. 338.

5   Arnold praised the performances of the Comédie Française at the Gaiety in 1879 – performances that were Sarah Bernhardt's first on an English stage.

6   Henry James, "The London Theatres," in *Scribner's*, January 1881, and "After the Play" in *New Review*, June 1889, both rpt. in James, *The Scenic Art: Notes on Acting and the Drama*, ed. Allan Wade (New Brunswick, N.J.: Rutgers University Press, 1948), pp. 134, 232.

7   James, "Henrik Ibsen: On the Occasion of Hedda Gabler" in *New Review*, June 1891, rpt. in James, *The Scenic Art*, p. 246.

8   *The Letters of Oscar Wilde*, ed. Rupert Hart-Davis (New York: Harcourt, Brace & World, 1962), p. 295; hereafter cited as *Letters*. This is not to deny that Wilde also wrote, as he once told the *Sketch*, "to please myself."

9   *Era*, 26 March 1892, p. 15.

10 Madge Kendal, *Dramatic Opinions* (Boston: Little, Brown, 1890), p. 116.

11 *Era*, 19 March 1892, p. 9.

12 *Era*, 23 July 1892, p. 8.

13 *Era*, 16 March 1895, p. 9. Richard Ellmann, for instance, calls *A Woman of No Importance* "the weakest of the plays Wilde wrote in the nineties" (*Oscar Wilde* [New York: Knopf, 1988], p. 378).

14 *More Letters of Oscar Wilde*, ed. Rupert Hart-Davis (New York: Vanguard, 1985), p. 181.

[15] James, *The Scenic Art*, p. 137. Not long after this passage first appeared, Pinero's plays began to be published by Heinemann (in 1893).

[16] Sydney Grundy, *The Play of the Future, by a Playwright of the Past* (London: French, 1914), p. 22.

[17] Quoted from an interview of Wilde in the *St. James's Gazette*, 18 January 1895, pp. 4–5; rpt. in *Oscar Wilde: Interviews and Recollections*, ed. E. H. Mikhail (2 vols., London: Macmillan, 1979), vol. 1, p. 249.

[18] Harold Bloom, *A Map of Misreading* (New York: Oxford University Press, 1975), p. 10.

[19] See Bloom, *The Anxiety of Influence: A Theory of Poetry* (New York: Oxford University Press, 1973), pp. 5–7, and *Oscar Wilde: Modern Critical Views* (New York: Chelsea, 1985), p. 1.

[20] See Isobel Murray, "Oscar Wilde's Absorption of Influences: The Case History of Chuang Tzu," *Durham University Journal*, 64 (1971), 2–13, and the introduction to her edition of *The Picture of Dorian Gray* (London: Oxford University Press, 1974).

[21] On Wilde's "rewriting" himself, see Donald Lawler and Charles E. Knott, "The Context of Invention: Suggested Origins of *Dorian Gray*" in *Modern Philology*, 73 (1976), 389–98, for a convincing argument that earlier works such as "The Portrait of Mr. W. H." and "The Fisherman and His Soul" were among the sources of Wilde's novel. Others have suggested a similar effect in the plays, by which, for example, *Salomé* is viewed as a further development of the radical characterization of women begun in *Vera* and continued through *The Duchess of Padua* and the sharp-tongued dowagers of *Lady Windermere's Fan*. See Katharine Worth, *Oscar Wilde* (New York: Grove, 1984), pp. 53–4.

[22] "The Critic as Artist" in *The Artist as Critic: Critical Writings of Oscar Wilde*, ed. Richard Ellmann (New York: Random House, 1968), p. 389.

[23] Bloom, *A Map of Misreading*, p. 10.

[24] G. R. Sims, *My Life: Sixty Years' Recollection of Bohemian London* (London: Nash, 1917), p. 203.

[25] *Letters*, p. 589.

[26] *Letters*, pp. 364, 369, 376.

[27] Will Rothenstein, *Men and Memories: A History of the Arts 1872–1922* (2 vols., New York: Tudor, n.d.), vol. 1, p. 132.

[28] W. Lestocq and E. M. Robson, *The Foundling: A Farce in Three Acts*, quoted from the manuscript in the Lord Chamberlain's collection of the British Library, Act I, pp. 16, 28–9.

[29] *Times*, 15 February 1895, p. 5.

[30] Rothenstein, *Men and Memories*, vol. 1, p. 184.

[31] *Lady Windermere's Fan: A Play about a Good Woman*, ed. Ian Small (London: Benn, 1980), p. 80.

[32] *The First Collected Edition of the Works of Oscar Wilde*, ed. Robert Ross (15 vols., London: Methuen, 1908–22), vol. 13 (*Reviews*), p. 488.

[33] See my article "Tom, Dick and Dorian Gray: Magic-Picture Mania in Late Victorian Fiction," *Philological Quarterly*, 62 (1983), 147–70, and "Hawthorne, Arlo Bates, and *The Picture of Dorian Gray*" in *Papers on Language & Literature*, 16 (1980), 403–16.

[34] *Letters*, p. 259.

35 *Collected Edition*, vol. 1, p. 82. Further quotation of *The Duke of Padua* refers to this edition.

36 Robert H. Sherard, *The Life of Oscar Wilde* (London: Laurie, 1906), pp. 320–21.

37 Richard Ellmann suggests that Wilde may have been indebted in a general way to Dostoevski and Turgenev, who coined the term "nihilism" in *Fathers and Sons*. Another influence could have been the historical Vera Zassoulich, who shot the chief of police of St. Petersburg in 1878 (*Oscar Wilde*, pp. 121–2).

38 *More Letters*, p. 44.

39 Nikolai Chernyshevski, *What Is To Be Done?* (1863) was available in French, but not translated in English when Wilde wrote *Vera*.

40 Rodney Shewan, "*A Wife's Tragedy*: An Unpublished Sketch for a Play by Oscar Wilde," *Theatre Research International*, 7 (1982), 75–131.

41 *Era*, 27 February 1892, p. 10. See William Archer, *The Old Drama and the New* (Boston: Small, Maynard, 1922), pp. 309–10, for a discussion of the importance of the copyright act in returning plays to their former "literary" status as printed works.

42 Grundy, *The Play of the Future, by a Playwright of the Past*, pp. 8–9.

43 Michael R. Booth, "East End and West End: Class and Audience in Victorian London," *Theatre Research International*, 2 (1977), 98–103; Joseph W. Donohue Jr., "The First Production of *The Importance of Being Earnest*: A Proposal for a Reconstructive Study" in *Nineteenth Century British Theatre*, ed. Kenneth Richards and Peter Thomson (London: Methuen, 1971), pp. 125–43.

44 *English Drama of the Nineteenth Century* (New Canaan, Conn.: Readex, 1965–). Until 1975 the series was edited by George Freedley and Allardyce Nicoll.

45 For Rodney Shewan, see especially *Oscar Wilde: Art and Egotism* (London: Macmillan, 1977), and his work on *A Wife's Tragedy*, cited above.

46 Regenia Gagnier, *Idylls of the Marketplace: Oscar Wilde and the Victorian Public* (Stanford University Press, 1986), p. 8.

47 John Stokes, *Resistible Theatres: Enterprise and Experiment in the Late Nineteenth Century* (London: Elek, 1972), especially chapter 2, pp. 31–68.

48 *The Picture of Dorian Gray*, p. 17. Citation of Wilde's novel refers to the 1974 edition, edited by Isobel Murray.

2 *Lady Windermere's fan* and the unmotherly mother

1 Ellmann, *Oscar Wilde*, pp. 333–4.

2 *Stage*, 25 February 1892, p. 12.

3 See, e.g., Frederick Wedmore's review in the *Academy*, A. B. Walkley's in the *Spectator*, and an unsigned review in *Black and White*. All are reprinted in *Oscar Wilde: The Critical Heritage*, ed. Karl Beckson (New York: Barnes & Noble, 1970), pp. 119–23, 126–9.

4 "A Gossip with Sydney Grundy," *Era*, 8 October 1892, p. 11.

5 Wendell Stacy Johnson, "Fallen Women, Lost Children: Wilde and the Theatre of the Nineties" in *Sexuality and Victorian Literature*, ed. Don Richard Cox, Tennessee Studies in Literature, vol. 27 (Knoxville: University of Tennessee Press, 1984), pp. 196–211.

6 Worth, *Oscar Wilde*, p. 95.

[7] Alan Bird, *The Plays of Oscar Wilde* (New York: Barnes & Noble, 1977), p. 113.

[8] See the fascinating discussion of this genre in Martin Meisel, *Shaw and the Nineteenth-Century Theatre* (Princeton University Press, 1963), pp. 226–33. The quotations are from Tom Taylor's *Still Waters Run Deep: An Original Comedy in Three Acts* (London: French, n.d.), p. 51.

[9] Tom Taylor, *The Victims: An Original Comedy, in Three Acts* (New York: French, n.d.), p. 25.

[10] See, for example, Epifanio San Juan Jr., *The Art of Oscar Wilde* (Princeton University Press, 1967), pp. 140–54; Philip K. Cohen, *The Moral Vision of Oscar Wilde* (Rutherford, N.J.: Fairleigh Dickinson University Press, 1978), pp. 182–92; and Cleanth Brooks and Robert B. Heilman, in *Understanding Drama* (New York: Holt, 1945), pp. 73–82.

[11] See, e.g., Edouard Roditi, *Oscar Wilde* (Norfolk, Conn.: New Directions, 1947), p. 128; Christopher S. Nassaar, *Into the Demon Universe: A Literary Exploration of Oscar Wilde* (New Haven, Conn.: Yale University Press, 1974), p. 75.

[12] Louis Kronenberger, *Oscar Wilde* (Boston: Little, Brown, 1976), pp. 126–7.

[13] Bird, *The Plays of Oscar Wilde*, p. 212.

[14] The delinquent father as a stock figure in nineteenth-century fiction is sketched by Dorothy Van Ghent in *The English Novel: Form and Function* (New York: Rinehart, 1953), pp. 139–52.

[15] See C. Haddon Chambers, *The Idler: A Play in Four Acts* (London: French, 1902). As in Wilde's drama, the concealment scene occurs in Act III.

[16] In *Oscar Wilde: Art and Egotism*, commenting on reviewers who linked *The Idler* and *Lady Windermere's Fan*, Rodney Shewan writes: "In fact, Chambers' device involved a bouquet, not a fan" (p. 221). Although a bouquet figures prominently in Act II, it is indeed a fan which becomes the chief prop in the concealment scene of Act III. Wilde referred to the play in a letter of January 1894.

[17] The relation to Sheridan's play was perhaps first made by A. B. Walkley in his review for the *Speaker*.

[18] Sydney Grundy and G. R. Sims, *The Glass of Fashion: An Original Comedy in Four Acts* (London: French, 1898), p. 49. As in Wilde's play, this development concludes Act III.

[19] It would be interesting to know what occasioned the changes in Grundy's attitude toward Wilde. In 1892 he viewed him as a literary thief who made off with *The Glass of Fashion*; in 1895 he protested in a letter to the press the removal of Wilde's name from the playbills of *The Importance of Being Earnest* as a result of the scandal that wrecked his career. Later, in *The Play of the Future, by a Playwright of the Past* (1914), Grundy sneered at Wilde as an immoralist and failed playwright.

[20] Wilde admired Sardou and apparently knew all his plays – or claimed to. When critics likened *An Ideal Husband* to Sardou's *Dora* because of the business of the diamond bracelet, Wilde complained that Sardou "is not understood in England." Such a scene, he explained to a newspaper reporter, "does not occur in any of Sardou's plays" (See "*An Ideal Husband* at the Haymarket Theatre: A Talk with Mr. Oscar Wilde," *The Sketch*, 9 January 1895, p. 495; reprinted in Mikhail, ed., *Oscar Wilde: Interviews and Recollections*, vol. 1, p. 241). Sardou's influence on Wilde is almost always discussed in terms of *Dora's* alleged impact upon *An Ideal Husband*. The relation of the little-known *Odette* to *Lady Windermere's Fan* has

gone unexplored. Although I can find no record of the play having been published in English, it was adapted in English stage versions for the Haymarket and Princess's theatres. "We entrusted the adaptation to Clement Scott, with whom, as usual, we worked in concert, although he modestly preferred that his name should not appear, the play being simply announced as written by Victorien Sardou," recalled Squire and Marie Bancroft of the 1882 production (*The Bancrofts: Recollections of Sixty Years* [1909; rpt. New York: Blom, 1969], p. 230). The 1894 production at the Princess's was advertised as Scott's, however.

21   One of the most accessible of the many stage adaptations of Mrs. Henry Wood's novel *East Lynne* is quoted here, that of the United States production of 1862 as reprinted in J. O. Bailey, ed., *British Plays of the Nineteenth Century* (New York: Odyssey, 1966), p. 317. See also Arthur Shirley, *Saved; or, a Wife's Peril: Comedy Drama in Four Acts* (Chicago: Dramatic Publishing, n.d.), p. 12; further references are to this text.

22   Jules Lemaître, *Révoltée: Pièce en quatre actes* (Paris: Lévy, 1889), pp. 80–1, Oscar Wilde, *Lady Windermere's Fan: A Play about a Good Woman*, ed. Ian Small (London: Benn, 1980), p. 49. Further references to *Lady Windermere's Fan* are to Small's edition.

23   Victorien Sardou, *Odette*, in *Théâtre complet*, 15 vols. (Paris: Michel, 1934–61), vol. 6, pp. 280, 419.

24   Arthur Shirley and Maurice Gally, *The Cross of Honour* (1892), quoted from the Lord Chamberlain's manuscript copy. The play was licensed on 22 October 1890 and had been performed outside London under the title *False Witness*.

25   Sardou, *Odette*, p. 423. As in Wilde's play, this material occurs in Act IV and leads to the denouement.

26   Estelle Burney and Arthur Benham's *The Awakening* was never published, but played the Garrick Theatre for twenty-five performances in October 1892. The Lord Chamberlain's manuscript is quoted (Act II, p. 12).

27   Henri Meilhac and Ludovic Halévy, *Frou-Frou* (New York: Rullman, n.d.), p. 48. Sarah Bernhardt often performed the title role of Gilberte (Frou-Frou) – indeed, she was acting the part in July 1892 at the Royal English Opera House while *Lady Windermere's Fan* was still engaged at the St. James's Theatre. *Frou-Frou* was performed in London frequently throughout the 1890s. (All reference to *Frou-Frou* is made to the English–French edition of Rullman.)

28   Pierre Leclerq's unpublished play *This Woman and That: A New Play in Three Acts* was staged at the Globe on 2 August 1890. It is somewhat similar in subject and treatment to his other play of 1890, *Illusion*. The Lord Chamberlain's manuscript is quoted (Act III, p. 11).

29   The full context of Wilde's letter to an unidentified correspondent makes clear in what he thinks the newness consists. "The psychological idea that suggested to me the play is this. A woman who has had a child, but never known the passion of maternity (there are such women), suddenly sees the child she has abandoned falling over a precipice. There wakes in her the maternal feeling – the most terrible of all emotions – a thing which weak animals and little birds possess. She rushes to rescue, sacrifices herself, does follies – and the next day she feels 'This passion is too terrible. It wrecks my life. I don't want to know it again. It makes me suffer too much. Let me go away. I don't want to be a mother

any more.' And so the fourth act is to me the psychological act, the act that is newest, most true." Quoted from *Letters*, pp. 331–2.

[30] *Letters*, p. 275. Here – in late 1890 – Wilde praises Saltus's *Mary Magdalen* and invites the American to dine while he is visiting London.

[31] Edgar Saltus, *Eden* (Chicago: Belford, Clark, 1888), p. 111.

[32] Saltus, *Eden*, p. 134.

[33] *Era*, 4 June 1892, p. 13.

[34] *Letters*, p. 291. Pierre Leclerq himself would write two more plays, both in the 1890s and both failures. Unlike other members of his famous family – including Rose and Carlotta Leclerq and his father and mother – the unremembered author of *Illusion* was not a performer himself. He died, long after the memory of his plays, in 1932 (see "The Death of Mr. Pierre Leclerq," *Times*, 29 January 1932, p. 10).

[35] *Stage*, 11 July 1890, p. 11.

[36] Pierre Leclerq, *Illusion: A New and Original Play in Three Acts*, is quoted from the typescript in the Lord Chamberlain's collection in the British Library, Act I, p. 13. Further citation will appear parenthetically in the text.

[37] Lady Windermere, of course, is seen arranging flowers – roses from Selby – in the first act of Wilde's play, and *Saved* opens with a presentation of flowers to Beatrice Fane from her six-year-old daughter.

[38] *East Lynne*, p. 318.

[39] Lord Augustus Lorton is reminiscent of Gussie Cholmondeley in Shirley's *Saved* – "a bit of a fool," Cholmondeley is also capable of wit ("Tailors never die – they can't afford it, people owe them too much"). He is "a modern swell" cleverly maneuvered into proposing marriage to the strong-minded, aging beauty of the play. If Gussie cannot find words to propose, says Mrs. Merryweather – "if he don't, I shall have to do it for him" (*Saved*, pp. 5–8).

[40] *Letters*, p. 308.

[41] *Era*, 27 February 1892, p. 11.

[42] *Era*, 26 March 1892, p. 10. George Alexander "knew audience mentality and was not going to offend it," writes W. MacQueen-Pope in *St. James's: Theatre of Distinction* (London: Allen, 1958), pp. 119–20. Wilde, he suggests, "was learning a new craft at the hands of a master." Against Wilde's desire to create a new effect, Alexander's insistence on an early disclosure of Mrs. Erlynne's secret is not impractical. Without it, Lord Windermere's insistence on inviting Mrs. Erlynne to his house, and the motive for Mrs. Erlynne's self-sacrifice, can only baffle the audience until the very end of the play.

[43] *Times*, 7 July 1890, p. 10; *Era*, 5 July 1890, p. 9.

[44] Morse Peckham, "What Did Lady Windermere Learn?" *College English*, 18 (1956), 11–14, makes this association in a convincing fashion.

[45] *A Doll's House*, trans. William Archer, in *The Collected Works of Henrik Ibsen* (New York: Scribner's, 1911), vol. 7, pp. 144, 147.

[46] G. B. Shaw, *Mrs. Warren's Profession*, in *The Works of Bernard Shaw* (33 vols., London: Constable, 1931), vol. 7, p. 216.

[47] Blanche Crackanthorpe, *The Turn of the Wheel*, quoted from the typed manuscript dated "1901" in the British Library file "Unlicensed Plays," vol. 1 (Act II, p. 20). In the end, like some of Wilde's dramas, the play is too weak to resist the genre it begins by undercutting. When the son has grown to be a dissipated

youth, Isabel experiences the upsurge of maternal interest so familiar to play-goers of the day. She seeks him out, and takes him under her care, unworthy though he is.

48 Mona Caird, *The Daughters of Danaus* (London: Bliss, 1894), p. 341.

49 Janet Achurch, *Mrs. Daintree's Daughter*, staged in Manchester in 1903, is quoted from the typescript in the Lord Chamberlain's collection of the British Library. For a discussion of Achurch's play in relation to Shaw's *Mrs. Warren's Profession*, see Geoffrey Bullough, "Literary Relations of Shaw's Mrs. Warren," *Philological Quarterly*, 41 (January 1962), pp. 339–58.

50 First, however, the heroine baptizes the baby – a sequence like that in Thomas Hardy's *Tess of the D'Urbervilles*. A Norwegian drama, *Karin* by Alfild Agrell, first staged in Stockholm in 1881 after the success of *A Doll's House*, ends with the wife cradling her dead child in her arms and announcing to her husband that she is about to leave him. *Karin* opened in London in May 1892 during the first engagement of *Lady Windermere's Fan*.

51 Mrs. Sarah Ellis, *The Daughters of England* (London: Fisher, 1842), p. 73.

52 Martha Vicinus, *Suffer and Be Still: Women in the Victorian Age* (Bloomington: Indiana University Press, 1972), p. ix.

53 Vicinus, *Independent Women: Work and Community for Single Women 1850–1920* (University of Chicago Press, 1985), p. 291.

54 Margaret Oliphant, "The Anti-Marriage League," *Blackwood's*, January 1896, pp. 135–49.

55 Shewan, *Oscar Wilde: Art and Egotism*, p. 163.

56 Jerome K. Jerome, *Stage-Land: Curious Habits and Customs of Its Inhabitants* (London: Chatto & Windus, 1890), p. 10.

57 Jerome, *Stage-Land*, p. 37.

58 Nassaar, *Into the Demon Universe: A Literary Exploration of Oscar Wilde*, p. 79.

59 San Juan, *The Art of Oscar Wilde*, pp. 141–2.

60 Gilbert Cross emphasizes the complex construction of morality in *East Lynne*. See *Next Week – East Lynne: Domestic Drama in Performance 1820–1874* (Lewisburg, Pa.: Bucknell University Press, 1977), pp. 221–2.

61 Gagnier, *Idylls of the Marketplace: Oscar Wilde and the Victorian Public*, p. 121.

62 For this observation I am indebted to Martin Meisel.

3 *Salomé*, the censor, and the divine Sarah

1 Kronenberger, *Oscar Wilde*, p. 140.

2 Nassaar, *Into the Demon Universe: A Literary Exploration of Oscar Wilde*, p. 109.

3 Philippe Jullian, *Oscar Wilde*, trans. Violet Wyndham (New York: Viking, 1969), p. 247.

4 John R. Stephens, *The Censorship of English Drama 1824–1901* (Cambridge University Press, 1980), p. 112.

5 Henry Arthur Jones, *The Renascence of the English Drama: Essays, Lectures, and Fragments* (London: Macmillan, 1895), p. 118.

6 Archer's estimate of the play's chance of being performed came in a letter to the *Pall Mall Gazette*, 1 July 1892, in which he protested the censor's action (*Letters*, p. 317).

7 From an interview in the *Pall Mall Budget*, 30 June 1892, p. 947 (reprinted in *Oscar Wilde: Interviews and Recollections*, vol. 1, pp. 186–8), and from

Wilde's letter to the *Times* of 2 March 1893, reprinted in *Letters*, pp. 335–6.

8 Gagnier, *Idylls of the Marketplace: Oscar Wilde and the Victorian Public*, p. 165. See also Jane Marcus, "Salomé: The Jewish Princess Was a New Woman," *Bulletin of the New York Public Library*, 78 (1974), 95–113. Marcus points to the play's "revolutionary content," remarking that "Salomé was Oscar Wilde's New Woman. She was a Biblical Hedda Gabler" (p. 105).

9 See Elliot L. Gilbert, " 'Tumult of Images': Wilde, Beardsley, and Salomé," *Victorian Studies*, 26 (1983), 133–59. A less sympathetic, but related point of view is that of Kate Millett, who calls *Salomé* "a drama of homosexual guilt and rejection," concluding with "a death of crushing and penetration under an army of males." By this interpretation Wilde's play is an "archaic slanderous accusation" against women, a herald of counterrevolution against the feminist movement. See *Sexual Politics* (Garden City, N.Y.: Doubleday, 1970), pp. 153–5.

10 Karen Horney, "The Dread of Woman" in *Feminine Psychology* (New York: Norton, 1967), p. 138.

11 Nina Auerbach, *Woman and the Demon: The Life of a Victorian Myth* (Cambridge, Mass.: Harvard University Press, 1982), especially chapter 3: "Angels and Demons: Woman's Marriage of Heaven and Hell," pp. 63–109.

12 Quoted from a transcription of Piggot's testimony published in the *Era*, 28 May 1892, p. 7. A recently published letter of Wilde to Pigott shows him to be well aware of the censor's protocol more than a decade before *Salomé*. "Dear Mr. Piggot," he writes after completing *Vera*, "I send you a copy of my first play . . . any suggestion, any helpful advice, your experience and very brilliant critical powers can give me I shall thank you very much for." (Quoted from *More Letters of Oscar Wilde*, p. 32.)

13 James M. Glover, *Jimmy Glover His Book* (London: Methuen, 1911), p. 20.

14 From the interview with the *Pall Mall Budget*, 30 June 1892.

15 From the "Theatrical Gossip" column, the *Era*, 2 July 1892, p. 8.

16 *Era*, 18 March 1893, p. 15.

17 From the review in the *Times*, 24 June 1890, p. 10; for a review of the production two years later, in French rather than Italian, see the *Era*, 2 July 1892, p. 13.

18 *Times*, 24 June 1890, p. 10.

19 *Era*, 16 June 1894, p. 15.

20 *Ibid.*

21 The phrase is Alan Bird's, in *The Plays of Oscar Wilde*, p. 82.

22 Archer's review appeared in *Black and White*, 11 May 1893, p. 290, and is reprinted in *Oscar Wilde: The Critical Heritage*, pp. 141–2.

23 *Letters*, p. 475. Vincent O'Sullivan writes that the bloody conclusion of *Salomé* was stimulated by some "wild and terrible music" that Wilde heard in a Parisian café (*Aspects of Wilde*, p. 33).

24 Richard Strauss, *Recollections and Reflections*, ed. Willi Schuh, trans. L. J. Lawrence (London: Boosey and Hawkes, 1949), p. 150; Norman Del Mar, *Richard Strauss: A Critical Commentary on His Life and Works* (3 vols., Philadelphia: Chilton, 1972), vol. 1, pp. 238–86; and George R. Marek, *Richard Strauss: The Life of a Non-Hero* (New York: Simon and Schuster, 1967), p. 156.

25 Nikolai A. Gorchakov, *The Theater in Soviet Russia*, trans. Edgar Lehrman (New York: Columbia University Press, 1957), pp. 224–5.

26 Initially the Lord Chamberlain's office denied the play a license, but Sir Thomas Beecham explained to Prime Minister Asquith "my little difficulty over Salomé"

and persuaded him to intervene, noting that "how being in German it would be comprehended by few" (Sir Thomas Beecham, *A Mingled Chime* [New York: Putman's, 1943], pp. 159–62, 167–73).

[27] Not listed in Allardyce Nicoll's *English Drama 1900–1930*, this English-language *Salomé* was reviewed in the *Strand* on 7 October 1909.

[28] See A. W. Pinero, *Dandy Dick: A Farce in Three Acts* (London: Heinemann, 1906), staged for the first time in 1887.

[29] Max Beerbohm, *"Salomé"* in *Around Theatres* (London: Hart-Davis, 1953), pp. 378–9.

[30] W. Graham Robertson, *Time Was: The Reminiscences of W. Graham Robertson* (London: Hamilton, 1931), p. 136.

[31] *Times*, 3 June 1892, p. 14. Even the few opponents of censorship did not always maintain their view energetically. For example, Augustus Filon says in *The English Stage* that although the censorship is absurd in principle, "in practice it is not wholly unreasonable" ([1897; rpt. Port Washington, N.Y.: Kennikat, 1970], p. 309). After all, comparatively few plays were denied licenses. From 1852 to 1912 there were 19,304 plays licensed, while only 103 were banned. In the turbulent years 1895–1909, only thirty plays were denied licenses (James Woodfield, *English Theatre in Transition 1881–1914* [London: Croom Helm, 1984], p. 112). Of course many plays were awarded licenses only after modifications, and some were never offered to the censor for fear of the result. Immediately after *Salomé* was banned, the *Era* reported the abandonment of a "gallant (if unnecessary) enterprise" of staging Shelley's *The Cenci*, another play with a murderous heroine whose performance by the Shelley Society had been favorably reviewed by Wilde in 1886 (*Reviews*, in *Collected Edition*, vol. 13, pp. 66–9). "No manager would lend his theatre for the performance," noted the *Era*, "– mainly, it is said, because the managers feared the vengeance of the Lord Chamberlain" (11 June 1892, p. 8).

[32] *Letters*, p. 336.

[33] Wilde made the offer in a letter believed to have been written *c.* 1 September 1892 (*Letters*, p. 320), but makes clear he already had discussed the play with Tree.

[34] For a reproduction, see Stuart Mason (C. S. Millard), *Bibliography of Oscar Wilde* (London: Laurie, n.d.), p. 328. In *The Days I Knew*, Lillie Langtry says of Wilde that "He called one afternoon with an important air and a roll of manuscript, placed it on the table, pointed to it with a sweeping gesture, and said: 'there is a play which I have written for you' " ([New York: Doran, 1925], p. 93). It was *Lady Windermere's Fan*, according to Langtry, but she refused the part of Mrs. Erlynne because she thought it too old for her.

[35] See Ross's introductory note to *Salomé* in the *Collected Edition*, vol. 2. For example, Donald H. Ericksen apparently accepts Wilde's denial of having written the play for Bernhardt (see *Oscar Wilde* [New York: Twayne, 1977], p. 124), while it is contradicted by Bird, *The Plays of Oscar Wilde*, p. 54, and Cornelia Otis Skinner, *Madame Sarah* (Boston: Houghton Mifflin, 1966), p. 123.

[36] Wilfrid Scawen Blunt, *My Diaries: Being a Personal Narrative of Events 1888–1914* (2 vols., New York: Knopf, 1922), vol. 1, p. 58. Richard Ellmann describes a written recollection in the papers of Mrs. Edgar Saltus describing her husband's meeting with Wilde some time in 1890. Impressed on this occasion by a picture

of Herodias dancing, Wilde supposedly announced that he would undertake to write about the dancer in the picture, while Edgar Saltus was already planning a novel on Mary Magdalen. "We will pursue the wantons together," Wilde is reported to have said (*Oscar Wilde*, p. 341). Saltus's novel came out in 1891, before *Salomé* was completed. Near the book's conclusion Mary Magdalen, contemplating revenge for the death of Christ, experiences a moonlit fantasy in which she brings about the crucifixions of Pilate, Judas, and Caiaphas (*Mary of Magdala: A Chronicle* [London: Greening, 1903], pp. 200–2).

37 O'Sullivan, *Aspects of Wilde*, pp. 32–3.
38 The surviving mss. are discussed by Clyde de L. Ryals in "Oscar Wilde's 'Salomé'," *Notes and Queries*, 204 (1959), 56–7.
39 Skinner, *Madame Sarah*, quoting the French critic Francisque Sarcey, p. 215.
40 Sarah Bernhardt, *My Double Life* (1907; rpt. London: Owen, 1977), p. 297. (Translated from the French *Ma Double Vie*.)
41 *Letters*, p. 65.
42 *Pall Mall Budget*, 30 June 1892, p. 947; *Letters*, p. 156.
43 *Pall Mall Budget*, 30 June 1892, p. 947.
44 Robert H. Sherard, *Oscar Wilde: The Story of an Unhappy Friendship* (1905; rpt. New York: Haskell House, 1970), pp. 135–44.
45 *Letters*, p. 392.
46 *Letters*, p. 834.
47 Arthur Symons, *Plays, Acting, and Music* (New York: Dutton, n.d.), pp. 27–8.
48 Murray is quoted in Bernhardt, *My Double Life*, p. 307; for Archer's comment, see the *Sketch*, 20 June 1894, p. 418.
49 *Era*, 18 June 1892, p. 8.
50 *Era*, 30 July 1892, p. 8.
51 Robertson, *Time Was*, p. 117.
52 *Era*, 18 June 1892, p. 9.
53 *Era*, 1 June 1895, p. 10.
54 Skinner, *Madame Sarah*, p. 204.
55 *Era*, 18 June 1892, p. 9.
56 *Era*, 23 June 1894, p. 11.
57 Jules Lemaître, "Madame Sarah Bernhardt" in *Literary Impressions*, trans. A. W. Evans (London: O'Connor, 1921), p. 284. Jean Lorrain also likened Sarah Bernhardt to a Moreau painting of Salomé (see Jullian, *Oscar Wilde*, p. 252).
58 *Letters*, pp. 399–400.
59 Worth, *Oscar Wilde*, pp. 54, 56.
60 Mario Praz, *The Romantic Agony*, trans. Angus Davidson (Cleveland: World, 1956), pp. 298–306.
61 See, e.g., Bird, *The Plays of Oscar Wilde*, p. 81.
62 *Pall Mall Gazette*, 27 February 1893, p. 3; reprinted in *Oscar Wilde: The Critical Heritage*, pp. 135–6.
63 Richard Ellmann, "Overtures to *Salomé*" in *Oscar Wilde: A Collection of Critical Essays*, ed. Richard Ellmann (Englewood Cliffs, N.J.: Prentice-Hall, 1969), pp. 73–91. Ellmann also brought attention to the Salomé of J. C. Heywood, whose *Herodias* Wilde reviewed (see *Reviews*, in *Collected Edition*, vol. 13, pp. 291–2). Heywood's Salomé, however, is a morally exemplary young girl with little in common with Wilde's.

[64] Shewan, *Oscar Wilde: Art and Egotism*, p. 147.

[65] "Pen Pencil and Poison" in *Intentions* (1891), reprinted in Ellmann, ed., *The Artist as Critic: Critical Writings of Oscar Wilde* (p. 338).

[66] "The Soul of Man under Socialism" in *The Artist as Critic*, p. 262.

[67] *Era*, 23 July 1892, p. 8.

[68] *Era*, 16 July 1892, p. 9.

[69] *Times*, 30 May 1892, p. 8.

[70] Maurice Maeterlinck, *La Princesse Maleine*, in *Théâtre* (3 vols., Paris: Slatkine, 1979), vol. 1, p. 4.

[71] *Salomé: Drame en un Acte* is quoted from the Ross edition – an exception in rejecting the English translation to print the French text. See *Collected Edition*, vol. 2, pp. 64–5. I cite the French version rather than English because Wilde himself conceived of *Salomé* as his "French" play; and while French friends such as Maurice Schwab may have made some changes in the text, Philippe Jullian has noted that the play's somewhat artificial and anglicized French gives it a strange although not unpleasing sound. "In order that certain words should stand out as the author intended, *Salomé* has to be acted with an English accent" (*Oscar Wilde*, p. 247). In addition, it is not clear how much of the English translation belongs to Lord Alfred Douglas and how much to Wilde, so that for a variety of reasons the French text seems to exert a superior claim. The English version of the passage above is as follows:

> *Herod*: Ah! Look at the moon! She has become red. She has become red as blood. Ah! the prophet prophesied truly. He prophesied that the moon would become red as blood. Did he not prophesy it? All of you heard him. And now the moon has become red as blood. Do ye not see it?
> *Herodias*: Oh, yes, I see it well, and the stars are falling like ripe figs, are they not? And the sun is becoming black like sackcloth of hair . . .
>
> (p. 569)

The English translation of passages cited in *Salomé* will be supplied in the notes. Their source is *Complete Works of Oscar Wilde* (London: Collins, 1966).

[72] "How beautiful is the Princess Salomé to-night!" "You are always looking at her. You look at her too much" (p. 553).

[73] Robertson, *Time Was*, p. 136.

[74] *Times*, 24 June 1890, p. 10.

[75] *Times*, 30 May 1892, p. 8.

[76] "Ah! I have kissed thy mouth, Jokanaan. I have kissed thy mouth. There was a bitter taste on thy lips. Was it the taste of blood . . .?" (p. 575).

[77] *Era*, 23 June 1894, p. 11.

[78] Symons, *Plays, Acting, and Music*, pp. 28, 32.

[79] Robertson, *Time Was*, pp. 117–18.

[80] *Era*, 4 June 1892, p. 9. John Stokes sums up the matter in this way: "Sardou's heroines (one should really say 'heroine', since they hardly change from one play to another) are women torn between uncontrollable impulses of power-hungry aggression and passive subservience. The plots are always designed to bring this divided nature to a crisis point by having the heroine fall in love with a man whom she must either sacrifice or destroy." Quoted from "Sarah Bern-

hardt" in John Stokes, Michael R. Booth, and Susan Bassnett, *Bernhardt, Terry, Duse: The Actress in Her Time* (Cambridge University Press, 1988), p. 36.

81 Robertson, *Time Was*, p. 126.

82 Quoted by Skinner, *Madame Sarah*, p. 247.

83 *Era*, 3 November 1894, p. 11.

84 "Ah! thou wouldst not suffer me to kiss thy mouth, Jokanaan. Well! I will kiss it now. I will bite it with my teeth as one bites a ripe fruit. Yes, I will kiss thy mouth, Jokanaan. I said it. Did I not say it? Ah! I will kiss it now . . ." (p. 573).

85 *Fédora: Drame en Quatre Actes*, in Victorien Sardou, *Théâtre complet* (15 vols., Paris: Michel, 1934–61), vol. 1, p. 445.

86 Sardou, *La Tosca: Pièce en Cinq Actes*, in *Théâtre complet*, vol. 1, 147.

87 George Bernard Shaw, *Our Theatres in the Nineties*, in *The Works of Bernard Shaw*, vol. 23, p. 145.

88 Sardou, *Fédora*, p. 537.

89 William Emboden, *Sarah Bernhardt* (London: Studio Vista, 1974), p. 85.

90 Walkley included this notice in *Playhouse Impressions* (London: Unwin, 1892), pp. 240–1.

91 *Ibid.*, p. 244.

92 *Ibid.*, p. 241.

93 *Ibid.*

94 "Give me the head of Jokanaan" (pp. 571ff.).

95 *Max Beerbohm's Letters to Reggie Turner*, ed. Rupert Hart-Davis (Philadelphia: Lippincott, 1965), p. 53.

96 "I am athirst for thy beauty. I am hungry for thy body" (p. 574).

97 G. B. Shaw, *Our Theatres in the Nineties*, in *The Works of Bernard Shaw*, vol. 23, p. 158.

98 Stokes, *Bernhardt, Terry, Duse*, p. 61.

99 For the pictorial quality of Victorian theatre – what James belittled as its merely "scenic" art – see Martin Meisel, *Realizations: Narrative, Pictorial, and Theatrical Arts in Nineteenth-Century England* (Princeton University Press, 1983), and Michael R. Booth, *Victorian Spectacular Theatre 1850–1910* (Boston: Routledge & Kegan Paul, 1981).

100 Robertson, *Time Was*, p. 136.

4 Unimportant women and men with a past

1 Henry Arthur Jones, "Our Modern Drama," a lecture to the Playgoers' Club, in *The Renascence of the English Drama*, p. 284. The talk was given a few months before Wilde's play made its debut. Wilde's other plays also fell short of Jones's standard, but for various reasons. *Salomé* was barred from performance by the censor, and both *The Importance of Being Earnest* and *An Ideal Husband* had their engagements curtailed by the scandal which destroyed Wilde's career in the spring of 1895. His longest-running production was *Lady Windermere's Fan*, which played 197 performances at the St. James's.

2 Revivals of *A Woman of No Importance* include those of 1916 in New York, and of 1907, 1953, and 1968 in London. A television production for ITV aired in 1960.

3 Eriksen, *Oscar Wilde*, p. 140.

[4] George Woodcock, *The Paradox of Oscar Wilde* (New York: Macmillan, 1950), p. 161.

[5] Philip K. Cohen, *The Moral Vision of Oscar Wilde* (Rutherford, N.J.: Fairleigh Dickinson University Press, 1978), p. 193.

[6] *A Woman of No Importance*, Ian Small, ed., in *Two Society Comedies* (London: Benn, 1983), p. 96. Further references are to this edition.

[7] See, e.g., Bird, *The Plays of Oscar Wilde*, pp. 126–9.

[8] Eriksen, *Oscar Wilde*, p. 140.

[9] Kelver Hartley, *Oscar Wilde: L'Influence française dans son oeuvre* (Paris: Librairie du Recueil Sirey, 1935), pp. 130–1.

[10] Albert Delpit, *Le Fils de Coralie* (Paris: Ollendorff, 1894), p. 190. The 29th edition of the novel is quoted here.

[11] Edouard Plouvier, *Madame Aubert: Drame en Quatre Actes* (Paris: Lévy, 1865), p. 81.

[12] *Ibid.*, p. 82.

[13] *Ibid.*, p. 87.

[14] "I work for hire, sewing," says Mrs. Arbuthnot in a manuscript draft and an early typescript version of the play, both in the British Museum, and both entitled *Mrs. Arbuthnot.* (See *Two Society Plays*, p. 110, note 308.) This line, posing a direct resemblance to both Hawthorne's Hester Prynne and Dumas's character, the seamstress Clara Vignot, was deleted in the Lord Chamberlain's ms. and in the first edition of the play.

[15] Alexandre Dumas *fils*, *Le Fils naturel*, in *Théâtre complet de Alexandre Dumas Fils* (7 vols., Paris: Lévy, 1898–9), vol. 3, p. 113.

[16] *Ibid.*, p. 189.

[17] *Ibid.*, p. 203.

[18] Quoted in Hesketh Pearson, *Beerbohm Tree: His Life and Laughter* (New York: Harper, 1956), p. 67.

[19] For these and other resemblances between Wilde's play and *The Scarlet Letter*, see Katharine Worth's *Oscar Wilde*, p. 110, and Elissa Guralnick and Paul M. Levitt, "Allusion and Meaning in Wilde's *A Woman of No Importance*," *Eire–Ireland*, 13 (1978), 45–51.

[20] Guralnick and Levitt, "Allusion and Meaning in Wilde's *A Woman of No Importance*," p. 45.

[21] Joseph Hatton, *The Scarlet Letter; or, Hester Prynne: A Drama in Three Acts* (London: Lindley, n.d.), p. 30.

[22] *Times*, 5 June 1888, p. 9.

[23] W. MacQueen-Pope, *Haymarket: Theatre of Perfection*, p. 338.

[24] *Letters*, p. 376.

[25] Doris A. Jones, *Taking the Curtain Call: The Life and Letters of Henry Arthur Jones* (New York: Macmillan, 1930), p. 156. See also Hesketh Pearson, *The Life of Oscar Wilde* (London: Methuen, 1946), p. 221.

[26] *Letters*, p. 320.

[27] Russell Jackson and Ian Small, "Some New Drafts of a Wilde Play," *English Literature in Transition 1880–1920*, 30 (1987), 7–15. The newly discovered drafts are in the Tree archive of the Bristol Theatre Collection.

[28] "Behold the First Lord Illingworth," *New York Times*, 30 April 1916, Section 2, p. 7.

[29] Pearson, *Beerbohm Tree: His Life and Laughter*, p. 70.

30 Henry Arthur Jones, *The Dancing Girl: A Drama in Four Acts* (London: French, 1907), p. 19.

31 *Ibid.*, p. 40.

32 *Ibid.*, p. 108.

33 Henry Arthur Jones, *Saints and Sinners: A New and Original Drama in Five Acts* (New York: Macmillan, 1908), p. 115.

34 D. C. Murray's *The Puritan*, never published, was performed at the Trafalgar Theatre. A typescript is in the Lord Chamberlain's collection at the British Library.

35 Sydney Grundy, *A Fool's Paradise* (London: French, 1898), p. 64.

36 See C. H. Hazlewood's adaptation of Braddon's novel, reprinted in George Rowell, ed., *Nineteenth Century Plays*, 2nd edn. (Oxford University Press, 1972), pp. 235–66.

37 A. W. Pinero, *The Second Mrs. Tanqueray*, in *The Social Plays of Arthur Wing Pinero*, ed. Clayton Hamilton (4 vols., New York: Dutton, 1917–22), vol. 1, p. 190.

38 Lady Violet Greville and Arthur Bourchier's *Justice: A Play in Four Acts* was never published. It is quoted from the Lord Chamberlain's manuscript, Act III, p. 10.

39 *Theatre*, 1 June 1893, pp. 332–3.

40 *Era*, 22 April 1893, p. 9.

41 Worth, *Oscar Wilde*, pp. 99, 125.

42 Mona Caird, *The Daughters of Danaus* (London: Bliss, 1894), p. 190. Further reference is to this text.

43 A. W. Pinero, *Sweet Lavender: A Domestic Drama in Three Acts* (London: Heinemann, 1908), p. 169.

44 Sydney Grundy, *Sowing the Wind: An Original Play in Four Acts* (London: French, 1901), p. 55.

45 Eugène Brieux, *Monsieur de Réboval: Pièce en trois actes*, in *Théâtre complet de Brieux* (9 vols., Paris: Librairie Stock, 1921), vol. 1, p. 263.

46 George Gissing, *The Odd Women* (New York: Norton, 1971), p. 61.

47 Wilkie Collins, *The New Magdalen: A Dramatic Story in a Prologue and Three Acts* (London: n.p., 1873), p. 81.

48 Martha Vicinus, " 'Helpless and Unfriended': Nineteenth-Century Domestic Melodrama," *New Literary History*, 13 (1981), 127–43.

49 Dion Boucicault, *Formosa ('The Most Beautiful'): or the Railroad to Ruin* (n.p.: n.p., n.d.), p. 15.

50 Shewan, *Oscar Wilde: Art and Egotism*, p. 177.

51 Mary Poovey, *The Proper Lady and the Woman Writer* (University of Chicago Press, 1984), p. xv.

52 The elite composition of Tree's audience is described by W. MacQueen-Pope in *Haymarket: Theatre of Perfection*, p. 336.

53 Shirley Foster, *Victorian Women's Fiction: Marriage, Freedom, and the Individual* (Beckenham: Croom Helm, 1985), p. 15.

5 Wilde and Ibsen

1 O'Sullivan, *Aspects of Wilde*, p. 145.

2 "The Collected Plays of Oscar Wilde," *Fortnightly Review*, 1 May 1908, pp. 791–802; reprinted in *Oscar Wilde: The Critical Heritage*, p. 293.

[3] So Wilde was quoted in the *St. James's Gazette* of 18 January 1895, pp. 4–5; reprinted in Mikhail, ed., *Oscar Wilde: Interviews and Recollections*, vol. 1, p. 249.

[4] E. H. Mikhail, "The French Influences on Oscar Wilde's Comedies," *Revue de Littérature Comparée*, 42 (1968), 220–33.

[5] Harley Granville-Barker, "The Coming of Ibsen" in *The Eighteen-Eighties*, ed. Walter de la Mare (Cambridge University Press, 1930), pp. 59–96.

[6] "Rita" was the pen name of Eliza M. J. Humphreys, whose novel *A Husband of No Importance* (London: Unwin, 1894), entitled with a turn on the name of Wilde's second comedy, has much to say about the theatre in the 1890s and the changing roles of the sexes.

[7] Herbert Beerbohm Tree, *Some Interesting Fallacies of the Modern Stage: An Address Delivered to the Playgoers' Club on Sunday, 6th December 1891* (London: Heinemann, 1892), pp. 22, 26–7.

[8] William Archer, "*Ghosts* and Gibberings," *Pall Mall Gazette*, 8 April 1891, p. 3; reprinted in Michael Egan, ed., *Ibsen: The Critical Heritage* (London: Routledge and Kegan Paul, 1972), pp. 209–14.

[9] William Archer, "Ibsen and English Criticism," *Fortnightly Review*, 1 July 1889, p. 30.

[10] Excellent accounts of Terry's and Irving's careers in relation to developments in the theatre and culture generally appear in Nina Auerbach, *Ellen Terry: Player in Her Time* (New York: Norton, 1987; p. 223 is quoted here) and in Michael R. Booth, "Ellen Terry" in *Bernhardt, Terry, Duse*, pp. 64–117.

[11] Louis N. Parker, *Several of My Lives* (London: Chapman and Hall, 1928), p. 148.

[12] Archer's review of *A Woman of No Importance* appeared in the *World* of 26 April 1893 and was reprinted in his *Theatrical 'World' for 1893* (London: W. Scott, 1894), pp. 105–13. The quotation comes from the first paragraph of the article.

[13] Grein's article appeared 9 and 16 December 1900 in the *Sunday Special* and is reprinted in *Oscar Wilde: The Critical Heritage*, pp. 233–6. The quotation appears on p. 234.

[14] *Letters*, p. 293.

[15] *Ibid.*, p. 332.

[16] *Ibid.*, p. 522. Norwegian was a language Wilde evidently never studied, so his knowledge of Ibsen's work came mainly from English translations and productions.

[17] Shaw, in a letter to the *Evening Standard*, 30 November 1944, called his play "a counterblast to Ibsen's *Doll's House*, showing that in the real typical doll's house it is the man who is the doll." Quoted by Margery Morgan, *The Shavian Playground* (London: Methuen, 1972), p. 65.

[18] Quoted from the Lord Chamberlain's manuscript of J. M. Barrie, *Ibsen's Ghost, or Toole up to Date*, p. 10.

[19] Quoted from the Lord Chamberlain's manuscript of Austin Fryers, *Beata*, Act III, p. 7. Austin Fryers was the pseudonym of William Edward Clery.

[20] *Era*, 23 April 1892, p. 8.

[21] Augustus Filon, *The English Stage: Being an Account of the Victorian Drama*, 1897 (rpt. Port Washington, N.Y.: Kennikat, 1970), p. 297.

[22] Henry Arthur Jones and Henry Herman, *Breaking a Butterfly: A Play in Three Acts* (n.p.: privately printed, n.d.), p. 65.

23 F. Anstey (Thomas Anstey Guthrie), *Mr. Punch's Pocket Ibsen* (New York: Macmillan, 1893), p. 87.

24 *Lady Windermere's Fan*, pp. 83–4. Henrik Ibsen, *Ghosts*, trans. William Archer, in *The Collected Works of Henrik Ibsen*, ed. William Archer (13 vols., New York: Scribner's, 1906–12), vol. 7, p. 222.

25 *The Importance of Being Earnest: A Trivial Comedy for Serious People*, ed. Russell Jackson (London: Benn, 1980), pp. 98, 100.

26 Clement Scott's review, in the *Illustrated London News* of 25 April 1891, pp. 551–2, is reprinted in *Ibsen: The Critical Heritage*, pp. 225–8.

27 Archer's article in *Black and White*, 11 May 1893, p. 290, is reprinted in *Oscar Wilde: The Critical Heritage*, pp. 141–2.

28 Egan, ed., *Ibsen: The Critical Heritage*, pp. 202–4, reprinted from a review of *Ghosts* in the *Licensed Victuallers' Mirror*, 17 March 1891, p. 128.

29 From the "Plays and Players" column in the *Sunday Times*, 15 March 1891, p. 7; reprinted in *Ibsen: The Critical Heritage*, p. 201.

30 James Woodfield, *English Theatre in Transition 1881–1914*, pp. 43–4. Woodfield provides valuable accounts of the Independent Theatre and the censorship.

31 *Letters*, p. 399.

32 A good account of these events is provided by N. Schoonderwoerd, *J. T. Grein: Ambassador of the Theatre 1862–1935* (Assen, the Netherlands: Van Gorcum, 1963), pp. 197–206.

33 G. B. Shaw, *The Quintessence of Ibsenism*, in *The Works of Bernard Shaw*, vol. 19, p. 69.

34 Shaw, *The Quintessence of Ibsenism*, p. 69. It has been suggested that Shaw may have influenced Wilde in providing fuller and more realistic stage directions for *An Ideal Husband* than in previous plays – or at least did so in the printed version. See Kristin Morrison, " 'Horrible Flesh and Blood,' " *Theatre Notebook*, 35 (1981), 7–9; Alan Andrew's rejoinder in *Theatre Notebook*, 36 (1982), 34–5; and Russell Jackson, *Theatre Notebook*, 37 (1983), 29–31.

35 *The Illustrated London News*, 12 January 1895, p. 35; reprinted in *Oscar Wilde: The Critical Heritage*, pp. 178–9.

36 Wilde denied all influence by Sardou, or anybody else, in an interview published in *The Sketch*, 9 January 1895, reprinted in *Interviews and Recollections*, vol. 1, 239–43.

37 Ibsen, *Pillars of Society*, trans. William Archer, in *Collected Works*, vol. 6, pp. 319, 397; Wilde, *An Ideal Husband*, ed. Russell Jackson, in *Two Society Comedies* (London: Benn, 1983), pp. 169, 172, 210. Further reference is to these texts.

38 *Letters*, p. 649.

39 The *O.E.D.* explains that the term "Chiltern Hundreds" refers to certain Crown lands in Oxfordshire and Buckinghamshire. It adds: "No member of parliament is by law at liberty to resign his seat, so long as he is duly qualified; on the other hand, a member who accepts an office of profit under the Crown must vacate his seat . . . A member desiring to resign therefore applies for the *stewardship of the Chiltern Hundreds* . . . which is, by a legal figment, held to be such an office; the appointment necessitates his resignation, and, having thus fulfilled its purpose, it is again resigned, so as to be ready for confinement upon the next member who wishes to make the same use of it."

40 *Collected Edition*, vol. 13, pp. 487–8.

[41] Archer's review appeared in the *Pall Mall Budget*, 10 January 1895, and was Ereprinted in *The Theatrical 'World' of 1895* (London: W. Scott, 1896), p. 16.

[42] Shaw's review of *An Ideal Husband* appeared in the *Saturday Review*, 12 January 1895, pp. 44–5, and is reprinted in *Oscar Wilde: The Critical Heritage*, pp. 176–8.

[43] See Sydney Grundy, *The Play of the Future, by a Playwright of the Past*.

[44] R. K. Miller, *Oscar Wilde* (New York: Ungar, 1982), p. 67.

6 *An Ideal Husband*: resisting the feminist police

[1] *Era*, 16 February 1895, p. 15.

[2] Michael R. Booth, *English Plays of the Nineteenth Century* (5 vols., Oxford: Clarendon, 1969–76), vol. 3, pp. 27–8.

[3] For example, see Dr. H. S. Pomeroy, *The Ethics of Marriage* (London: Funk & Wagnalls, 1889), p. 174.

[4] Sydney Grundy, *A Debt of Honour: An Original Play in One Act* (London: Scott, n.d.), p. 13.

[5] A. W. Pinero, *Lady Bountiful: A Story of Years: A Play in Four Acts* (London: Heinemann, 1891), p. 18.

[6] Joseph Conrad, *Heart of Darkness* (New York: Norton, 1963), p. 78.

[7] Carol Christ, "Victorian Masculinity and the Angel in the House" in *A Widening Sphere: Changing Roles of Victorian Women* (Bloomington: Indiana University Press, 1977), pp. 146–62. See "An Angel in the House" in *The Poems of Coventry Patmore*, ed. Frederick Page (Cambridge University Press, 1949), p. 79, and *The Princess*, in *The Complete Poetical Works of Tennyson*, ed. W. J. Rolfe (Cambridge, Mass.: Riverside, 1898), p. 159.

[8] Elaine Showalter, *A Literature of Their Own: British Women Novelists from Brontë to Lessing* (Princeton University Press, 1977), pp. 187–90.

[9] Sarah Grand, *The Heavenly Twins* (New York: Cassell, 1893), pp. 78–80.

[10] Kathleen Blake, *Love and the Woman Question in Victorian Literature: The Art of Self-Postponement* (Totowa, N.J.: Barnes & Noble, 1983), p. ix.

[11] Henry Fielding, *Joseph Andrews* (Middletown, Conn.: Wesleyan University Press, 1967), p. 41.

[12] Harry Quilter, *Is Marriage A Failure? A Modern Symposium* (Chicago: Rand, McNally, 1889). The English edition came out a year earlier from Sonnenschein.

[13] E. M. S., "Some Modern Ideas about Marriage," *Westminster Review*, 143 (1895), 520.

[14] *How To Be Happy Though Married: Being a Handbook to Marriage* (London: Unwin, 1885), pp. 242–3.

[15] This title was announced by Marshall, but I can find no record of its having been published.

[16] Pomeroy, *The Ethics of Marriage*, p. 174.

[17] Annie Besant, *Marriage; As It Was, As It Is, And As It Should Be* (New York: Butts, n.d.), pp. 12, 29–30.

[18] *The Subjection of Women*, in *Essays on Sex Equality: John Stuart Mill and Harriet Taylor Mill*, ed. Alice S. Rossi (University of Chicago Press, 1970), p. 236.

[19] Mona Caird, "Ideal Marriage," *Westminster Review*, 130 (1888), 624, 634–5.

[20] Sydney Grundy, *The New Woman: An Original Comedy, in Four Acts* (London: Chiswick, 1894), Act I, p. 28.

21 William Archer, *The Old Drama and the New* (Boston: Small, Maynard, 1922), p. 288.

22 Henry Arthur Jones, *The Case of Rebellious Susan: A Comedy in Three Acts* (London: Chiswick, 1894), pp. 51, 81, 87.

23 Charles Rogers's *The Future Woman, or Josiah's Dream* is quoted from the Lord Chamberlain's manuscript, Act IV, pp. 15, 17.

24 F. C. Philips and Percy Fendall, *Husband and Wife*, in F. C. Philips, *A Barrister's Courtship* (Leipzig: Tauchnitz, 1907), p. 103.

25 *Ibid.*, p. 237.

26 James Payn, *The Best of Husbands* (3 vols., London: Bentley, 1874), vol. 3, pp. 216, 221.

27 *Divorce; or, Faithful and Unfaithful* (New York: Lovell, 1889), p. 373. Wilde's review in *Woman's World* is reprinted in the *Collected Edition*, vol. 13, pp. 486–8.

28 George Gissing, *The Odd Women* (New York: Norton, 1971), p. 254.

29 *The Philanderer*, in *The Works of Bernard Shaw*, vol. 7, p. 125.

30 Gissing, *The Odd Women*, pp. 61, 87, 99.

31 Pierre Leclerq, *This Woman and That: A New Play in Three Acts* is quoted from the manuscript in the Lord Chamberlain's collection of the British Library, Act I, pp. 5, 16–17; Act III, p. 12.

32 Tom Taylor, *The House or the Home; A Comedy in Two Acts* (London: Lacy, n.d.), p. 6.

33 *Ibid*, p. 41.

34 *The M.P.'s Wife* is quoted from the Lord Chamberlain's manuscript in the British Library, p. 26.

35 Nancy Armstrong argues the existence of a feminine, domestic power – which polices and complements male political and economic authority rather than undermines it – in *Desire and Domestic Fiction: A Political History of the Novel* (New York: Oxford University Press, 1987).

36 Justin H. McCarthy's *The Candidate* is quoted from the Lord Chamberlain's manuscript, p. 123. The play, an adaptation of Alexandre Bisson's *Le Député de Bombignac*, was revived with great success in 1894.

37 These are among the last lines given Mr. Egerton-Bompas, M.P., the central character of A. W. Pinero's *The Times: A Comedy in Four Acts* (London: Heinemann, 1891).

38 F. C. Philips and Sydney Grundy, *The Dean's Daughter* (London: Trischler, 1891), pp. 64, 69.

39 Neville Doone, *A Modern Marriage* is quoted from the Lord Chamberlain's manuscript, Act IV, p. 37.

40 Henry Arthur Jones, *The Liars*, in *Late Victorian Plays 1890–1914*, ed. George Rowell, 2nd edn (Oxford University Press, 1972), p. 104.

41 Charles Dickens, *Martin Chuzzlewit* (Oxford University Press, 1951), p. 256.

42 J. P. Wooler, *A Model Husband: A Farce in One Act* (London: Lacy, n.d.).

43 *George Mandeville's Husband* (New York: Appleton, 1894), p. 216. Elizabeth Robins wrote the novel under the pseudonym "C. E. Raimond."

44 Doyle's play survives in manuscript in the Lord Chamberlain's collection.

45 A. W. Pinero, *The Cabinet Minister: A Farce in Four Acts* (Boston: Baker, 1892), pp. 40, 154.

46 C. Haddon Chambers, *The Idler: A Play in Four Acts* (London: French, 1902), p. 8. As if to capitalize on the obvious similarities with *An Ideal Husband*, this play was

revived in the summer of 1895 at the St. James's, just after the success of Wilde's comedy at the Haymarket.

47 *Ibid.*, pp. 53, 61.

48 Sydney Grundy, *A Bunch of Violets: A Play in Four Acts* (London: French, 1901), p. 40.

49 *Ibid.*, p. 35.

50 Maurice Barrès had been Deputy for Nancy and wrote against the background of the great Panama Scandal, in which a number of his fellow parliamentarians were implicated. In the 1880s he had been an aesthete and admirer of Wilde. On one occasion he arranged a banquet in Paris in Wilde's honor at the Restaurant Voisin, according to the painter Jacques-Emile Blanche in *Portraits of a Lifetime*, trans. Walter Clement (London: Dent, 1937), reprinted in *Oscar Wilde: Interviews and Recollections*, vol. 2, pp. 351–3.

51 Wilde claimed in *De Profundis* that he finished "the three remaining acts" of *An Ideal Husband* soon after Lord Alfred Douglas left the country in December 1893. The typescript from Mrs. Marshall's Typing Agency bears a stamped date of 19 February 1894. See *Letters*, pp. 349, 426–7.

52 Maurice Barrès, *Une Journée parlementaire* (Paris: Charpentier et Fasquelle, 1894), pp. 58, 72.

53 R. C. Carton, *The Home Secretary*, quoted from a typescript copy in New York Public Library, Act IV, pp. 27–9. "R. C. Carton" was the pseudonym of Richard Claude Critchett.

54 *Ibid.*, Act I, p. 11.

55 *Ibid.*, Act IV, p. 29.

56 Archer's review appeared in the *Pall Mall Budget*, 10 January 1895, and later in his *The Theatrical 'World' of 1895* (London: Scott, 1896), pp. 15–19.

57 *Era*, 5 January 1895, p. 13. In observing that "this kind of thing happens every day, and the results are duly reported in the newspapers," perhaps the critic had in mind the Panama Canal scandal which had recently broken over France.

58 *Times*, 24 April 1890, p. 5.

59 Peter Raby, *Oscar Wilde* (Cambridge University Press, 1988), p. 99.

60 *Era*, 5 January 1895, p. 13.

61 Ian Gregor, "Comedy and Oscar Wilde," *Sewanee Review*, 74 (1966), 501–21.

62 Linda Dowling, "The Decadent and the New Woman in the 1890s," *Nineteenth-Century Fiction*, 33 (1979), 434–53. Julia Neilson, the actress who created the role of Lady Chiltern, felt little sympathy for the New Drama or "advanced" women. Of Lady Chiltern she wrote: "she was an impossible prig . . . – and I hated her" (*This for Remembrance* [London: Hurst & Blackett, 1940], p. 139). Nevertheless, after *An Ideal Husband* closed she would play a part very similar to Lady Chiltern's – that of Rhoda Trendel in R. C. Carton's *The Home Secretary*.

63 John Stokes, *Oscar Wilde* (London: Longman, 1978), pp. 39–40. (Writers & Their Work, no. 264.)

64 E. H. Mikhail, "Self-Revelation in An Ideal Husband," *Modern Drama*, 11 (1968), 180–86. Cf. Rodney Shewan, *Oscar Wilde: Art and Egotism*, p. 178: "The Chilterns' plight can be understood as the plight of the Wildes of Tite Street."

65 "Rita," *A Husband of No Importance* (London: Unwin, 1894), p. 48. "Rita" was a pen name of Eliza M. J. Humphreys.

66 See D. G. Ritchie, *Darwinism and Politics* (London: Sonnenschein, 1889), p. 89.

Wilde cites Ritchie's argument with approval in a review for *Woman's World*, reprinted in *Collected Edition*, vol. 13, pp. 486–8. Wilde in fact uses Ritchie's language, without troubling to give the author credit: "The family ideal of the State may be difficult of attainment, but as an ideal it is better than the policeman theory. It would mean the moralisation of politics. The cultivation of separate sorts of virtues and separate ideals of duty in men and women has led to the whole social fabric being weaker and unhealthier than it need be."

[67] Mill, *The Subjection of Women*, in *Essays on Sex Equality*, p. 141.

[68] Gagnier, *Idylls of the Marketplace: Oscar Wilde and the Victorian Public*, p. 129.

7 The importance of being at Terry's

[1] W. Lestocq was the pseudonym of William Lestocq Boileau Woolridge, who died in 1920 at age sixty-nine. His other plays included *Uncles and Aunts* (with Walter Everard), 1888; *The Sportsman* (an adaptation from the French), 1893; and *Jane* (with Harry Nicholls), his most successful play, a farce which ran for 191 performances after its opening in 1890 at the Comedy Theatre and was revived in 1892 at the Comedy and in 1899 at Terry's.

[2] Review of *The Foundling* in the *Era*, 1 September 1894, p. 7. Terry's Theatre, which specialized in farces and other light comedy, opened in 1887 at 105–106 The Strand. It closed in 1910, and its building was demolished in 1923.

[3] A. W. Pinero, whose *Sweet Lavender* played at Terry's and was hailed as the most popular play of 1889, said in an interview with the *Era* that "a hundred nights would perfectly content me" (in "A Morning with Mr. Pinero," the *Era*, 12 November 1892). Lestocq, however, was no Pinero, and a span of fifty-eight performances perhaps seemed quite satisfactory to an actor-author who had not achieved fame. Few plays ran longer at Terry's, which apparently favored rapid turnover in its offerings.

[4] The New York typescript is in the Billy Rose Theatre Collection of the New York Public Library.

[5] *Letters*, p. 359.

[6] *Ibid.*

[7] Frank Harris, *Oscar Wilde* (East Lansing: Michigan State University Press, 1959), p. 107.

[8] Acts III and IV are stamped 19 September 1894. Acts I and II of this first typescript, however, have disappeared. A revised four-act typescript was produced in October 1894 and another in November. The Lord Chamberlain's typed manuscript, dated 30 January 1895, is a shorter three-act version. Since its first publication in 1899 the play has usually been printed in three acts, omitting considerable material that Wilde included in the original manuscript draft.

[9] Russell Jackson, introduction, *The Importance of Being Earnest: A Trivial Comedy for Serious People* (London: Benn, 1980), p. xlii; Bird, *The Plays of Oscar Wilde*, p. 161.

[10] *Letters*, p. 360.

[11] *Letters*, p. 364.

[12] See, for example, *Letters*, p. 369.

[13] Ricketts, *Oscar Wilde: Recollections by Jean Paul Raymond and Charles Ricketts*, p. 15. *Earnest*'s original title – *Lady Lancing* – has no evident connection with the play

as Wilde finally wrote it. In a manuscript as late as the Lord Chamberlain's, *Lady Lancing* appears as the title on the cover sheet, but lined through and replaced in script by the words *The Importance of Being Earnest*.

[14] *Theatre*, 1 October 1894, pp. 191–2.

[15] On the other hand Wilde would not have wanted to bring out his own work at a theatre so comparatively undistinguished as Terry's, even though farces enjoyed great success there (for instance, Arthur Law's *The New Boy* had been a major hit earlier in 1894). From the beginning he had in mind the prestigious St. James's, where Henry James's *Guy Domville* was the predecessor of *Earnest*.

[16] From a review in *Truth*, 21 February 1895, pp. 464–5; rpt. in *Oscar Wilde: The Critical Heritage*, pp. 191–3.

[17] Eric Bentley, *The Life of the Drama* (New York: Atheneum, 1964), p. 234.

[18] G. B. Shaw, "The Farcical Comedy Outbreak" in *Our Theatres in the Nineties*, in *The Works of Bernard Shaw*, vol. 24, p. 124.

[19] Charles Lamb, "On the Artificial Comedy of the Last Century" in *The Collected Essays of Charles Lamb* (2 vols. New York: Dutton, 1929), vol. 1, p. 166.

[20] Brandon Thomas's spectacularly popular farce *Charley's Aunt* ran for 1,469 performances from 1892 to 1895. John Maddison Morton's frequently revived *Box and Cox*, first performed in 1847, was adapted as an operetta by Burnand and Sullivan under the title *Cox and Box*.

[21] See especially Act III of Eugène Labiche and Alfred Delacour's *Célimare le bien-aimé*, in *Oeuvres complètes de Labiche* (8 vols., Paris: Club de l'Honnête Homme, 1966–), vol. 6, pp. 190–219. The play has been suggested as a likely source for Wilde (see Bird, *The Plays of Oscar Wilde*, p. 172).

[22] C. B. Paul and J. L. Heilbrun translated *Il ne faut jurer de rien* at the end of their article, "The Importance of Reading Alfred: Oscar Wilde's Debt to Alfred de Musset," *Bulletin of the New York Public Library*, 75 (1971), 506–72.

[23] John Maddison Morton, *A Husband to Order: A Serio-Comic Drama in Two Acts* (Boston: Baker, n.d.), p. 24. Gilbert's *Engaged*, first acted in 1877, is sometimes similar in tone, as well as action, to *The Importance of Being Earnest*. The ingenue Minnie, e.g., sounds much like Wilde's self-indulgent heroines Cecily and Gwendolen when she says of her fiancé: "He tells me that his greatest happiness is to see me happy. So it will be my duty – my *duty* . . . to devote my life, my whole life, to making myself as happy as I possibly can." (*Engaged: An Entirely Original Farcical Comedy* can be found in *Original Plays by W. S. Gilbert* [London: Chatto & Windus, 1925], pp. 39–85; here, p. 57 is quoted). The relation of Wilde's play to Gilbert's is more important than that of many suggested "sources." Lynton Hudson first proposed a connection between *Earnest* and *Engaged* in *The English Stage 1850–1950* (London: Harrap, 1951), pp. 99–105.

[24] Wilde's play has even been called an "adaptation" of Musset's *Jurer*. See Paul and Heilbrun, "The Importance of Reading Alfred," p. 513.

[25] *The Importance of Being Earnest: A Trivial Comedy for Serious People*, ed. Russell Jackson (London: Benn, 1980), pp. 31–2. Except as noted, further references to the play will appear parenthetically and cite this text, which for the most part reflects Wilde's last revisions of *Earnest*.

[26] W. Lestocq and E. M. Robson, *The Foundling: A Farce in Three Acts*, typescript in the Lord Chamberlain's Collection, p. 15. Except as noted, further references to *The Foundling* will cite this ms. and appear parenthetically.

[27] The manuscript draft of August and/or September 1894 is transcribed in vol. 1 of Sarah Augusta Dickson, ed., *The Importance of Being Earnest: A Trivial Comedy for Serious People in Four Acts as Originally Written by Oscar Wilde* (2 vols., New York: New York Public Library, 1956). The quotation is from p. 29. This edition will be referred to hereafter as the "manuscript draft."

[28] *Era*, 1 September 1894, p. 7.

[29] Mrs. Moncrieff's husband, Jack's father, was a general who served in India; Dick Pennell's father left for an unidentified post in India shortly after his son was born.

[30] The Indian background occurs in other farces, too, including Pinero's *The Magistrate*, where it also provides a key to a character's real identity.

[31] G. B. Shaw, review of *Earnest* in *Saturday Review*, 23 February 1895, pp. 249–50; rpt. in *Our Theatres in the Nineties*, in *The Complete Works of Bernard Shaw*, vol. 24, pp. 43–6.

[32] *Times*, 31 August 1894, p. 3.

[33] *Times*, 15 February 1895, p. 5.

[34] *The Picture of Dorian Gray*, ed. Isobel Murray (Oxford University Press, 1974), pp. 142–3.

[35] Brandon Thomas, *Charley's Aunt: A Play in Three Acts* (London: French, 1962), p. 140.

[36] This is the ideal expressed in "The Decay of Lying."

[37] "The Playhouses" in *Illustrated London News*, 19 March 1892, p. 376.

[38] Quoted by T. Edgar Pemberton, *The Criterion Theatre* (London: Eyre & Spottiswoode, n.d.), p. 9.

[39] *Stage*, 6 September 1894, p. 12, from a review of *The Foundling*.

[40] See, e.g., the *Era*, 8 December 1894, in which a reviewer says of Georges Feydeau and Maurice Desvallières's *Hôtel du Libre Echange*, a farce just opened in Paris: "To analyze it is out of the question. Such a compound of whimsicality cannot be transferred to paper, and all I shall be able to do is sketch its outlines" (p. 11).

[41] For example, C. Haddon Chambers was accused in letters to the *Era* in 1894 of having stolen a bomb incident in his play *The Fatal Card*. Pinero was accused by Thomas Hardy of taking *Far From the Madding Crowd* and turning it into a play of his own, *The Squire*. The *Era* summarized the Pinero case, deciding against Hardy, in a leader of 13 May 1893 (p. 15). In 1893 playwright Walter Sapte was acquitted of a complaint that his play *A Lucky Dog* was plagiarized from an earlier work called *The Picture Dealer* (as reported in the *Era*, 29 July 1891, p. 13).

[42] Quoted from the American typescript of *The Foundling* in the New York Public Library, Act I, p. 18.

8 Algernon's other brothers

[1] See, e.g., Edouard Roditi in *Oscar Wilde* (Norfolk, Conn.: New Directions, 1947), pp. 138–9; Shaw's review of *Earnest*, in *Saturday Review*, 23 February 1895, pp. 249–50; and Arthur Symons's "An Artist in Attitudes: Oscar Wilde" in *Studies in Prose and Verse* (London: Dent, [1904], pp. 124–8), which calls *Earnest* a "sublime" but "meaningless" farce. Mary McCarthy, "The Unimportance of Being Oscar," voices an influential complaint against *Earnest*'s alleged triviality

(in Ellmann, ed., *Oscar Wilde: A Collection of Critical Essays*, pp. 107–10); Louis Kronenberger, *Oscar Wilde*, p. 140, offers a more tolerant view of the play as "proudly but unconquerably trivial."

2 Richard Ellmann, "Romantic Pantomime in Oscar Wilde," *Partisan Review*, 30 (1963), 342–55. James M. Ware finds Algernon to be an "artificer" whose "artifact" is his own life ("Algernon's Appetite: Oscar Wilde's Hero as Restoration Dandy," *English Literature in Transition 1880–1920*, 13 [1970], 17–26). Rodney Shewan notes that Jack and Algernon finally confront their *alter egos* in such a way as to unite them with their actual selves (*Oscar Wilde: Art and Egotism*, p. 187).

3 Gagnier, *Idylls of the Marketplace: Oscar Wilde and the Victorian Public*, p. 113.

4 Eric Bentley, *The Playwright as Thinker* in *Oscar Wilde: Modern Critical Views*, ed. Bloom, pp. 15–19.

5 Worth, *Oscar Wilde*, p. 155. Arthur Ganz stresses the subversiveness of Algernon in making ordinary morality seem ridiculous ("The Meaning of *The Importance of Being Earnest*," *Modern Drama*, 6 [1963], 42–52).

6 Worth, *Oscar Wilde*, p. 155.

7 For a discussion of the domestic nature of Victorian farce, see the introduction to *English Plays of the Nineteenth Century*, ed. Booth, vol. 4. Other useful discussions of Victorian farce include Martin Meisel, *Shaw and the Nineteenth-Century Theater*, chapter 10; and Jeffrey H. Huberman, *Late Victorian Farce* (Ann Arbor: UMI Research Press, 1986).

8 See W. E. Suter, *The Lost Child: or, Jones's Baby: An Original Farce in One Act* (London: French, n.d.), and Mrs. R. Pacheco, *Tom, Dick, and Harry: A Farcical Comedy* (London: French, n.d.), which ran for 105 performances at the Trafalgar Square Theatre in 1893–4.

9 Lestocq and Robson, *The Foundling: A Farce in Three Acts*, p. 4.

10 The typescript of *An Innocent Abroad*, by W. Stokes Craven, is in the Lord Chamberlain's collection of the British Library. The play had sixty-four performances at Terry's in 1895.

11 *Mr. Boodle's Predicament*, by C. J. Hamilton, was published in *Original Plays for the Drawing-Room* (London: Ward, Lock, 1890).

12 The typescript of *Crime & Christening: A Farce* is in the Lord Chamberlain's collection. Richard Henry was the pseudonym of Richard Butler and H. Chance Newton. The play had 112 performances at the Opera Comique, from October to July 1891.

13 Richard Henry's *Adoption: A Farce in One Act* (London: French, n.d.) ran for thirty-six performances at Toole's Theatre, and was revived for sixty more at the Prince of Wales's in 1893–4.

14 A. W. Pinero's *The Magistrate: A Farce in Three Acts* is reprinted in *English Plays of the Nineteenth Century*, ed. Booth, vol. 4. The play was revived in 1892 at Terry's, where it had fifty-three performances.

15 Arthur Law, *The New Boy: A Farcical Play in Three Acts* (New York: French, 1904), pp. 19, 25. The return to childhood was one of the devices of farcical comedy which Shaw incorporated in *Mrs. Warren's Profession*. Bright but frivolous Frank Gardner, who expresses himself in baby talk to Vivie Warren, embodies the insubstantial cleverness so common in late Victorian farce, and for which Shaw expressed contempt.

[16] F. C. Philips and Charles H. E. Brookfield, *Godpapa: A Farcical Comedy in Three Acts*, Act I, p. 30, is quoted from the typescript in the Lord Chamberlain's collection. The play, apparently never published, ran for seventy-two performances at the Comedy from October 1891 to January 1892. The hero's double life was an obsession, not an innovation, of late Victorian farce. It had been common in plays of an earlier time, from Etherege's *The Man of Mode* to Sheridan's *The Rivals*. Bunbury's name, like so many in Wilde's plays, is difficult to pin down in terms of its source. Names like Chiltern, Bracknell, Worthing, and even Bunbury are place-names, but reverberate with associations and meanings that have little to do with the map. On Bunbury's name, see William Green, "Wilde and the Bunburys," *Modern Drama*, 21 (1978), 67–80.

[17] *Jane* ran for 191 performances at the Comedy in 1890–1. It was revived in 1892 at the same theatre, and in 1899 at Terry's.

[18] A. W. Pinero, *The Schoolmistress: A Farce in Three Acts* (London: Heinemann, 1907), p. 23.

[19] Mrs. H. Musgrave, *Our Flat: Farcical Comedy in 3 Acts*, is quoted from the first act of the Lord Chamberlain's manuscript. The play was performed at the Strand 118 times in 1894. I have been unable to determine Mrs. Musgrave's full name.

[20] Fred Horner, *The Late Lamented*, an adaptation of Alexandre Bisson's *Feu Topinel*, remains unpublished, but the Lord Chamberlain's collection contains a typescript of the play. It ran for 230 performances at the Court and Strand in 1891–2.

[21] Sydney Grundy, *The Arabian Nights: A Farcical Comedy in Three Acts* (Chicago: Dramatic Publishing, n.d.), p. 8. The play, founded on Gustav von Moser's *Haroun Alraschid*, was revived in 1892 at the Comedy and 1896 at the Novelty.

[22] Philips and Brookfield, *Godpapa*, Act III, pp. 9, 15.

[23] A typescript of Alfred Murray's *Mistaken Identity* is in the Lord Chamberlain's collection. It was produced at the Gaiety.

[24] Brandon Thomas, *Charley's Aunt: A Play in Three Acts* (London: French, 1962), pp. 49–50. The play had 1,469 performances at the Royalty and Globe Theatres 1892–6.

[25] Walter Everard and W. Lestocq, *Uncles and Aunts: A Farcical Comedy in Three Acts*, played at the Comedy Theatre.

[26] W. S. Gilbert, *Tom Cobb; or Fortune's Toy*, in *English Plays of the Nineteenth Century*, ed. Booth, vol. 4, p. 281.

[27] Lestocq and Robson, *The Foundling*, p. 14.

[28] Fred Horner's *Two Johnnies* was an adaptation of Albert Valabrègue and Maurice Ordonneau, *Durand et Durand*. Never published, it played the Trafalgar Square Theatre for a brief run in 1893.

[29] Seymour Hicks, *A Night Out*, adapted from Maurice Desvallières and Georges Feydeau's *Hôtel du Libre Echange*, ran for 525 performances at the Vaudeville in 1896–7. The Lord Chamberlain's manuscript is quoted, Act II.

[30] Jerome K. Jerome, *New Lamps for Old*, never published, ran for 160 performances at Terry's, from February to July 1890; p. 138 of the Lord Chamberlain's manuscript is quoted.

[31] F. C. Burnand, *Mrs. Ponderbury's Past*, an adaptation of Ernest Blum and Raoul Touché's *Madame Mongodin*, played at the Avenue Theatre for ninety performances in 1895–6. The play, unpublished, is quoted from the Lord Chamberlain's manuscript, Act III, p. 24.

[32] Pacheco, *Tom, Dick, and Harry*, p. 3.

[33] Israel Zangwill, *Six Persons* (New York: French, 1898), p. 3. The play ran for ninety-two performances at the Haymarket in 1893–4.

[34] A. W. Pinero, *Dandy Dick: A Farce in Three Acts* (London: Heinemann, 1906), p. 139.

[35] Sydney Grundy, *Man Proposes: An Original Comedietta in One Act* (New York: French, n.d.), pp. 14–15. The play had 102 performances when it was revived at the Avenue Theatre in 1890–1. In Sheridan's *The Rivals* (1775) Lydia Languish provides an earlier instance of the heroine's writing romantic letters to herself.

[36] Horner, *Two Johnnies*, Act I, p. 11.

[37] Philips and Brookfield, *Godpapa*, Act I, p. 8.

[38] Harry Nicholls and W. Lestocq, *Jane: A Farce in Three Acts* (New York: French, 1900), p. 43.

[39] Richard Henry, *Adoption*, p. 19.

[40] *Letters*, p. 586.

[41] Review of *Bootle's Baby*, in the *Times*, 11 May 1888, p. 13.

[42] Lestocq and Robson, *The Foundling*, p. 17.

[43] Suter, *The Lost Child*, p. 15. By contrast, eighteenth-century comedies treat the foundling with an almost Dickensian respect. Not only is this true of *Tom Jones*, but also of such stage productions as Edward Moore's *The Foundling* and John O'Keeffe's *Wild Oats*, revived in 1891 at the Criterion. In both plays the foundling's dilemma is made to seem pathetic, and resolved when his rightful parents are discovered. The mockery of family ties, so distinctive of 1890s farce, is absent.

[44] Henry Arthur Jones, "Preface to *Saints and Sinners*" in *The Renascence of the English Drama*, p. 317.

[45] Pinero, *The Magistrate*, pp. 333–4. The romantic mixups in the Hôtel des Princes in *The Magistrate* perhaps derive from James Albery's extremely popular *Pink Dominos* (1877; revived in 1892). The comedy of marital infidelity was often, like Albery's, adapted from a French model and considerably toned down (so that no adultery is ever committed, or seriously intended). See Jeffrey Huberman, *Late Victorian Farce*, chapter 2, for a good account of the heyday of French adaptation, 1875–83. Adaptation waned in popularity when copyright protection was extended in 1887 to foreign dramas.

[46] Horner, *Two Johnnies*, Act I, p. 7.

[47] Pinero, *The Schoolmistress*, p. 23.

[48] J. H. McCarthy, *Your Wife*, is quoted from Act II, p. 6 of the Lord Chamberlain's typescript.

[49] Mark Melford, *Kleptomania* (London: French, n.d.), pp. 15, 17.

[50] By contrast, Pinero's farces dealt with deans, magistrates, and Cabinet ministers, Brandon Thomas's with young Oxonians, and Wilde's with aristocratic dandies and their families. In this milieu, comic language was certain to prevail at the expense of slapstick gags. An interesting account of some alterations in class representation appears in Jeffrey Huberman, *Late Victorian Farce*, pp. 104–27.

[51] Jones, "Relations of the Drama to Education" in *The Renascence of the English Drama*, p. 305.

[52] "Myself and M/others," *Sub-stance*, no. 32 (1981), pp. 6–14.

[53] See Camille A. Paglia, "Oscar Wilde and the English Epicene," *Raritan*, 4

(1985), 85–109, for a discussion of "the iron rod of classification" in Wilde's rhetoric.

[54] Grundy, *Man Proposes*, p. 16; McCarthy, *Your Wife*, Act III, p. 23.

[55] Hicks, *A Night Out*, Act II, p. 28.

[56] *Never Again*, an anonymous adaptation of Maurice Desvallières and Anthony Mars's, *Le Truc d'Arthur*, was licensed on 10 September 1897 and ran for 117 performances at the Vaudeville Theatre.

Epilogue

[1] Grundy, *The Play of the Future, by a Playwright of the Past*, pp. 19–21.

[2] Melford, *Kleptomania*, p. 27.

[3] Katharine Worth, e.g., writes that Wilde's prison ordeal "damaged his creative energy irretrievably" (*Oscar Wilde*, p. 183). Robert Sherard writes in *The Real Oscar Wilde*: "During two years in prison, Wilde's brain had been driven beyond powers of recuperation. . . he was simply unable to produce, and writhed in despair as this fact forced itself upon him" ([London: Laurie, n.d.], p. 397).

[4] *Letters*, p. 649.

[5] *Letters*, p. 775.

[6] André Gide, *Oscar Wilde* (Paris: Mercure de France, 1947), p. 46.

[7] *Letters*, p. 583.

[8] *A Florentine Tragedy*, in the *Collected Edition*, vol. 2, p. 105.

[9] *La Sainte Courtesane; or, the Woman Covered with Jewels*, in the *Collected Edition*, vol. 14, p. 237. Wilde claimed he lost the manuscript in a cab in Paris in 1897 or 1898 (*Letters*, p. 390), but this explanation sounds too much like an incident in *The Importance of Being Earnest* to be believed. Another scenario, drafted in 1894 as *The Cardinal of Avignon* (printed in Mason's *Bibliography of Oscar Wilde*, pp. 583–4), returns to the premise of *A Woman of No Importance*, blending it with the romantic-exotic mode of *Salomé*. The Cardinal of the title, newly elected Pope, is his son's rival in love, a conflict which leads the Pope to tell the son for the first time of their real relation. In an ending reminiscent of *Romeo and Juliet*, the girl whom both love, forbidden to wed the son, kills herself, whereupon the Pope's son throws himself on her bier and stabs himself.

[10] Ricketts, *Oscar Wilde: Recollections by Jean Paul Raymond and Charles Ricketts*, p. 16.

[11] Lord Alfred Douglas, *Oscar Wilde: A Summing-Up* (London: Richards, 1940), p. 113.

Bibliography

Periodicals such as the theatrical newspaper the *Era*, the *Times* of London, the *Theatre*, the *Stage*, and others have been cited repeatedly in the preceding chapters for their play reviews, obituaries of playwrights, and general theatrical news. Each of these references is documented in the footnotes, but with only a few exceptions (full-scale interviews with playwrights, for instance) are not mentioned here.

Achurch, Janet. *Mrs. Daintree's Daughter*. Lord Chamberlain's manuscript, British Library.

Adams, W. Davenport. *A Dictionary of the Drama*. London: Chatto & Windus, 1904.

Anstey, F. (Thomas Anstey Guthrie). *Mr. Punch's Pocket Ibsen*. New York: Macmillan, 1893.

Archer, William. "Ibsen and English Criticism," *Fortnightly Review*, 1 July 1889, pp. 30–7.

The Old Drama and the New. Boston: Small, Maynard, 1922.

The Theatrical 'World' for 1893–7. London: W. Scott, 1894–8.

Armstrong, Nancy. *Desire and Domestic Fiction: A Political History of the Novel*. New York: Oxford University Press, 1987.

Auerbach, Nina. *Ellen Terry: Player in Her Time*. New York: Norton, 1987.

Woman and the Demon: The Life of a Victorian Myth. Cambridge, Mass.: Harvard University Press, 1982.

Bailey, J. O., ed. *British Plays of the Nineteenth Century*. New York: Odyssey, 1966.

Bancroft, Squire and Marie. *The Bancrofts: Recollections of Sixty Years*. 1909; rpt. New York: Blom, 1969.

Barrès, Maurice. *Une Journée parlementaire*. Paris: Charpentier et Fasquelle, 1894.

Barrie, James M. *Ibsen's Ghost, or Toole up to Date*. Lord Chamberlain's manuscript, British Library.

Beckson, Karl, ed. *Oscar Wilde: The Critical Heritage*, New York: Barnes & Noble, 1970.

Beecham, Sir Thomas. *A Mingled Chime*. New York: Putnam's, 1943.

Beerbohm, Max. *Around Theatres*. London: Hart-Davis, 1953.

Max Beerbohm's Letters to Reggie Turner, ed. Rupert Hart-Davis. Philadelphia: Lippincott, 1965.

"Behold the First Lord Illingworth," *New York Times*, 30 April 1916, sec. 2, p. 7.

Bell, Florence E. E., and Elizabeth Robins. *Alan's Wife: A Dramatic Study in Three Scenes*. Introduction by William Archer. London: Henry, 1893.

Bibliography

Bentley, Eric. *The Life of the Drama*. New York: Atheneum, 1964.

Bernhardt, Sarah. *My Double Life*. 1907; rpt. London: Owen, 1977.

Besant, Annie. *Marriage; As It Was, As It Is, And As It Should Be*. New York: Butts, n.d.

Bird, Alan. *The Plays of Oscar Wilde*. New York: Barnes & Noble, 1977.

Blake, Kathleen. *Love and the Woman Question in Victorian Literature: The Art of Self-Postponement*. Totowa, N.J.: Barnes & Noble, 1983.

Bloom, Harold. *The Anxiety of Influence: A Theory of Poetry*. New York: Oxford University Press, 1973.

A Map of Misreading. New York: Oxford University Press, 1975.

ed. *Oscar Wilde: Modern Critical Views*, New York: Chelsea, 1985.

Blunt, Wilfrid Scawen. *My Diaries: Being a Personal Narrative of Events 1888–1914*. 2 vols. New York: Knopf, 1922.

Booth, Michael R. "East End and West End: Class and Audience in Victorian London," *Theatre Research International*, 2 (1977), 98–103.

Victorian Spectacular Theatre 1850–1910. Boston: Routledge & Kegan Paul, 1981.

ed. *English Plays of the Nineteenth Century*. 5 vols. Oxford: Clarendon, 1969–76.

Boucicault, Dion. *Formosa ('The Most Beautiful'): or The Railroad to Ruin*. N.p.: n.p., n.d.

Brieux, Eugène. *Théâtre complet de Brieux*. 9 vols. Paris: Librairie Stock, 1921– .

Brooks, Cleanth, and Robert Heilman. *Understanding Drama*. New York: Holt, 1945.

Bullough, Geoffrey. "Literary Relations of Shaw's Mrs. Warren," *Philological Quarterly*, 41 (1962), 339–58.

Burnand, F. C. *Mrs. Ponderbury's Past*. Lord Chamberlain's manuscript, British Library.

Burney, Estelle, and Arthur Benham. *The Awakening*. Lord Chamberlain's manuscript, British Library.

Caird, Mona. *The Daughters of Danaus*. London: Bliss, 1894.

"Ideal Marriage," *Westminster Review*, 130 (1888), 617–36.

Carton, R. C. (Richard Claude Critchett). *The Home Secretary*. Manuscript in the New York Public Library.

Chambers, C. Haddon. *The Idler: A Play in Four Acts*. London: French, 1902.

Chernyshevski, Nikolai. *What Is To Be Done? A Romance*, trans. Benjamin R. Tucker. Boston: Tucker, 1886.

Christ, Carol. "Victorian Masculinity and the Angel in the House" in *A Widening Sphere: Changing Roles of Victorian Women*, ed. Martha Vicinus. Bloomington: Indiana University Press, 1977, pp. 146–62.

Cohen, Philip K. *The Moral Vision of Oscar Wilde*. Rutherford, N.J.: Fairleigh Dickinson University Press, 1978.

Collins, Wilkie. *The New Magdalen: A Dramatic Story in a Prologue and Three Acts*. London: n.p., 1873.

Conrad, Joseph. *Heart of Darkness*. New York: Norton, 1963.

Crackanthorpe, Mrs. Montague (Blanche Alethea). *The Turn of the Wheel*. Lord Chamberlain's manuscript, British Library.

Craven, W. Stokes. *An Innocent Abroad*. Lord Chamberlain's manuscript, British Library.

Bibliography

Cross, Gilbert. *Next Week – East Lynne: Domestic Drama in Performance 1820–1874.* Lewisburg, Pa.: Bucknell University Press, 1977.

De la Mare, Walter, ed. *The Eighteen-Eighties.* Cambridge University Press, 1930.

Del Mar, Norman. *Richard Strauss: A Critical Commentary on His Life and Works.* 3 vols. Philadelphia: Chilton, 1972.

Delpit, Albert. *Le Fils de Coralie.* Paris: Ollendorf, 1894.

Dickens, Charles. *Martin Chuzzlewit.* Oxford University Press, 1951.

Divorce; or, Faithful and Unfaithful. New York: Lovell, 1889.

Donohue, Joseph, Jr. "The First Production of *The Importance of Being Earnest*: A Proposal for Reconstructive Study" in *Nineteenth Century British Theatre*, eds. Kenneth Richards and Peter Thomson. London: Methuen, 1971, pp. 125–43.

Donohue, Joseph, Jr., and James Ellis (succeeding Allardyce Nicoll and George Freedley), eds. *English Drama of the Nineteenth Century* (New Canaan, Conn.: Readex, 1965–).

Doone, Neville. *A Modern Marriage.* Lord Chamberlain's manuscript, British Library.

Douglas, Lord Alfred. *Oscar Wilde: A Summing Up.* London: Richards, 1940.

Dowling, Linda. "The Decadent and the New Woman in the 1890s," *Nineteenth-Century Fiction*, 33 (1979), 434–53.

Doyle, Arthur Conan. *Foreign Policy.* Lord Chamberlain's manuscript, British Library.

Dumas, Alexandre, *fils. Théâtre complet de Alexandre Dumas Fils.* 7 vols. Paris: Lévy, 1898–9.

Egan, Michael, ed. *Ibsen: The Critical Heritage.* London: Routledge & Kegan Paul, 1972.

Ellis, Mrs. Sarah. *The Daughters of England.* London: Fisher, 1842.

Ellmann, Richard, ed. *The Artist as Critic: Critical Writings of Oscar Wilde.* New York: Random House, 1968.

Oscar Wilde. New York: Knopf, 1988.

"Romantic Pantomime in Oscar Wilde," *Partisan Review*, 30 (1963), 342–55.

ed. *Oscar Wilde: A Collection of Critical Essays.* Englewood Cliffs: Prentice-Hall, 1969.

Emboden, William. *Sarah Bernhardt.* London: Studio Vista, 1974.

Ericksen, Donald H. *Oscar Wilde.* New York: Twayne, 1977.

Everard, Walter, and W. Lestocq. *Uncles and Aunts: A Farcical Comedy in Three Acts.* London: French, n.d.

Fielding, Henry. *Joseph Andrews.* Middletown, Conn.: Wesleyan University Press, p. 41.

Filon, Augustus. *The English Stage: Being an Account of the Victorian Drama.* 1897; rpt. Port Washington, N.Y.: Kennikat, 1970.

Foster, Shirley. *Victorian Women's Fiction: Marriage, Freedom, and the Individual.* Beckenham: Croom Helm, 1985.

Fryers, Austin (William Edward Clery). *Beata.* Lord Chamberlain's manuscript, British Library.

Gagnier, Regenia. *Idylls of the Marketplace: Oscar Wilde and the Victorian Public.* Stanford University Press, 1986.

Ganz, Arthur. "The Meaning of *The Importance of Being Earnest*," *Modern Drama*, 6 (1963), 42–52.

Bibliography

Gide, André. *Oscar Wilde*. Paris: Mercure de France, 1947.

Gilbert, Elliot L. " 'Tumult of Images': Wilde, Beardsley and Salomé," *Victorian Studies*, 26 (1983), 133–59.

Gilbert, W.S. *Original Plays by W. S. Gilbert*. London: Chatto & Windus, 1925.

Gissing, George. *The Odd Women*. New York: Norton, 1971.

Glover, James M. *Jimmy Glover His Book*. London: Methuen, 1911.

Gorchakov, Nikolai A. *The Theater in Soviet Russia*. Edgar Lehrman, trans. New York: Columbia University Press, 1957.

Grand, Sarah (Frances Elizabeth Macfall). *The Heavenly Twins*. New York: Cassell, 1893.

Granville-Barker, Harley. "The Coming of Ibsen" in *The Eighteen-Eighties*, ed. Walter de la Mare. Cambridge University Press, 1930.

Green, William. "Wilde and the Bunburys," *Modern Drama*, 21 (1978), 67–80.

Gregor, Ian. "Comedy and Oscar Wilde," *Sewanee Review*, 74 (1966), 501–21.

Greville, Lady Violet, and Arthur Bourchier. *Justice: A Play in Four Acts*. Lord Chamberlain's manuscript, British Library.

Grundy, Sydney. *The Arabian Nights: A Farcical Comedy in Three Acts*. Chicago: Dramatic Publishing, n.d.

A Bunch of Violets: A Play in Four Acts. London: French, 1901.

A Debt of Honour: An Original Play in Four Acts. London: Scott, n.d.

A Fool's Paradise: An Original Play in Three Acts. London: French, 1898.

Man Proposes: An Original Comedietta in One Act. New York: French, n.d.

The New Woman: An Original Comedy, in Four Acts. London: Chiswick, 1894.

The Play of the Future, by a Playwright of the Past. London: French, 1914.

Sowing the Wind: An Original Play in Four Acts. London: French, 1901.

Grundy, Sydney, and G. R. Sims. *The Glass of Fashion: An Original Comedy in Four Acts*. London: French, 1898.

Guralnick, Elissa, and Paul M. Levitt. "Allusion and Meaning in Wilde's *A Woman of No Importance*," *Eire–Ireland*, 13 (45–51).

Hamilton, C. J. *Mr. Boodle's Predicament*. In *Original Plays for the Drawing-Room*. London: Ward, Lock, 1890.

Harris, Frank. *Oscar Wilde*. East Lansing: Michigan State University Press, 1959.

Hartley, Kelver. *Oscar Wilde: L'Influence française dans son oeuvre*. Paris: Librairie du Recueil Sirey, 1935.

Hatton, Joseph. *The Scarlet Letter; or, Hester Prynne: A Drama in Three Acts*. London: Lindley, n.d.

Henry, Richard (H. Chance Newton and Richard Butler). *Adoption: A Farce in One Act*. London: French, n.d.

Crime & Christening: A Farce. Lord Chamberlain's manuscript, British Library.

Hicks, Seymour. *A Night Out*. Lord Chamberlain's manuscript, British Library.

Horner, Fred. *The Late Lamented*. Lord Chamberlain's manuscript, British Library.

Two Johnnies. Lord Chamberlain's manuscript, British Library.

Horney, Karen. *Feminine Psychology*. New York: Norton, 1967.

How To Be Happy Though Married: Being a Handbook to Marriage. London: Unwin, 1885.

Huberman, Jeffrey H. *Late Victorian Farce*. Ann Arbor: UMI Research Press, 1986.

Hudson, Lynton. *The English Stage 1850–1950*. London: Harrap, 1951.

Ibsen, Henrik. *The Collected Works of Henrik Ibsen*, ed. William Archer. 13 vols. New York: Scribner's, 1906–12.

Bibliography

Illustrated London News.

Jackson, Russell, and Ian Small. "Some New Drafts of a Wilde Play," *English Literature in Transition 1880–1920,* 30 (1987), 7–15.

James, Henry. *The Scenic Art: Notes on Acting and the Drama,* ed. Allan Wade. New Brunswick, N.J.: Rutgers University Press, 1948.

Jerome, Jerome K. *New Lamps for Old.* Lord Chamberlain's manuscript, British Library.

    Stage-Land: Curious Habits and Customs of Its Inhabitants. London: Chatto & Windus, 1890.

Johnson, Wendell Stacy. "Fallen Women, Lost Children: Wilde and the Theatre of the Nineties" in *Sexuality and Victorian Literature,* ed. Don Richard Cox. Knoxville: University of Tennessee Press, 1984, pp. 196–211.

Jones, Doris A. *Taking the Curtain Call: The Life and Letters of Henry Arthur Jones,* New York: Macmillan, 1930.

Jones, Henry Arthur. *The Case of Rebellious Susan: A Comedy in Three Acts.* London: Chiswick, 1894.

    The Dancing Girl: A Drama in Four Acts. London: French, 1907.

    The Renascence of the English Drama: Essays, Lectures, and Fragments. London: Macmillan, 1895.

    Saints and Sinners: A New and Original Drama in Five Acts. New York: Macmillan, 1908.

Jones, Henry Arthur, and Henry Herman. *Breaking a Butterfly: A Play in Three Acts.* N.p.: privately printed, n.d.

Jullian, Philippe. *Oscar Wilde.* Violet Wyndham, trans. New York: Viking, 1969.

Kendal, Madge. *Dramatic Opinions.* Boston: Little, Brown, 1890.

Kronenberger, Louis. *Oscar Wilde.* Boston: Little, Brown, 1976.

Labiche, Eugène. *Oeuvres complètes de Labiche.* 8 vols. Paris: Club de l'Honnête Homme, 1966– .

Lamb, Charles. "On the Artificial Comedy of the Last Century" in *The Collected Essays of Charles Lamb.* 2 vols. New York: Dutton, 1929.

Langtry, Lillie. *The Days I Knew.* New York: Doran, 1925.

Law, Arthur. *The New Boy: A Farcical Play in Three Acts.* New York: French, 1904.

Lawler, Donald, and Charles E. Knott. "The Context of Invention: Suggested Origins of *Dorian Gray,*" *Modern Philology,* 73 (1976), 389–98.

Leclerq, Pierre. *Illusion: A New and Original Play in Three Acts.* Lord Chamberlain's manuscript, British Library.

    This Woman and That: A New Play in Three Acts. Lord Chamberlain's manuscript, British Library.

Lemaître, Jules. *Literary Impressions,* trans. A. W. Evans. London: O'Connor, 1921.

    Révoltée. Paris: Lévy, 1889.

Lestocq, W. (William Lestocq Boileau Woolridge), and E. M. Robson. *The Foundling: A Farce in Three Acts.* Manuscripts in the Lord Chamberlain's Collection in the British Library and in the New York Public Library.

Lydon, Mary. "Myself and M/others," *Sub-stance,* no. 32 (1981), pp. 6–14.

McCarthy, Justin H. *The Candidate.* Lord Chamberlain's manuscript, British Library.

    Your Wife. Lord Chamberlain's manuscript, British Library.

MacQueen-Pope, W. *Haymarket: Theatre of Perfection.* London: Allen, 1948.

    St. James's: Theatre of Distinction. London: Allen, 1958.

Maeterlinck, Maurice. *La Princesse Maleine*. In *Théâtre*. 3 vols. Paris: Slatkine, 1979.

Marcus, Jane. "Salomé: The Jewish Princess Was a New Woman," *Bulletin of the New York Public Library*, 78 (1974), 95–113.

Marek, George R. *Richard Strauss: The Life of a Non-Hero*. New York: Simon and Schuster, 1967.

Mason, Stuart (C. S. Millard). *Bibliography of Oscar Wilde*. London: Laurie, n.d.

Meilhac, Henri, and Ludovic Halévy. *Frou-Frou*. New York: Rullman, n.d.

Meisel, Martin. *Realizations: Narrative, Pictorial, and Theatrical Arts in Nineteenth-Century England*. Princeton University Press, 1983.

Shaw and the Nineteenth-Century Theater. Princeton University Press, 1963.

Melford, Mark. *Kleptomania*. London: French, n.d.

Mikhail, E. H. "The French Influences on Oscar Wilde's Comedies," *Revue de Littérature Comparée*, 42 (1968), 220–33.

Oscar Wilde: An Annotated Bibliography. London: Macmillan, 1978.

"Self-Revelation in *An Ideal Husband*," *Modern Drama*, 11 (1968), 180–6.

ed. *Oscar Wilde: Interviews and Recollections*. London: Macmillan, 1979.

Mill, John Stuart, and Harriet Taylor Mill. *Essays on Sex Equality: John Stuart Mill and Harriet Taylor Mill*, ed. Alice S. Rossi. University of Chicago Press, 1970.

Miller, R. K. *Oscar Wilde*. New York: Ungar, 1982.

Millett, Kate. *Sexual Politics*. Garden City, N.Y.: Doubleday, 1970.

Morgan, Margery. *The Shavian Playground*. London: Methuen, 1972.

Morrison, Kristin. " 'Horrible Flesh and Blood,' " *Theatre Notebook*, 35 (1981), 7–9.

Morton, John Maddison. *Box and Cox*. London: Lacy, n.d.

A Husband to Order: A Serio-Comic Drama in Two Acts. Boston: Baker, n.d.

An M.P.'s Wife. Lord Chamberlain's manuscript, British Library.

Mullin, Donald. *Victorian Plays: A Record of Significant Productions on the London Stage, 1837–1901*. New York: Greenwood, 1987.

Murray, Alfred. *Mistaken Identity*. Lord Chamberlain's manuscript, British Library.

Murray, D. C. *The Puritan*. Lord Chamberlain's manuscript, British Library.

Murray, Isobel. "Oscar Wilde's Absorption of 'Influences': The Case History of Chuang Tzu," *Durham University Journal*, 44 (1971), 2–13.

Introduction to *The Picture of Dorian Gray*. London: Oxford University Press, 1974.

Musgrave, Mrs. H. *Our Flat: Farcical Comedy in 3 Acts*. Lord Chamberlain's manuscript, British Library.

Nassaar, Christopher S. *Into the Demon Universe: A Literary Exploration of Oscar Wilde*. New Haven, Conn.: Yale University Press, 1974.

Neilson, Julia. *This for Remembrance*. London: Hurst & Blackett, 1940.

Never Again. Lord Chamberlain's manuscript, British Library.

Nicholls, Harry, and W. Lestocq. *Jane: A Farce in Three Acts*. New York: French, 1900.

Nicoll, Allardyce. *Late Nineteenth Century Drama 1850–1900*. (Vol. 5 of *A History of English Drama 1660–1900*). 2nd edn. Cambridge University Press, 1959.

Oliphant, Margaret. "The Anti-Marriage League," *Blackwood's*, January 1896, pp. 135–49.

O'Sullivan, Vincent. *Aspects of Oscar Wilde*. London: Constable, 1936.

Pacheco, Mrs. R. *Tom, Dick, and Harry: A Farcical Comedy*. London: French, n.d.

Paglia, Camille. "Oscar Wilde and the English Epicene," *Raritan*, 4 (1985), 85–109.

Bibliography

Parker, John, ed. *The Green Room Book, or, Who's Who on the Stage.* London: T. Sealey Clark, 1906–9.

Parker, Louis N. *Several of My Lives.* London: Chapman and Hall, 1928.

Patmore, Coventry. *The Poems of Coventry Patmore*, ed. Frederick Page. Cambridge University Press, 1949.

Paul, C. B., and J. L. Heilbrun. "The Importance of Reading Alfred: Oscar Wilde's Debt to Alfred de Musset," *Bulletin of the New York Public Library*, 75 (1971), 506–72.

Payn, James. *The Best of Husbands.* 3 vols. London: Bentley, 1874.

Pearson, Hesketh. *Beerbohm Tree: His Life and Laughter.* New York: Harper, 1956.

The Life of Oscar Wilde. London: Methuen, 1946.

Pemberton, T. Edgar. *The Criterion Theatre.* London: Eyre & Spottiswoode, n.d.

Philips, F. C., and Charles H. E. Brookfield, *Godpapa: A Farcical Comedy in Three Acts.* Lord Chamberlain's manuscript, British Library.

Philips, F. C., and Percy Fendall. *Husband and Wife.* In F. C. Philips, *A Barrister's Courtship.* Leipzig: Tauchnitz, 1907.

Philips, F. C., and Sydney Grundy. *The Dean's Daughter.* London: Trischler, 1891.

Pinero, Arthur W. *Dandy Dick: A Farce in Three Acts.* London: Heinemann, 1906.

Lady Bountiful, A Story of Years: A Play in Four Acts. London: Heinemann, 1891.

The Magistrate: A Farce in Three Acts. In Michael R. Booth, *English Plays of the Nineteenth Century*, vol. 4, pp. 299–384.

The Schoolmistress: A Farce in Three Acts. London: Heinemann, 1907.

The Social Plays of Arthur Wing Pinero, ed. Clayton Hamilton. 4 vols. New York: Dutton, 1917.

Sweet Lavender: A Domestic Drama in Four Acts. London: Heinemann, 1908.

The Times: A Comedy in Four Acts. London: Heinemann, 1891.

Plouvier, Edouard. *Madame Aubert: Drame en Quatre Actes.* Paris: Lévy, 1865.

Pomeroy, H. S. *The Ethics of Marriage.* London: Funk & Wagnalls, 1889.

Poovey, Mary. *The Proper Lady and the Woman Writer.* University of Chicago Press, 1984.

Powell, Kerry. "Hawthorne, Arlo Bates, and *The Picture of Dorian Gray*," *Papers on Language & Literature*, 16 (1980), 403–16.

"Tom, Dick, and Dorian Gray: Magic-Picture Mania in Late Victorian Fiction," *Philological Quarterly*, 62 (1983), 147–70.

Praz, Mario. *The Romantic Agony.* Angus Davidson, trans. Cleveland: World, 1956.

Quilter, Harry. *Is Marriage A Failure? A Modern Symposium.* Chicago: Rand, McNally, 1889.

Raby, Peter. *Oscar Wilde.* Cambridge University Press, 1988.

Reid, Erskine, and Herbert Compton. *The Dramatic Peerage.* London: General, 1891.

Rigdon, Walter, ed. *Biographical Encyclopedia and Who's Who of the American Theatre.* New York: Heinemann, 1966.

"Rita" (Eliza M. J. Humphreys). *A Husband of No Importance.* London: Unwin, 1894.

Ritchie, D. G. *Darwinism and Politics.* London: Sonnenschein, 1889.

Robertson, W. Graham. *Time Was: The Reminiscences of W. Graham Robertson.* London: Hamilton, 1931.

Robins, Elizabeth ("C. E. Raimond"). *George Mandeville's Husband.* New York: Appleton, 1894.

Roditi, Edouard. *Oscar Wilde*. Norfolk, Conn.: New Directions, 1947.

Rogers, Charles. *The Future Woman, or Josiah's Dream*. Lord Chamberlain's manuscript, British Library.

Rothenstein, Will. *Men and Memories: A History of the Arts 1872–1922*. 2 vols. New York: Tudor, n.d.

Rowell, George, ed. *Late Victorian Plays 1890–1914*. 2nd edn. London: Oxford University Press.

Nineteenth Century Plays. 2nd edn. Oxford University Press, 1972.

The Victorian Theatre 1792–1914: A Survey. 2nd edn. Cambridge University Press, 1978.

Ryals, Clyde de L. "Oscar Wilde's Salomé," *Notes and Queries*, 204 (1959), 56–7.

Saltus, Edgar. *Eden*. Chicago: Belford, Clarke, 1888.

Mary of Magdala: A Chronicle. London: Greening, 1903.

Oscar Wilde: An Idler's Impression. Chicago: Brothers of the Book, 1917.

San Juan, Epifanio, Jr. *The Art of Oscar Wilde*. Princeton University Press, 1967.

Sardou, Victorien. *Théâtre complet*. 15 vols. Paris: Michel, 1934–61.

Schoonderwoerd, N. *J. T. Grein: Ambassador of the Theatre 1862–1935*. Assen, the Netherlands: Van Gorcum, 1963.

Scott, Clement. *The Drama of Yesterday and Today*. 2 vols. 1899; rpt. New York: Garland, 1986.

Shaw, George Bernard. *The Works of Bernard Shaw*. 33 vols. London: Constable, 1931.

Sherard, Robert H. *The Life of Oscar Wilde*. London: Laurie, 1906.

Oscar Wilde: The Story of an Unhappy Friendship. 1905; rpt. New York: Haskell House, 1970.

The Real Oscar Wilde. London: Laurie, n.d.

Shewan, Rodney. *Oscar Wilde: Art and Egotism*. London: Macmillan, 1977.

"*A Wife's Tragedy*: An Unpublished Sketch for a Play by Oscar Wilde," *Theatre Research International*, 7 (1982), 75–131.

Shirley, Arthur. *Saved; or, A Wife's Peril: Comedy Drama in Four Acts*. Chicago: Dramatic Publishing, n.d.

Shirley, Arthur, and Maurice Gally. *The Cross of Honour*. Lord Chamberlain's manuscript, British Library.

Showalter, Elaine. *A Literature of Their Own: British Women Novelists from Brontë to Lessing*. Princeton University Press, 1977.

Sims, G. R. *My Life: Sixty Years' Recollection of Bohemian London*. London: Nash, 1917.

Skinner, Cornelia Otis. *Madame Sarah*. Boston: Houghton Mifflin, 1966.

'The Stage' Cyclopaedia: A Bibliography of Plays. London: The Stage, 1909.

Stephens, John R. *The Censorship of English Drama 1824–1901*. Cambridge University Press, 1980.

Stokes, John. *Oscar Wilde*. London: Longman, 1978. [Writers & Their Work, no. 264.]

Resistible Theatres: Enterprise and Experiment in the Late Nineteenth Century. London: Elek, 1972.

Stokes, John, Michael R. Booth, and Susan Bassnett, *Bernhardt, Terry, Duse: The Actress in Her Time*. Cambridge University Press, 1988.

Strauss, Richard. *Recollections and Reflections*, ed. Willi Shuh, trans. L. J. Lawrence.London: Boosey and Hawkes, 1949.

Bibliography

Suter, W. E. *The Lost Child; or, Jones's Baby: An Original Farce in One Act*. London: French, n.d.

Symons, Arthur. *Plays, Acting, and Music*. New York: Dutton, n.d.

Studies in Prose and Verse. London: Dent, [1904].

Taylor, Tom. *The House or the Home; A Comedy in Two Acts*. London: Lacy, n.d..

Still Waters Run Deep: An Original Comedy in Three Acts. London: French, n.d.

The Victims: An Original Comedy, in Three Acts. New York: French, n.d.

Tennyson, Alfred. *The Complete Poetical Works of Tennyson*. ed. W. J. Rolfe. Cambridge, Mass.: Riverside, 1898.

Thomas, Brandon. *Charley's Aunt: A Play in Three Acts*. London: French, 1962.

Tree, Herbert Beerbohm. *Some Interesting Fallacies of the Modern Stage: An Address Delivered to the Playgoers' Club on Sunday, 6th December, 1891*. London: Heinemann, 1892.

Van Ghent, Dorothy. *The English Novel: Form and Function*. New York: Rinehart, 1953.

Vicinus, Martha. " 'Helpless and Unfriended': Nineteenth-Century Domestic Melodrama," *New Literary History*, 13 (1981), 127–43.

Independent Women: Work and Community for Single Women, 1850–1920. University of Chicago Press, 1985.

Suffer and Be Still: Women in the Victorian Age. Bloomington: Indiana University Press, 1972.

Walkley, A. B. *Playhouse Impressions*. London: Unwin, 1892.

Ware, James M. "Algernon's Appetite: Oscar Wilde's Hero as Restoration Dandy," *English Literature in Transition 1880–1920*, 13 (1970), 17–26.

Wearing, J. P. *American and British Theatrical Biography: A Directory*. Metuchen, N.J.: Scarecrow, 1979.

The London Stage 1890–1899: A Calendar of Plays and Players. Metuchen, N.J.: Scarecrow, 1976.

Who's Who in the Theatre. 14th edn. London: Pitman, 1967.

Who Was Who (1897–1970). London: Black, 1920–72.

Who Was Who in the Theatre: 1912–76. Rpt.; Detroit: Gale Research, 1978.

Wilde, Oscar. *Complete Works of Oscar Wilde*. London: Collins, 1966.

The First Collected Edition of the Works of Oscar Wilde, ed. Robert Ross. 15 vols. London: Methuen, 1908–22.

An Ideal Husband, ed. Russell Jackson. In *Two Society Comedies*. London: Benn, 1983.

The Importance of Being Earnest: A Trivial Comedy for Serious People, ed. Russell Jackson. London: Benn, 1980.

The Importance of Being Earnest: A Trivial Comedy for Serious People in Four Acts as Originally Written by Oscar Wilde, ed. Sarah Augusta Dickson. 2 vols. New York Public Library, 1956.

Lady Windermere's Fan: A Play about a Good Woman, ed. Ian Small. London: Benn, 1980.

The Letters of Oscar Wilde, ed. Rupert Hart-Davis. New York: Harcourt, Brace & World, 1962.

More Letters of Oscar Wilde, ed. Rupert Hart-Davis. New York: Vanguard, 1985.

The Picture of Dorian Gray, ed. Isobel Murray. London: Oxford University Press, 1974.

Bibliography

A Woman of No Importance, ed. Ian Small. In *Two Society Comedies*. London: Benn, 1983.

Woodcock, George. *The Paradox of Oscar Wilde*. New York: Macmillan, 1950.

Woodfield, James. *English Theatre in Transition 1881–1914*. London: Croom Helm, 1984.

Wooler, J. P. *A Model Husband: A Farce in One Act*. London: Lacy, n.d.

Worth, Katharine. *Oscar Wilde*. New York: Grove, 1984.

Zangwill, Israel. *Six Persons*, London: French, 1898.

Index

196

Index

200